DOCTOR STRANGE

DOCTOR STRANGE VOL. 4: MR. MISERY. Contains material originally
published in magazine form as DOCTOR STRANGE #17-20 and ANNUAL #1. First
printing 2017. ISBN# 978-1-302-90587-3. Published by MARVEL WORLDWIDE,
INC., a subsidiary of MARVEL ENTERTAINMENT, LLC. OFFICE OF PUBLICATION: 135
West 50th Street, New York, NY 10020. Copyright © 2017 MARVEL No similarity between any of the names, characters, persons, and/or institutions in this magazine with those
of any living or dead person or institution is intended, and any such similarity which may exist is
purely coincidental. **Printed in the U.S.A.** DAN BUCKLEY, President, Marvel Entertainment; JOE QUESADA,
Chief Creative Officer; TOM BREVOORT, SVP of Publishing; DAVID BOGART, SVP of Business Affairs & Operations,
Publishing & Partnership; C.B. CEBULSKI, VP of Brand Management & Development, Asia; DAVID GABRIEL, SVP of Sales
& Marketing, Publishing; JEFF YOUNGQUIST, VP of Production & Special Projects; DAN CARR, Executive Director of Publishing
Technology; ALEX MORALES, Director of Publishing Operations; SUSAN CRESPI, Production Manager; STAN LEE, Chairman Emer-
itus. For information regarding advertising in Marvel Comics or on Marvel.com, please contact Jonathan Parkhideh, VP of Digital Media
& Marketing Solutions, at jparkhideh@marvel.com. For Marvel subscription inquiries, please call 888-511-5480. **Manufactured between
10/27/2017 and 11/28/2017 by LSC COMMUNICATIONS INC., KENDALLVILLE, IN, USA.**

10 9 8 7 6 5 4 3 2 1

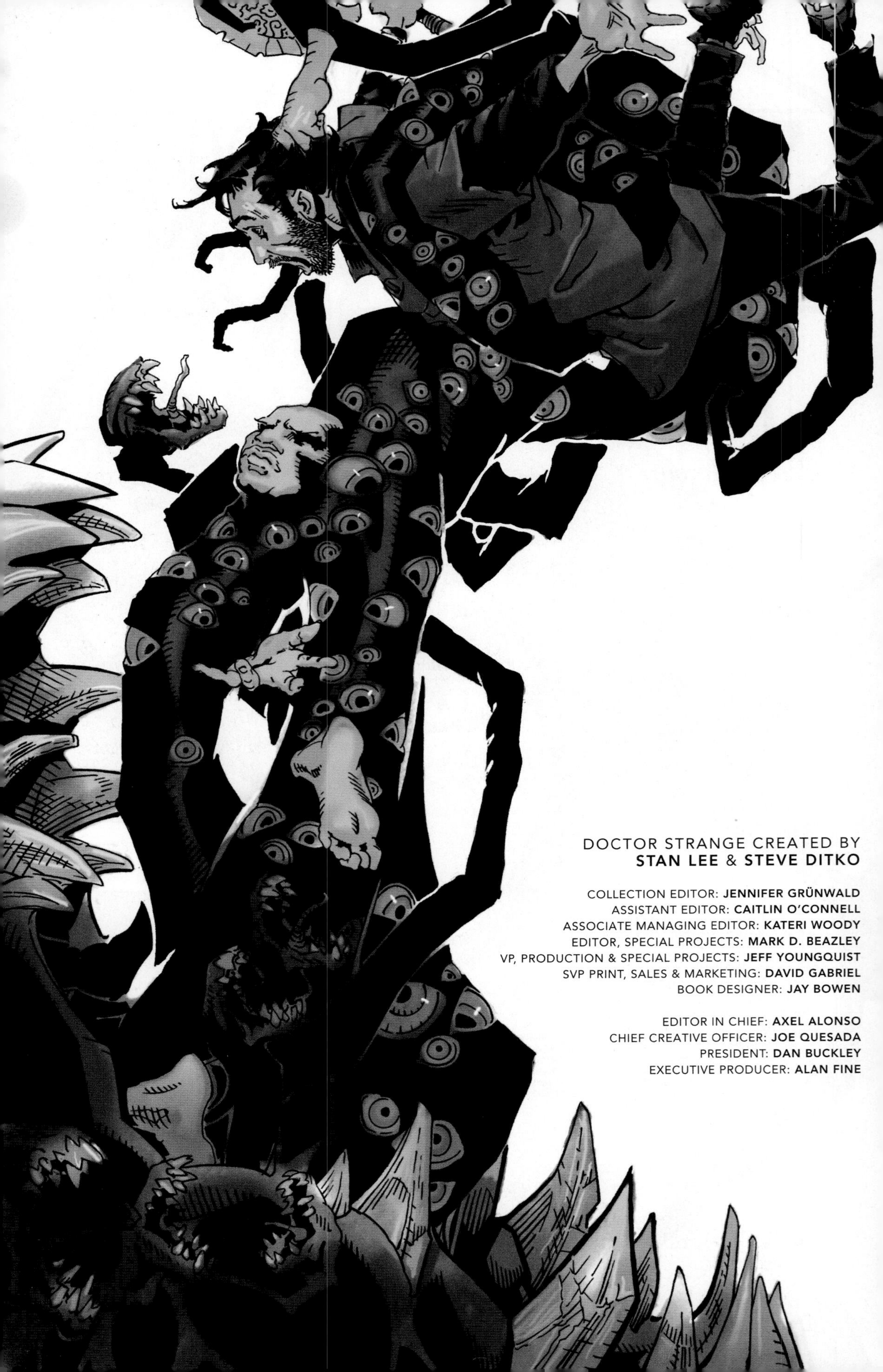

DOCTOR STRANGE CREATED BY
STAN LEE & **STEVE DITKO**

COLLECTION EDITOR: **JENNIFER GRÜNWALD**
ASSISTANT EDITOR: **CAITLIN O'CONNELL**
ASSOCIATE MANAGING EDITOR: **KATERI WOODY**
EDITOR, SPECIAL PROJECTS: **MARK D. BEAZLEY**
VP, PRODUCTION & SPECIAL PROJECTS: **JEFF YOUNGQUIST**
SVP PRINT, SALES & MARKETING: **DAVID GABRIEL**
BOOK DESIGNER: **JAY BOWEN**

EDITOR IN CHIEF: **AXEL ALONSO**
CHIEF CREATIVE OFFICER: **JOE QUESADA**
PRESIDENT: **DAN BUCKLEY**
EXECUTIVE PRODUCER: **ALAN FINE**

DOCTOR STRANGE

Mr. Misery

ISSUE #17

Jason Aaron
WRITER

Frazer Irving
ARTIST

Kevin Nowlan
COVER ART

ISSUES #18-19

Jason Aaron
WRITER

Chris Bachalo
PENCILER/COLORIST

Al Vey, Tim Townsend, John Livesay, Victor Olazaba, Jamie Mendoza & Wayne Faucher
INKERS

Patrick Brown (#18) *& Kevin Nowlan* (#19)
COVER ART

ISSUE #20

Jason Aaron
WRITER

Chris Bachalo & Kevin Nowlan
ARTISTS/COLORISTS

Al Vey, John Livesay, Tim Townsend, Jaime Mendoza, Victor Olazaba & Kevin Nowlan
INKERS

Chris Bachalo & Tim Townsend
COVER ART

ANNUAL #1

"TO GET HER. FOREVER."

KATHRYN IMMONEN
WRITER

LEONARDO ROMERO
ARTIST

JORDIE BELLAIRE
COLORIST

"STRANGE TALES: YAO, THE NOT-QUITE-ANCIENT ONE"

ROBBIE THOMPSON
WRITER

JONATHAN MARKS
ARTIST

LEE LOUGHRIDGE
COLORS

W. SCOTT FORBES
COVER ART

VC's Cory Petit
LETTERER

Allison Stock
ASSISTANT EDITOR

Darren Shan
ASSOCIATE EDITOR

Nick Lowe
EDITOR

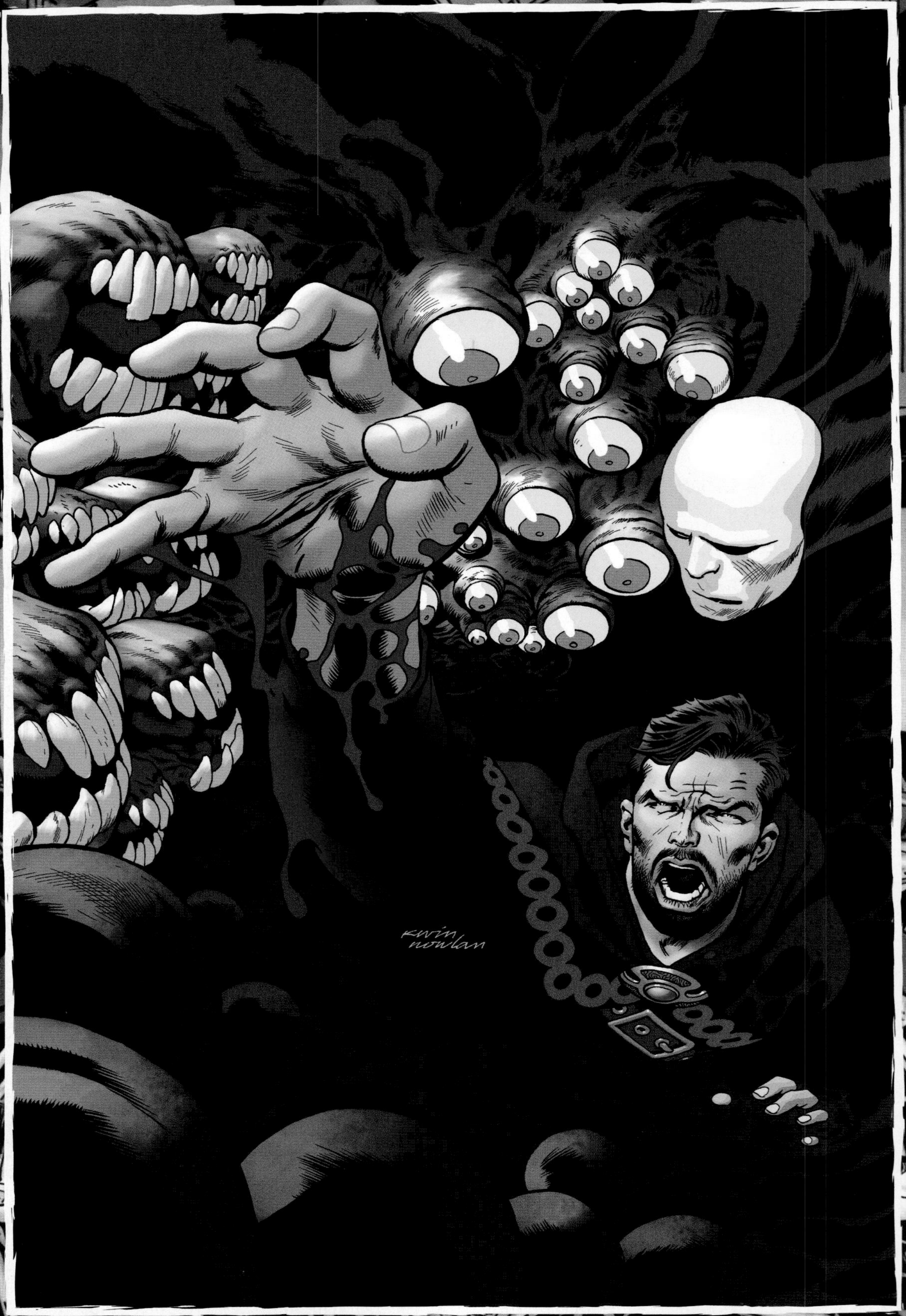
kevin nowlan

DOCTOR STRANGE 17 STATE OF MISERY

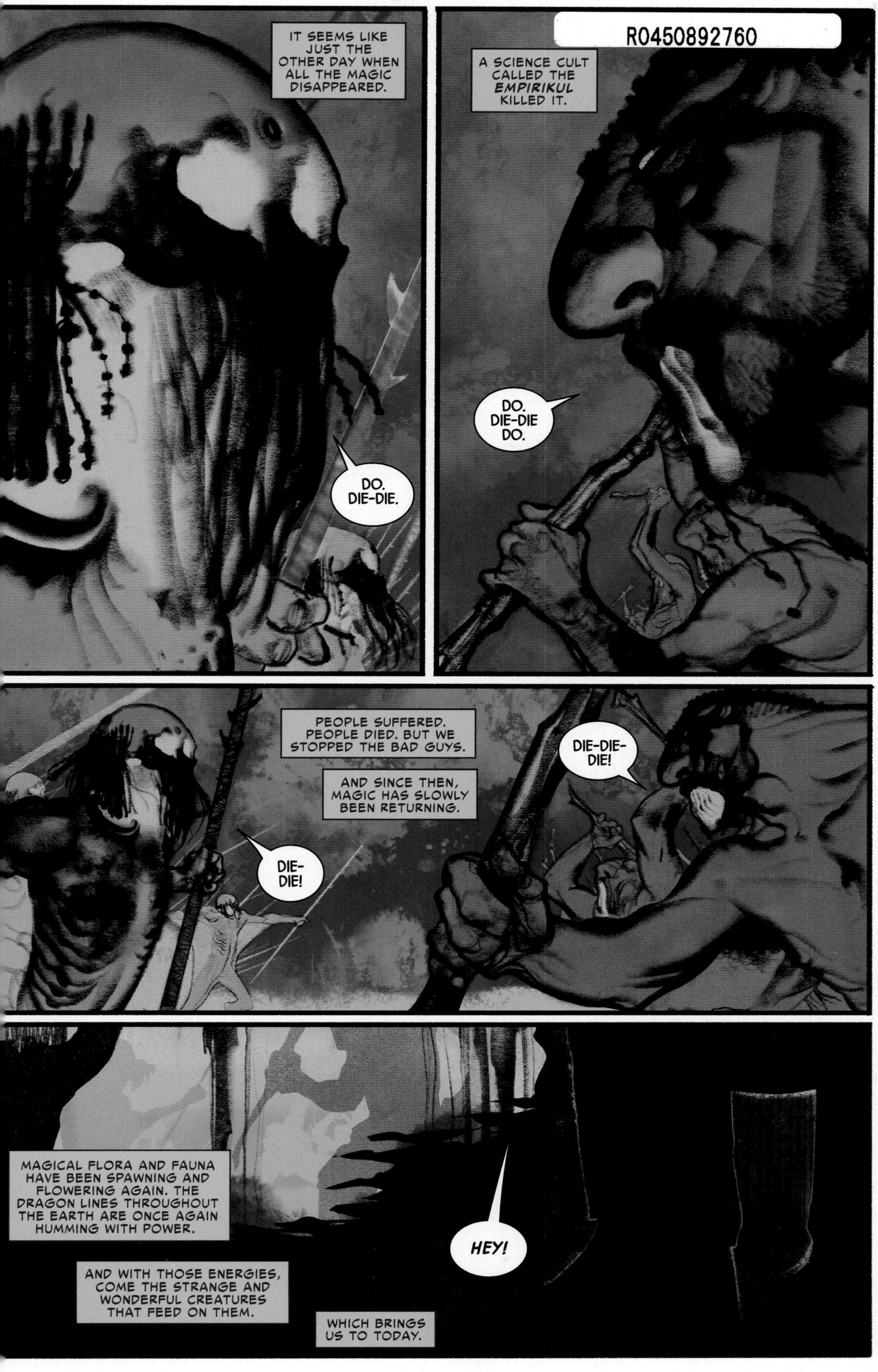
R0450892760
IT SEEMS LIKE JUST THE OTHER DAY WHEN ALL THE MAGIC DISAPPEARED.
DO. DIE-DIE.
A SCIENCE CULT CALLED THE *EMPIRIKUL* KILLED IT.
DO. DIE-DIE DO.
PEOPLE SUFFERED. PEOPLE DIED. BUT WE STOPPED THE BAD GUYS.
AND SINCE THEN, MAGIC HAS SLOWLY BEEN RETURNING.
DIE-DIE!
DIE-DIE-DIE!
MAGICAL FLORA AND FAUNA HAVE BEEN SPAWNING AND FLOWERING AGAIN. THE DRAGON LINES THROUGHOUT THE EARTH ARE ONCE AGAIN HUMMING WITH POWER.
AND WITH THOSE ENERGIES, COME THE STRANGE AND WONDERFUL CREATURES THAT FEED ON THEM.
WHICH BRINGS US TO TODAY.
HEY!

LET'S GET THIS OVER WITH, GUYS. I'VE GOT SOMEWHERE I NEED TO BE.

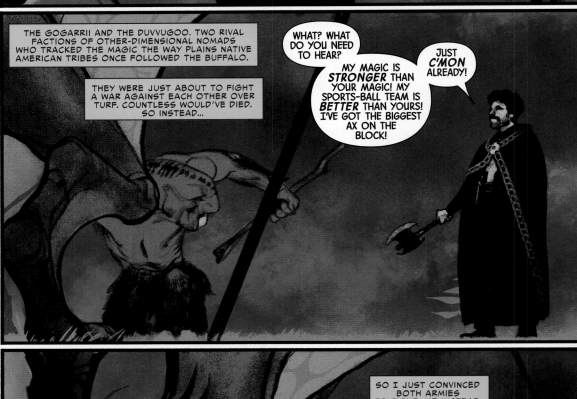

THE GOGARRII AND THE DUVVUGOO. TWO RIVAL FACTIONS OF OTHER-DIMENSIONAL NOMADS WHO TRACKED THE MAGIC THE WAY PLAINS NATIVE AMERICAN TRIBES ONCE FOLLOWED THE BUFFALO.

THEY WERE JUST ABOUT TO FIGHT A WAR AGAINST EACH OTHER OVER TURF. COUNTLESS WOULD'VE DIED. SO INSTEAD...

WHAT? WHAT DO YOU NEED TO HEAR?

MY MAGIC IS *STRONGER* THAN YOUR MAGIC! MY SPORTS-BALL TEAM IS *BETTER* THAN YOURS! I'VE GOT THE BIGGEST AX ON THE BLOCK!

JUST *C'MON* ALREADY!

SO I JUST CONVINCED BOTH ARMIES TO FIGHT *ME* INSTEAD.

NOW THESE TWO WARRING FACTIONS ARE UNITED. UNITED IN THEIR DESIRE TO SEE ME PAINFULLY AND REPEATEDLY MURDERED.

I NEVER SAID IT WAS A FOOL-PROOF PLAN.

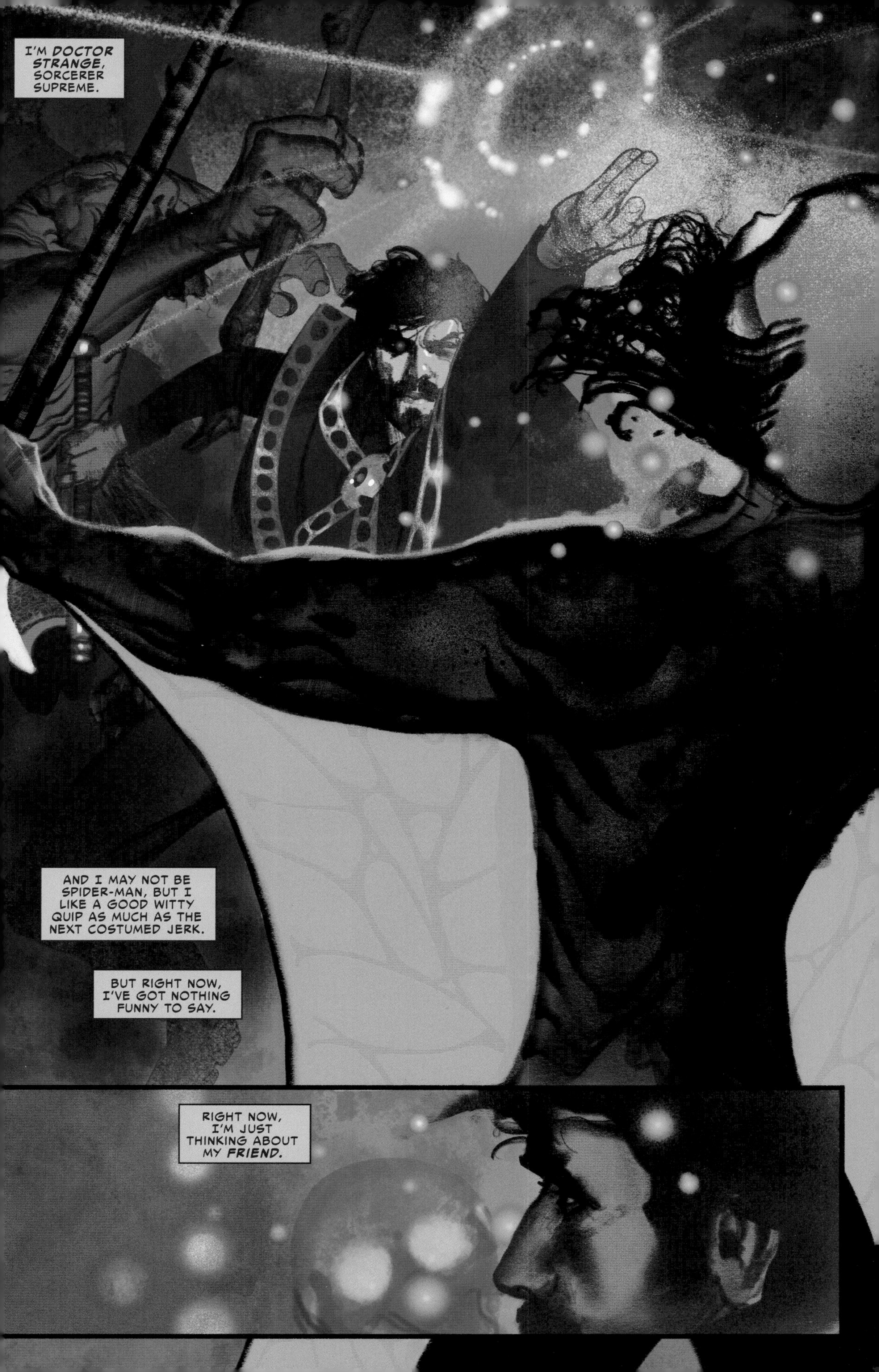
I'M DOCTOR STRANGE, SORCERER SUPREME.
AND I MAY NOT BE SPIDER-MAN, BUT I LIKE A GOOD WITTY QUIP AS MUCH AS THE NEXT COSTUMED JERK.
BUT RIGHT NOW, I'VE GOT NOTHING FUNNY TO SAY.
RIGHT NOW, I'M JUST THINKING ABOUT MY FRIEND.

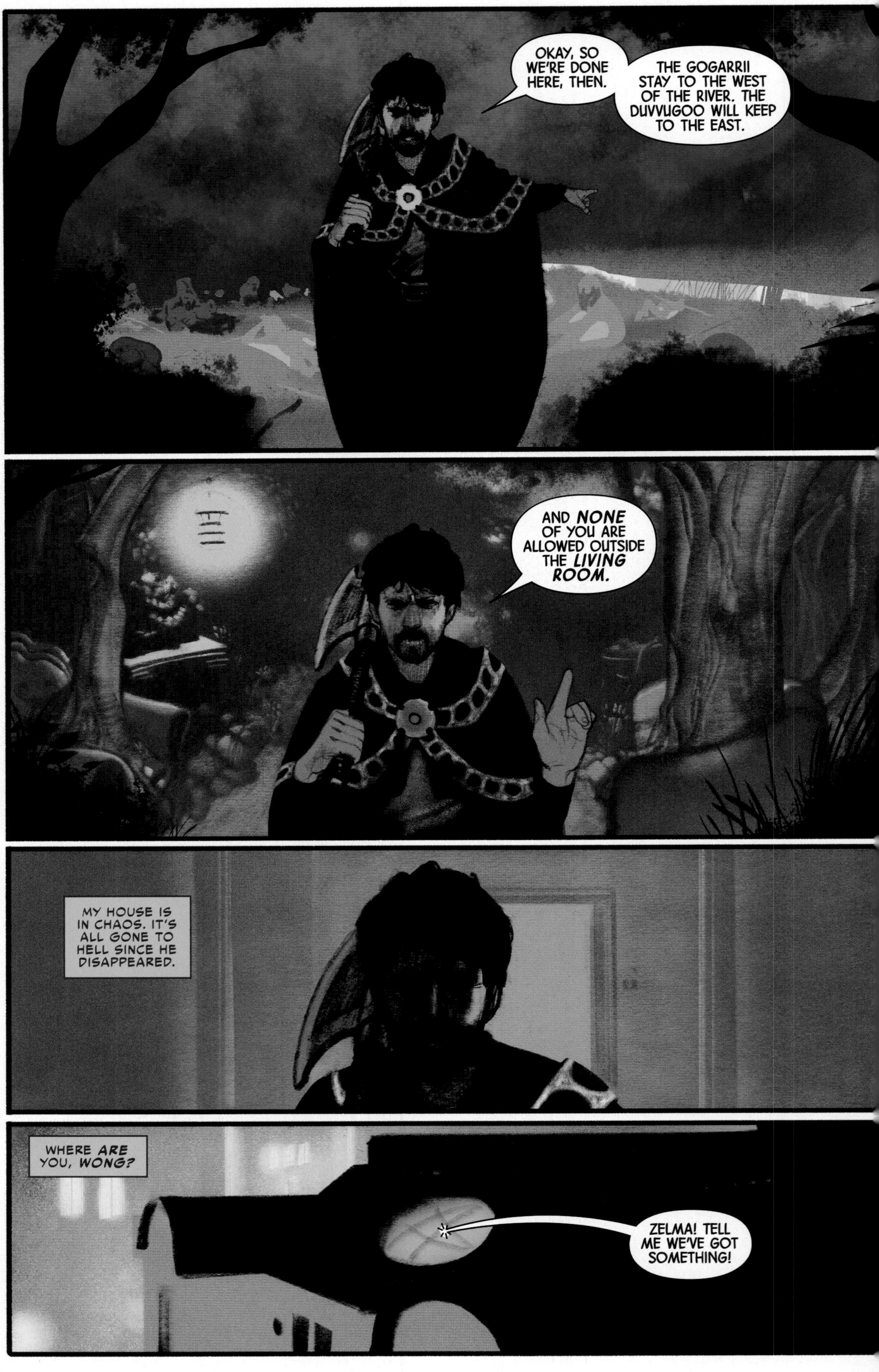
OKAY, SO WE'RE DONE HERE, THEN.
THE GOGARRII STAY TO THE WEST OF THE RIVER. THE DUVVUGOO WILL KEEP TO THE EAST.
AND *NONE* OF YOU ARE ALLOWED OUTSIDE THE *LIVING ROOM.*
MY HOUSE IS IN CHAOS. IT'S ALL GONE TO HELL SINCE HE DISAPPEARED.
WHERE *ARE* YOU, *WONG?*
ZELMA! TELL ME WE'VE GOT SOMETHING!

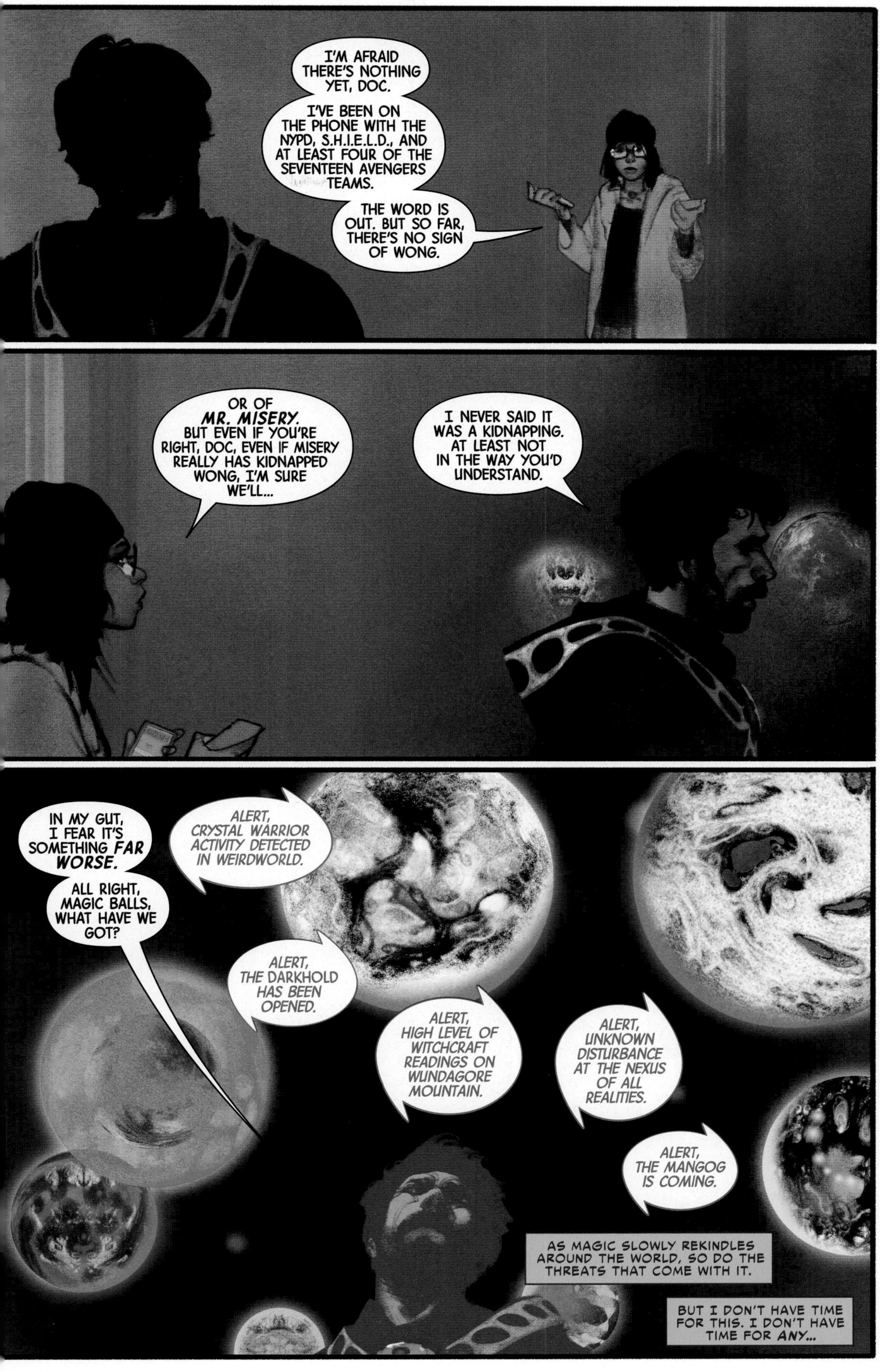
I'M AFRAID THERE'S NOTHING YET, DOC.
I'VE BEEN ON THE PHONE WITH THE NYPD, S.H.I.E.L.D., AND AT LEAST FOUR OF THE SEVENTEEN AVENGERS TEAMS.
THE WORD IS OUT. BUT SO FAR, THERE'S NO SIGN OF WONG.
OR OF MR. MISERY. BUT EVEN IF YOU'RE RIGHT, DOC, EVEN IF MISERY REALLY HAS KIDNAPPED WONG, I'M SURE WE'LL...
I NEVER SAID IT WAS A KIDNAPPING. AT LEAST NOT IN THE WAY YOU'D UNDERSTAND.
IN MY GUT, I FEAR IT'S SOMETHING FAR WORSE.
ALL RIGHT, MAGIC BALLS, WHAT HAVE WE GOT?
ALERT, CRYSTAL WARRIOR ACTIVITY DETECTED IN WEIRDWORLD.
ALERT, THE DARKHOLD HAS BEEN OPENED.
ALERT, HIGH LEVEL OF WITCHCRAFT READINGS ON WUNDAGORE MOUNTAIN.
ALERT, UNKNOWN DISTURBANCE AT THE NEXUS OF ALL REALITIES.
ALERT, THE MANGOG IS COMING.
AS MAGIC SLOWLY REKINDLES AROUND THE WORLD, SO DO THE THREATS THAT COME WITH IT.
BUT I DON'T HAVE TIME FOR THIS. I DON'T HAVE TIME FOR ANY...

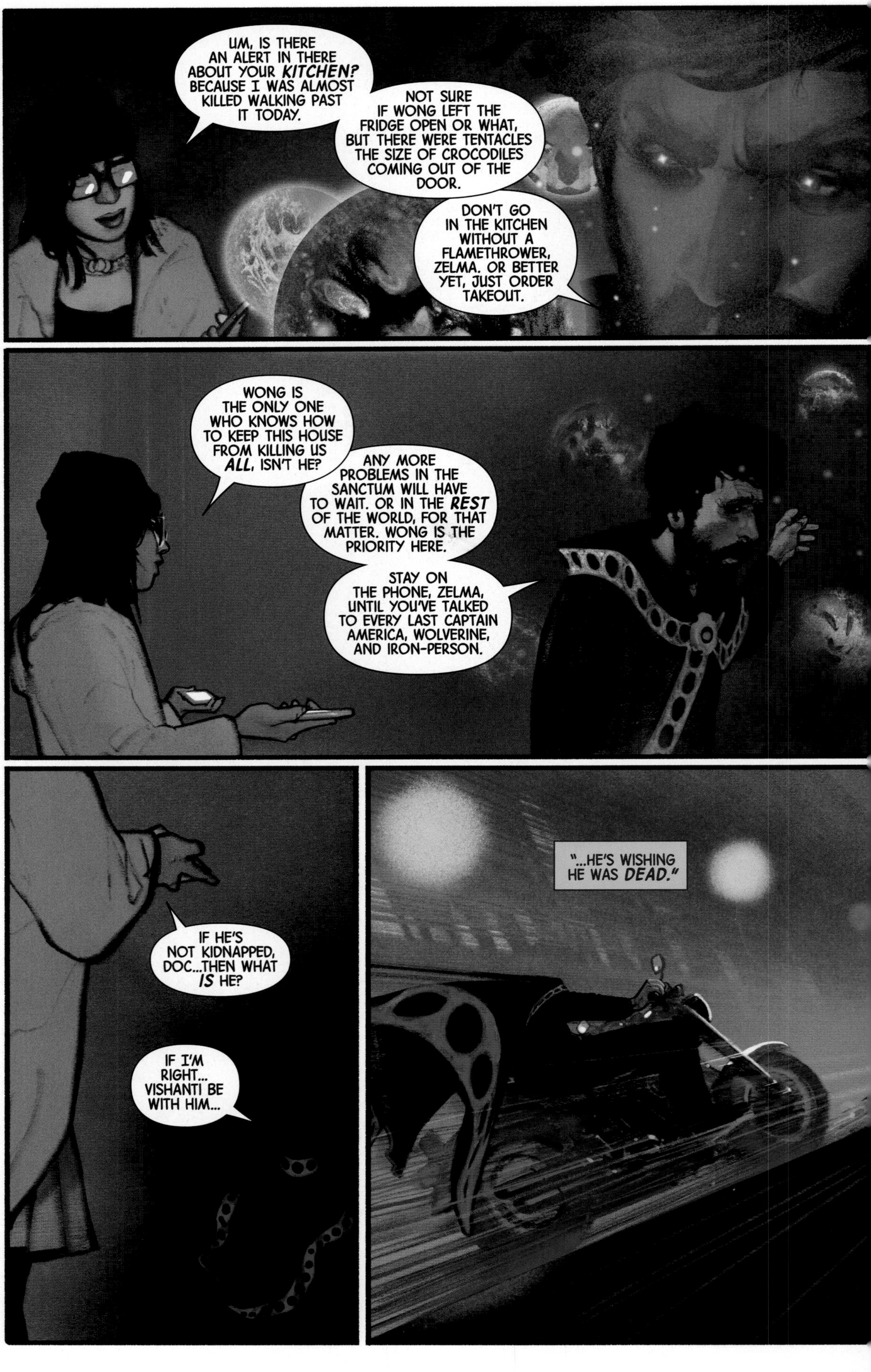
UM, IS THERE AN ALERT IN THERE ABOUT YOUR KITCHEN? BECAUSE I WAS ALMOST KILLED WALKING PAST IT TODAY.
NOT SURE IF WONG LEFT THE FRIDGE OPEN OR WHAT, BUT THERE WERE TENTACLES THE SIZE OF CROCODILES COMING OUT OF THE DOOR.
DON'T GO IN THE KITCHEN WITHOUT A FLAMETHROWER, ZELMA. OR BETTER YET, JUST ORDER TAKEOUT.
WONG IS THE ONLY ONE WHO KNOWS HOW TO KEEP THIS HOUSE FROM KILLING US ALL, ISN'T HE?
ANY MORE PROBLEMS IN THE SANCTUM WILL HAVE TO WAIT. OR IN THE REST OF THE WORLD, FOR THAT MATTER. WONG IS THE PRIORITY HERE.
STAY ON THE PHONE, ZELMA, UNTIL YOU'VE TALKED TO EVERY LAST CAPTAIN AMERICA, WOLVERINE, AND IRON-PERSON.
IF HE'S NOT KIDNAPPED, DOC...THEN WHAT IS HE?
IF I'M RIGHT... VISHANTI BE WITH HIM...
"...HE'S WISHING HE WAS DEAD."

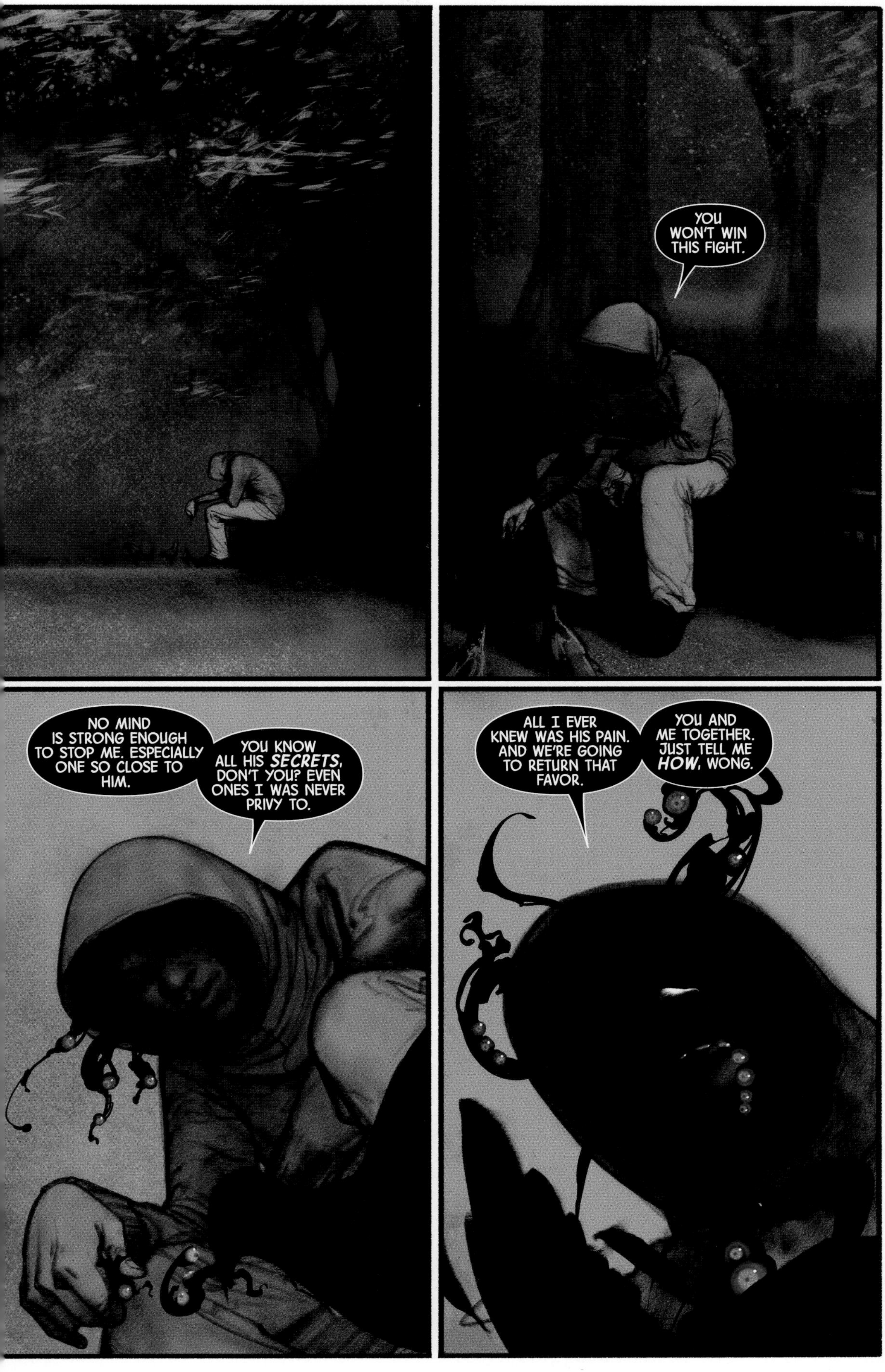
YOU WON'T WIN THIS FIGHT.
NO MIND IS STRONG ENOUGH TO STOP ME. ESPECIALLY ONE SO CLOSE TO HIM.
YOU KNOW ALL HIS SECRETS, DON'T YOU? EVEN ONES I WAS NEVER PRIVY TO.
ALL I EVER KNEW WAS HIS PAIN. AND WE'RE GOING TO RETURN THAT FAVOR.
YOU AND ME TOGETHER. JUST TELL ME HOW, WONG.

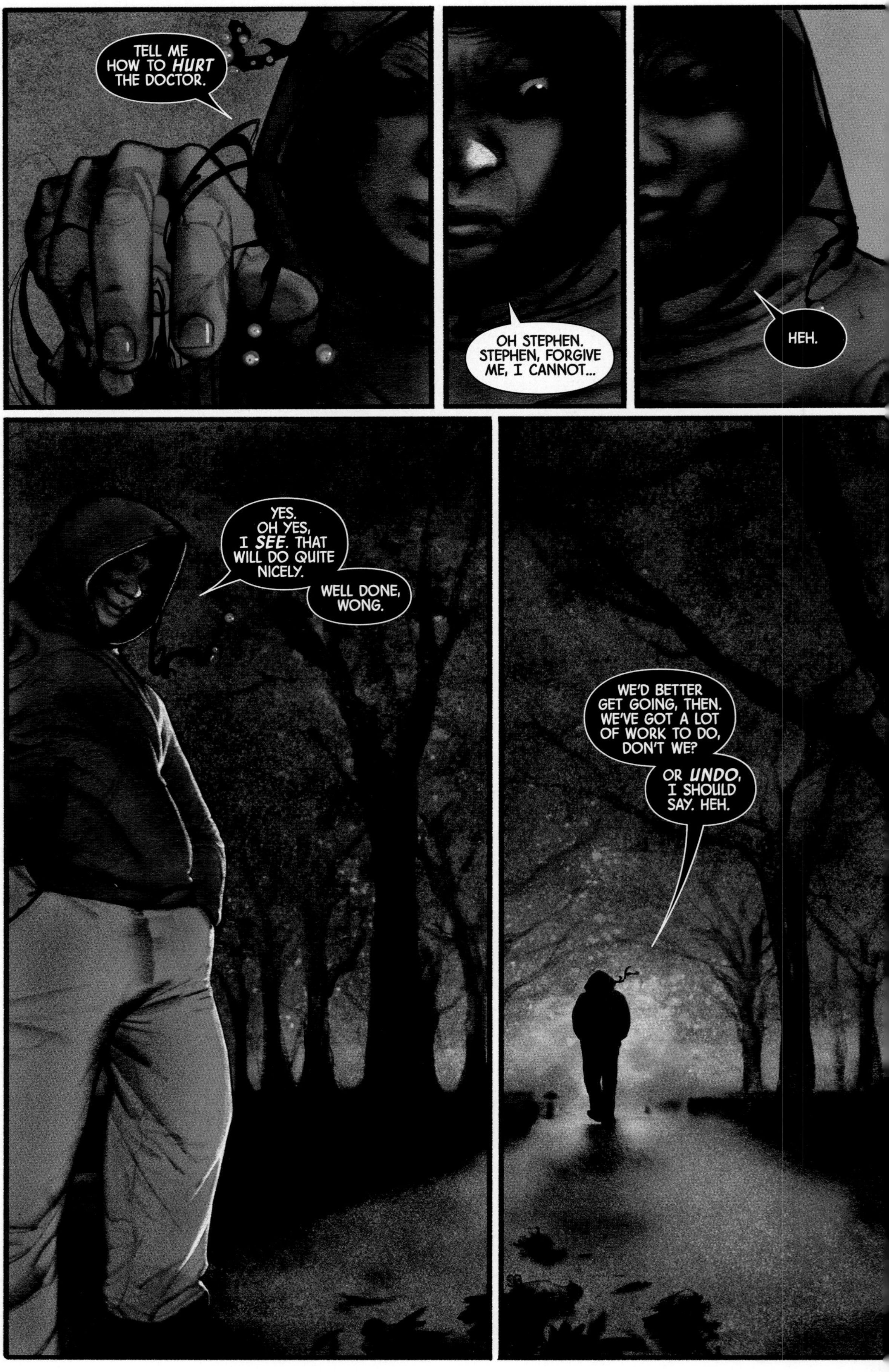
TELL ME HOW TO *HURT* THE DOCTOR.
OH STEPHEN. STEPHEN, FORGIVE ME, I CANNOT...
HEH.
YES. OH YES, I *SEE*. THAT WILL DO QUITE NICELY.
WELL DONE, WONG.
WE'D BETTER GET GOING, THEN. WE'VE GOT A LOT OF WORK TO DO, DON'T WE?
OR *UNDO*, I SHOULD SAY. HEH.

THE BAR WITH NO DOORS.

"NICE *WHEELS,* DOC! AND I IMAGINE IT'S LESS TAXING THAN A FLIGHT SPELL."

BUT, I MUST SAY, YOU NEVER STRUCK ME AS A HARLEY KINDA GUY.

IF I LIKED TO DRIVE THINGS THAT WENT SLOW, I'D STILL BE LIVING ON THE UPPER EAST SIDE AND CUTTING INTO PEOPLE'S BRAINS FOR $1,000 AN HOUR.

INSTEAD, I'M *HERE.* PLEASE TELL THIS WAS WORTH MY TIME.

WISH WE COULD, DOC. BUT NONE OF US HAVE HEARD SO MUCH AS A MYSTICAL PEEP ON THE STREETS.

NOTHING ABOUT WONG OR THIS MR. MISERY GUY.

AND, IN CASE YOU HAVEN'T NOTICED, BUSINESS IS REALLY PICKING UP OUT THERE THESE DAYS. FOR *ALL* OF US.

IN SIBERIA, IT RAIN DEAD BIRDS. THEN BIRDS COME BACK AS *ZOMBIES.* EAT BEAR. *COUNT KAOZ* HERE MISSING ALL THE FUN.

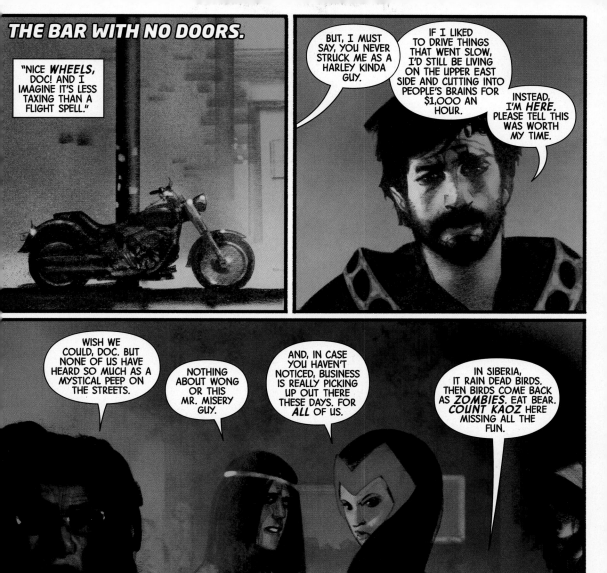

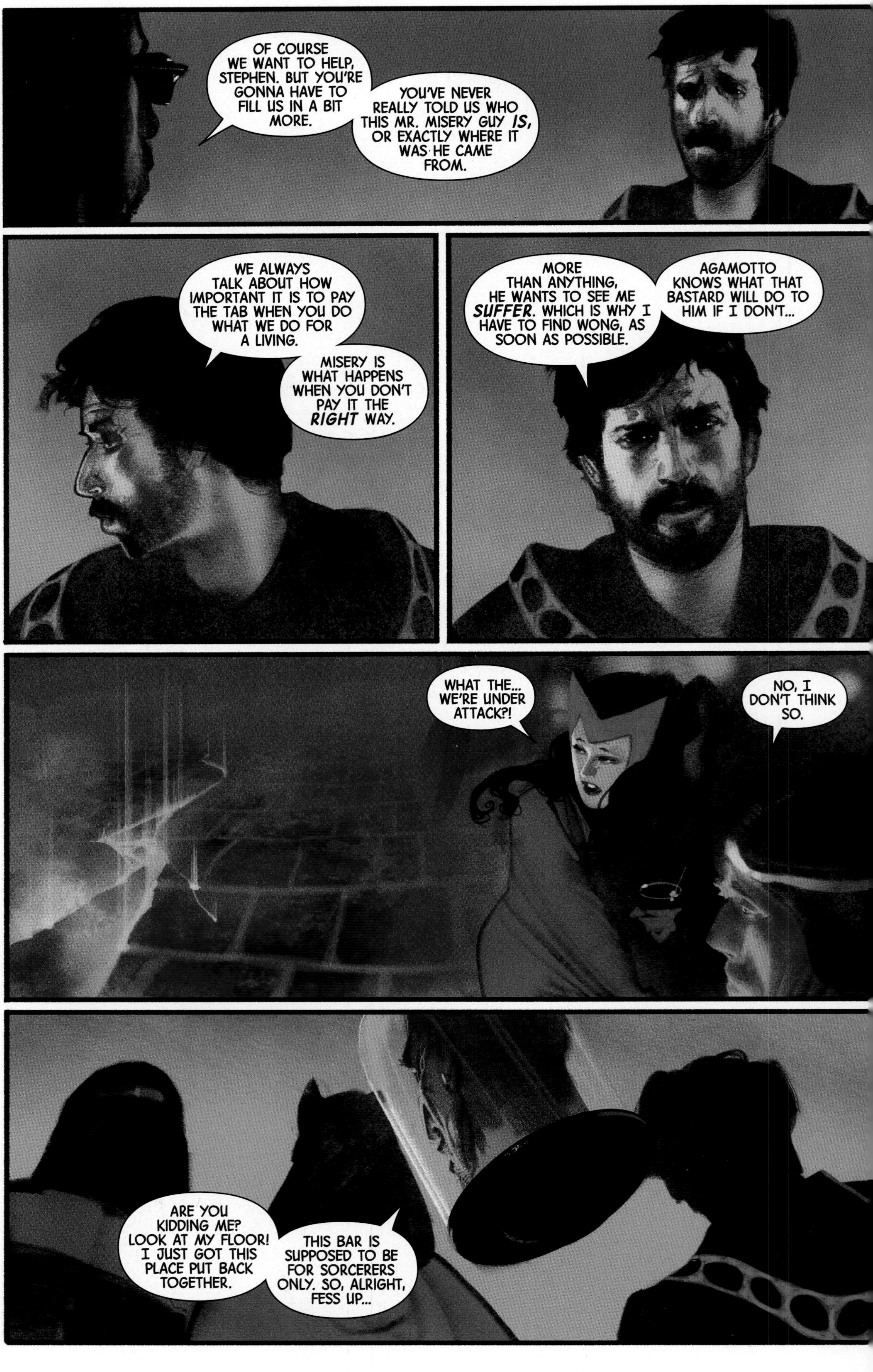
OF COURSE WE WANT TO HELP, STEPHEN. BUT YOU'RE GONNA HAVE TO FILL US IN A BIT MORE.
YOU'VE NEVER REALLY TOLD US WHO THIS MR. MISERY GUY IS, OR EXACTLY WHERE IT WAS HE CAME FROM.
WE ALWAYS TALK ABOUT HOW IMPORTANT IT IS TO PAY THE TAB WHEN YOU DO WHAT WE DO FOR A LIVING.
MISERY IS WHAT HAPPENS WHEN YOU DON'T PAY IT THE RIGHT WAY.
MORE THAN ANYTHING, HE WANTS TO SEE ME SUFFER. WHICH IS WHY I HAVE TO FIND WONG, AS SOON AS POSSIBLE.
AGAMOTTO KNOWS WHAT THAT BASTARD WILL DO TO HIM IF I DON'T...
WHAT THE... WE'RE UNDER ATTACK?!
NO, I DON'T THINK SO.
ARE YOU KIDDING ME? LOOK AT MY FLOOR! I JUST GOT THIS PLACE PUT BACK TOGETHER.
THIS BAR IS SUPPOSED TO BE FOR SORCERERS ONLY. SO, ALRIGHT, FESS UP...

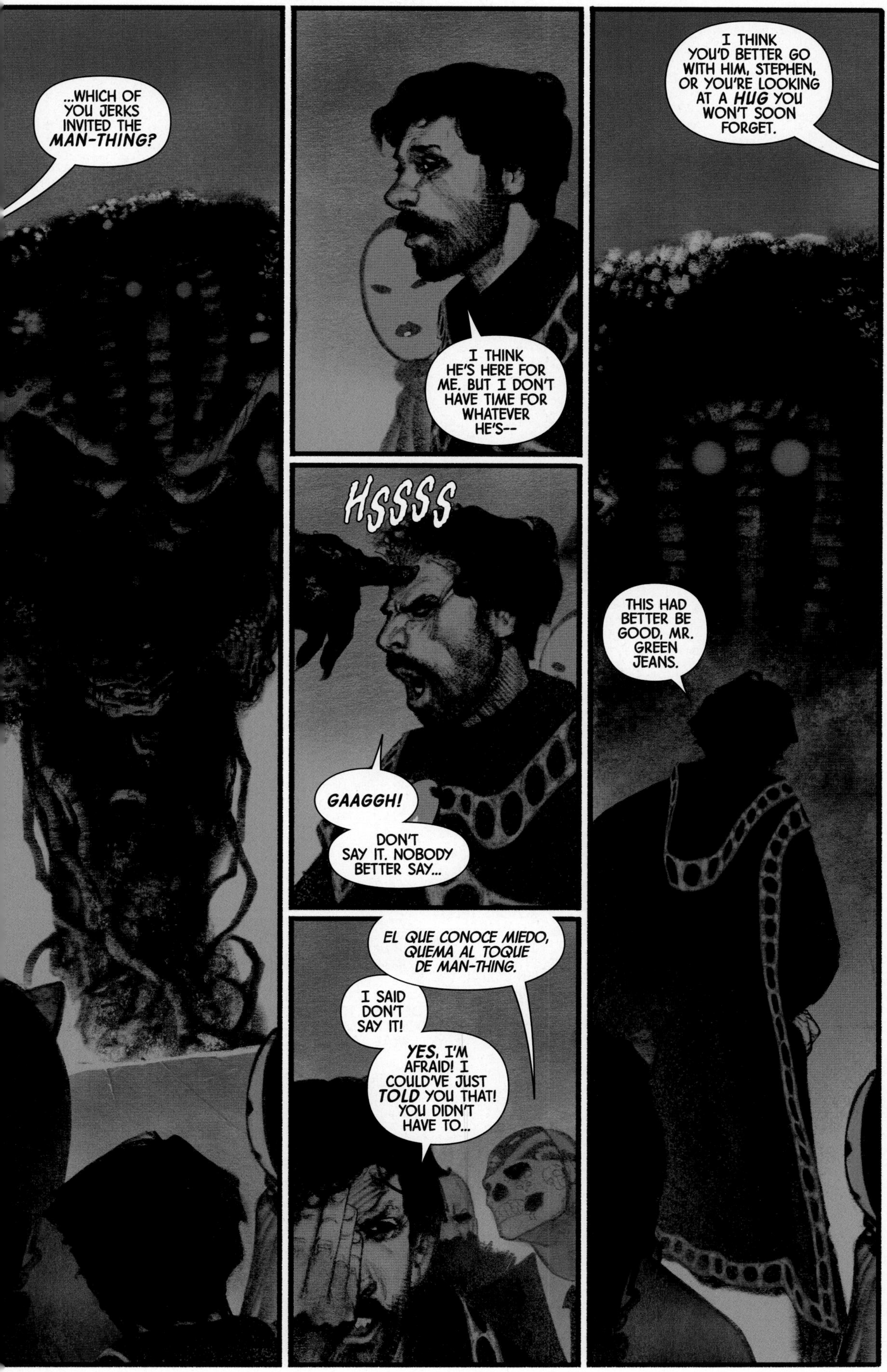
...WHICH OF YOU JERKS INVITED THE *MAN-THING?*
I THINK HE'S HERE FOR ME. BUT I DON'T HAVE TIME FOR WHATEVER HE'S--
HSSSS
GAAGGH!
DON'T SAY IT. NOBODY BETTER SAY...
EL QUE CONOCE MIEDO, QUEMA AL TOQUE DE MAN-THING.
I SAID DON'T SAY IT!
YES, I'M AFRAID! I COULD'VE JUST *TOLD* YOU THAT! YOU DIDN'T HAVE TO...
I THINK YOU'D BETTER GO WITH HIM, STEPHEN, OR YOU'RE LOOKING AT A *HUG* YOU WON'T SOON FORGET.
THIS HAD BETTER BE GOOD, MR. GREEN JEANS.

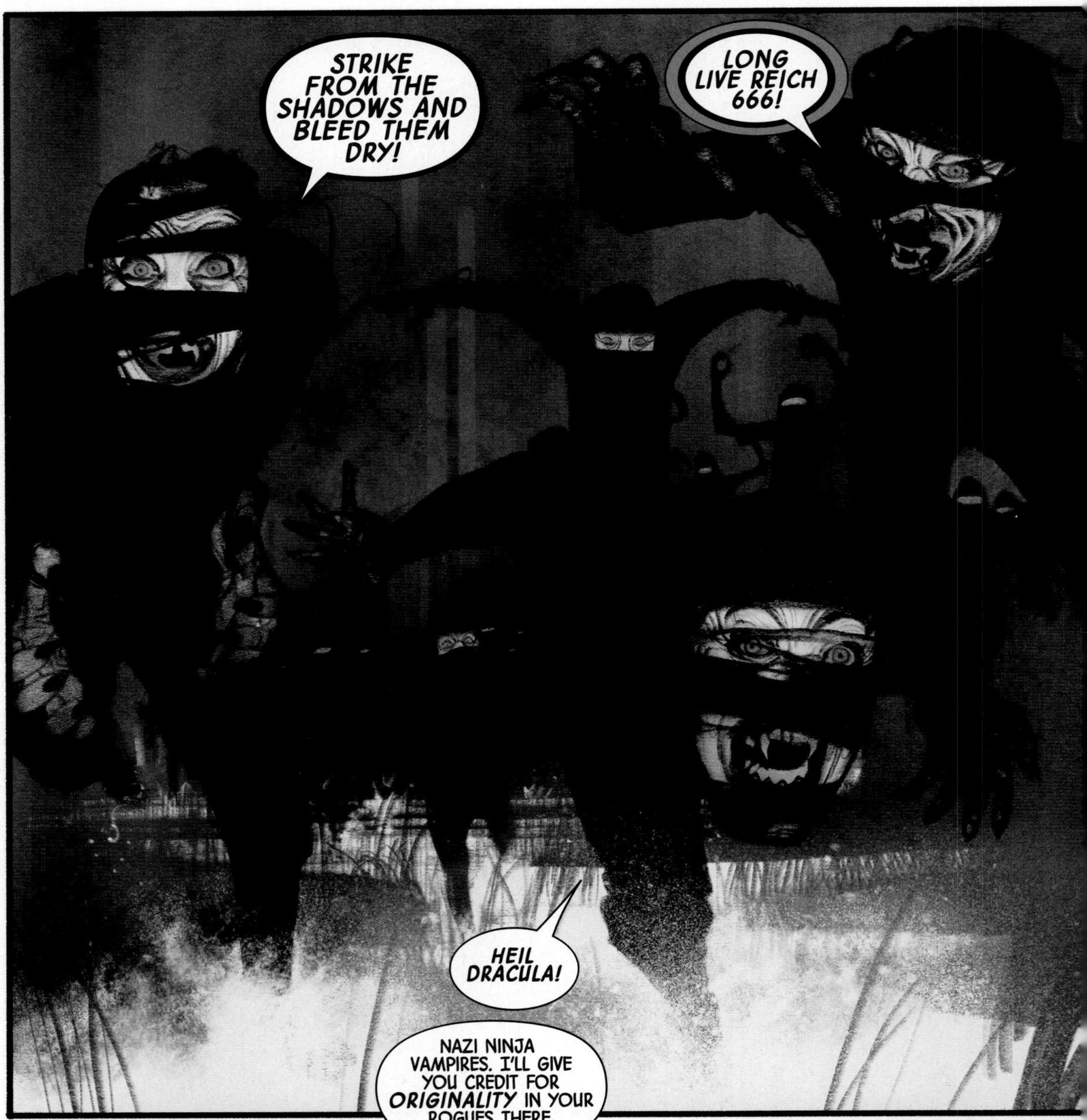
STRIKE FROM THE SHADOWS AND BLEED THEM DRY!
LONG LIVE REICH 666!
HEIL DRACULA!
NAZI NINJA VAMPIRES. I'LL GIVE YOU CREDIT FOR ORIGINALITY IN YOUR ROGUES THERE, MANNY.

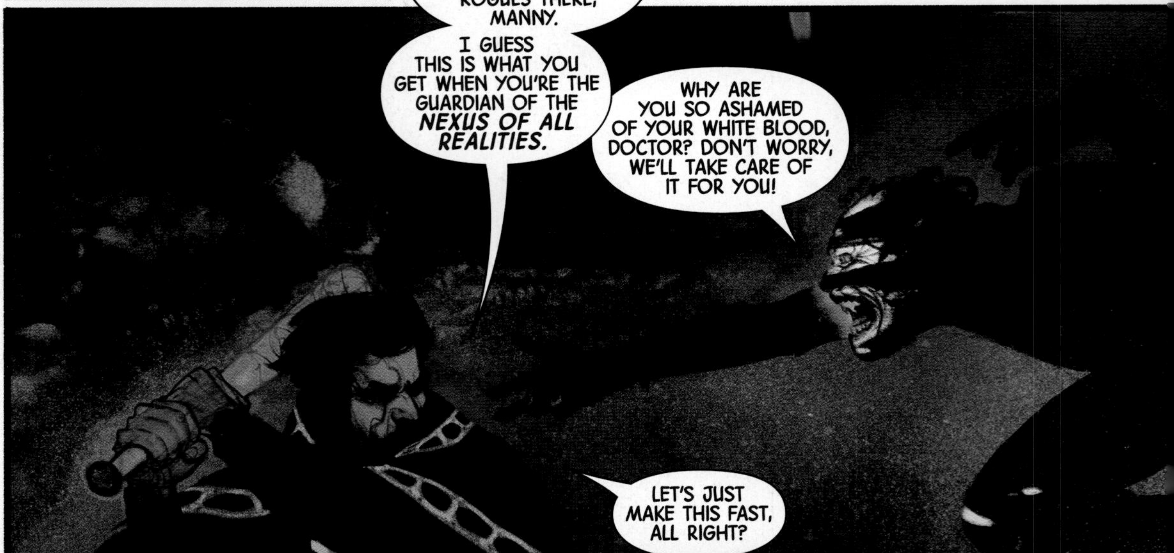
I GUESS THIS IS WHAT YOU GET WHEN YOU'RE THE GUARDIAN OF THE NEXUS OF ALL REALITIES.
WHY ARE YOU SO ASHAMED OF YOUR WHITE BLOOD, DOCTOR? DON'T WORRY, WE'LL TAKE CARE OF IT FOR YOU!
LET'S JUST MAKE THIS FAST, ALL RIGHT?

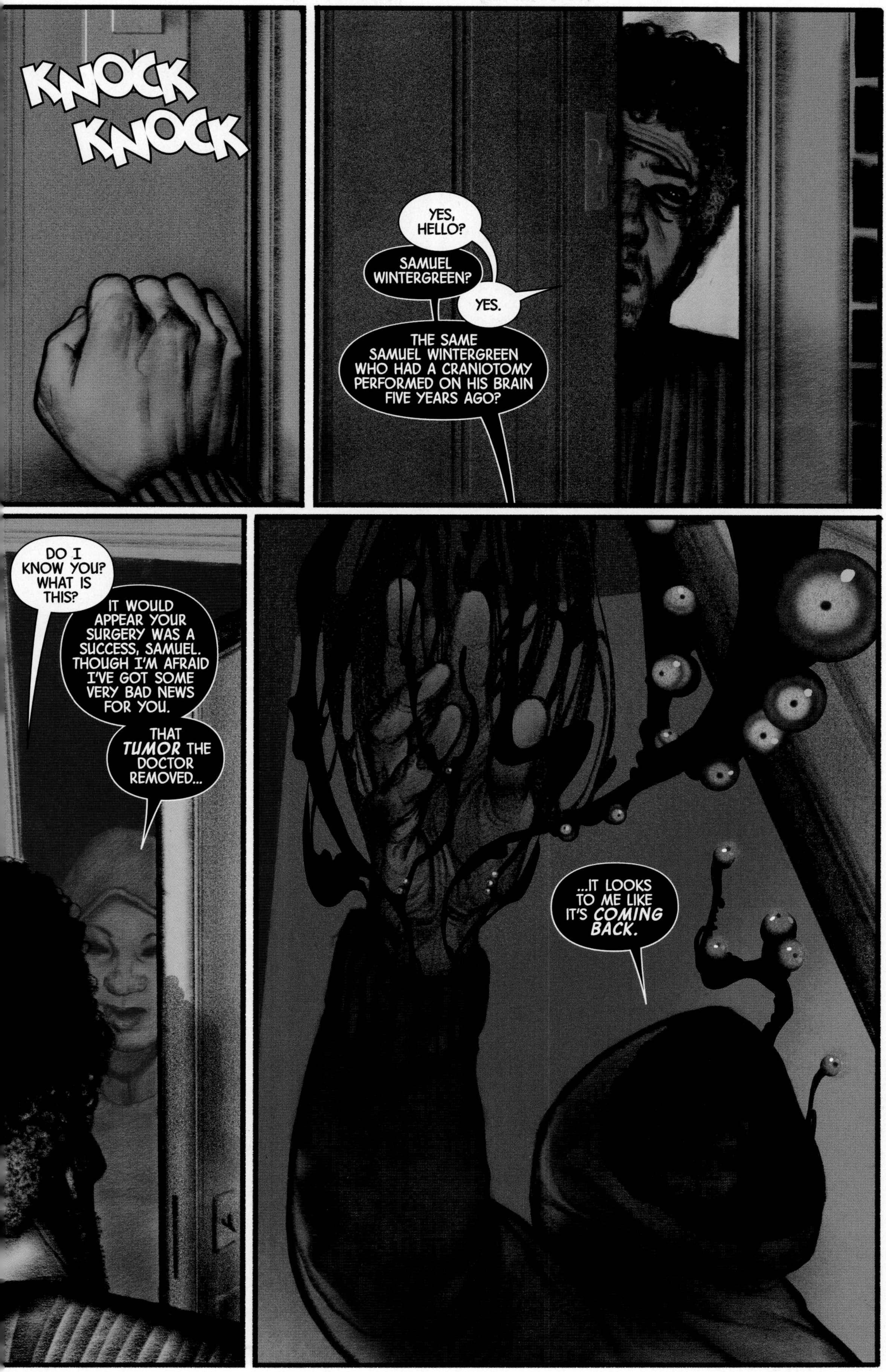
KNOCK KNOCK
YES, HELLO?
SAMUEL WINTERGREEN?
YES.
THE SAME SAMUEL WINTERGREEN WHO HAD A CRANIOTOMY PERFORMED ON HIS BRAIN FIVE YEARS AGO?
DO I KNOW YOU? WHAT IS THIS?
IT WOULD APPEAR YOUR SURGERY WAS A SUCCESS, SAMUEL. THOUGH I'M AFRAID I'VE GOT SOME VERY BAD NEWS FOR YOU.
THAT *TUMOR* THE DOCTOR REMOVED...
...IT LOOKS TO ME LIKE IT'S *COMING BACK.*

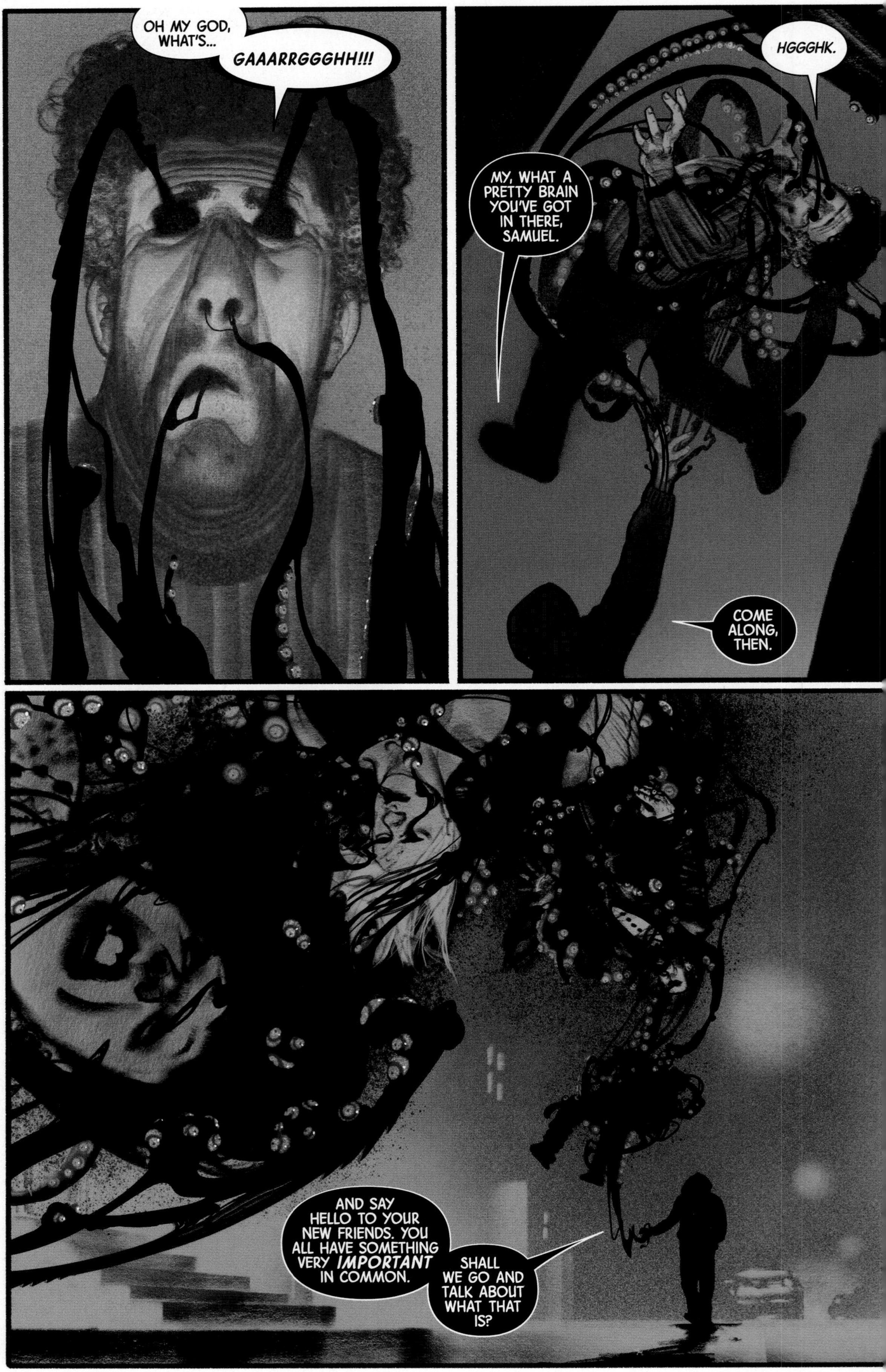
OH MY GOD, WHAT'S...
GAAARRGGGHH!!!
HGGGHK.
MY, WHAT A PRETTY BRAIN YOU'VE GOT IN THERE, SAMUEL.
COME ALONG, THEN.
AND SAY HELLO TO YOUR NEW FRIENDS. YOU ALL HAVE SOMETHING VERY IMPORTANT IN COMMON.
SHALL WE GO AND TALK ABOUT WHAT THAT IS?

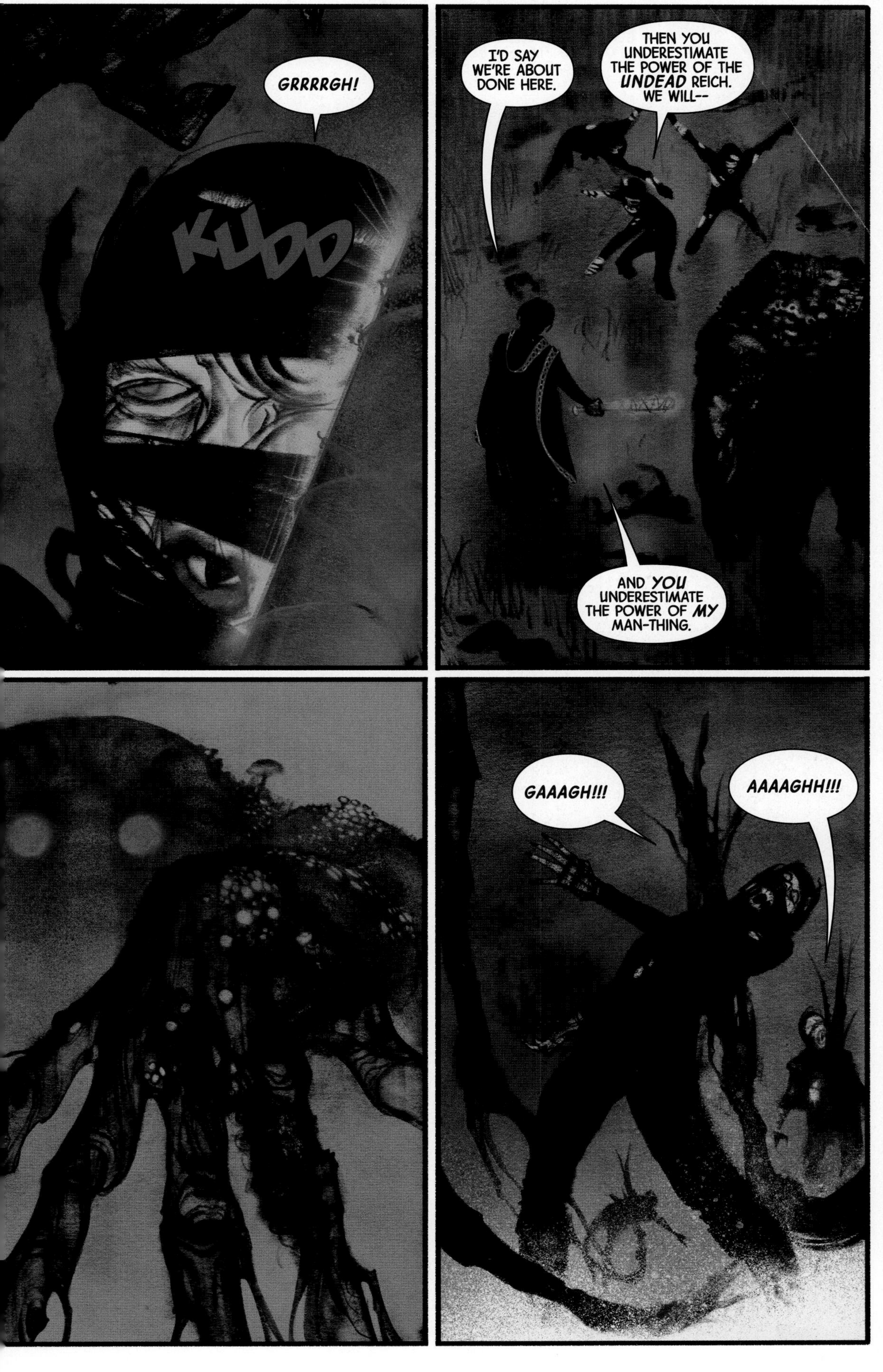
GRRRRGH!
KLUDD
I'D SAY WE'RE ABOUT DONE HERE.
THEN YOU UNDERESTIMATE THE POWER OF THE *UNDEAD* REICH. WE WILL--
AND *YOU* UNDERESTIMATE THE POWER OF *MY* MAN-THING.
GAAAGH!!!
AAAAGHH!!!

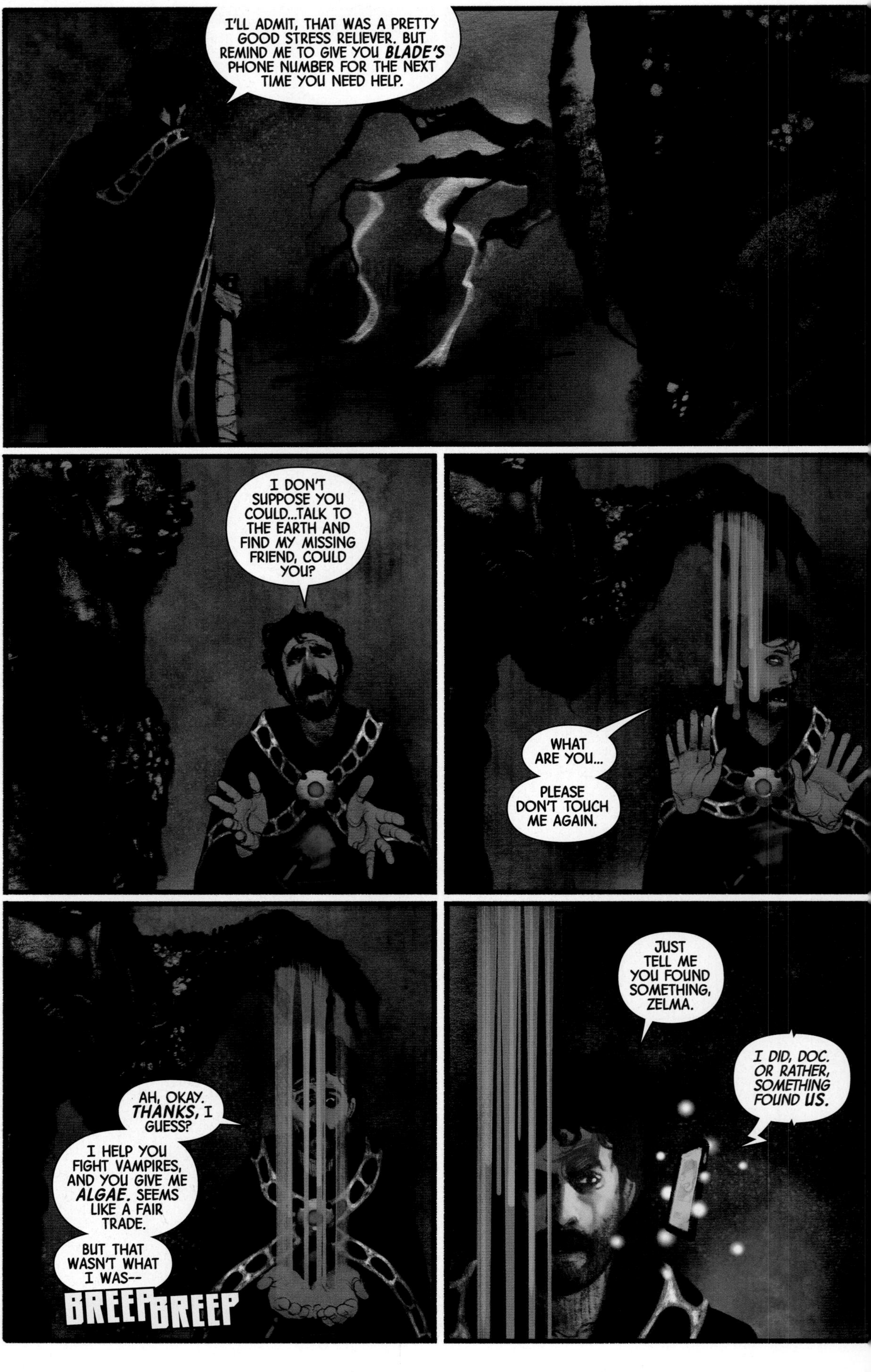
I'LL ADMIT, THAT WAS A PRETTY GOOD STRESS RELIEVER. BUT REMIND ME TO GIVE YOU BLADE'S PHONE NUMBER FOR THE NEXT TIME YOU NEED HELP.
I DON'T SUPPOSE YOU COULD...TALK TO THE EARTH AND FIND MY MISSING FRIEND, COULD YOU?
WHAT ARE YOU...
PLEASE DON'T TOUCH ME AGAIN.
AH, OKAY. THANKS, I GUESS?
I HELP YOU FIGHT VAMPIRES, AND YOU GIVE ME ALGAE. SEEMS LIKE A FAIR TRADE.
BUT THAT WASN'T WHAT I WAS--
BREEP BREEP
JUST TELL ME YOU FOUND SOMETHING, ZELMA.
I DID, DOC. OR RATHER, SOMETHING FOUND US.

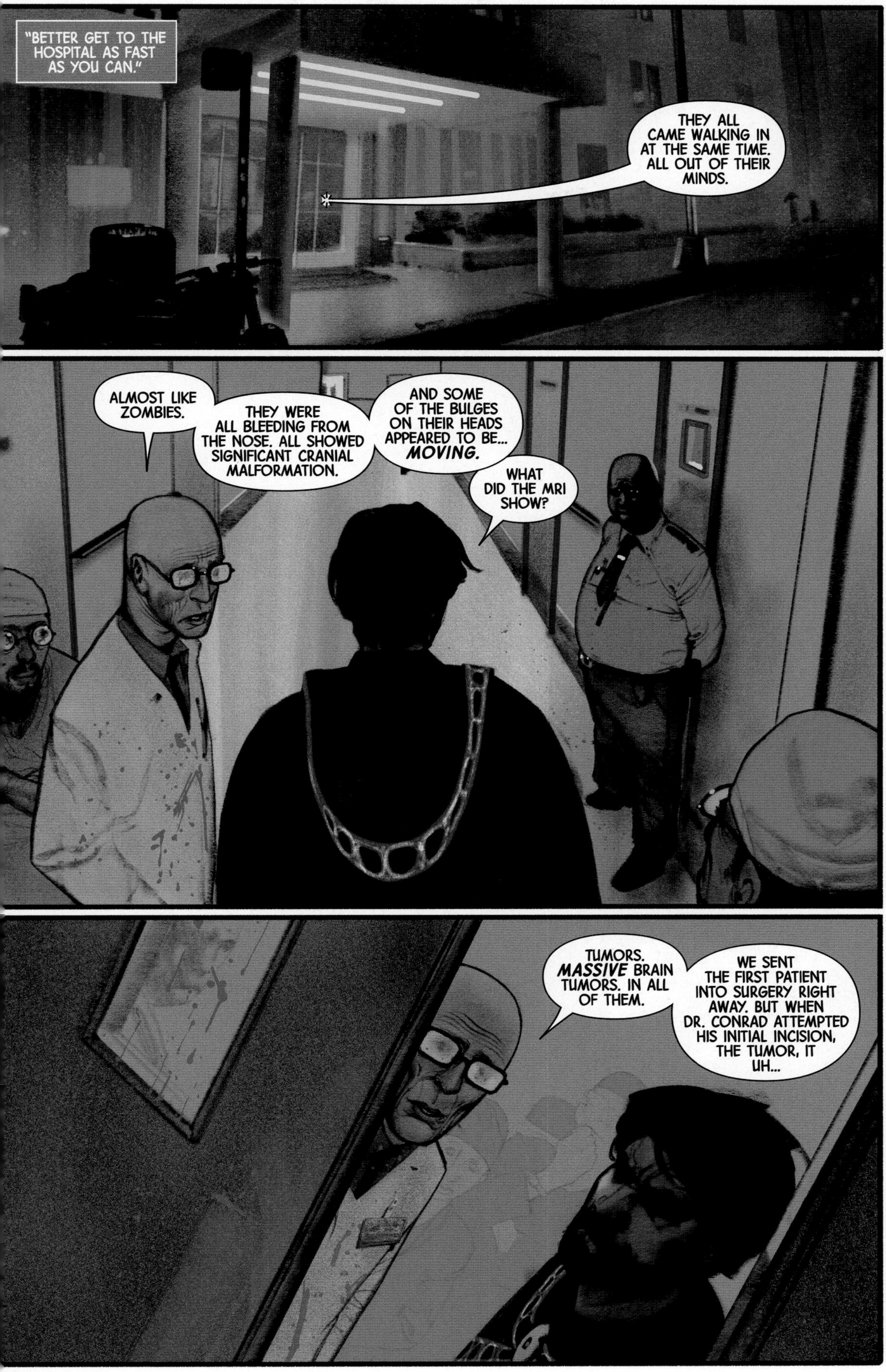
"BETTER GET TO THE HOSPITAL AS FAST AS YOU CAN."
THEY ALL CAME WALKING IN AT THE SAME TIME. ALL OUT OF THEIR MINDS.
ALMOST LIKE ZOMBIES.
THEY WERE ALL BLEEDING FROM THE NOSE. ALL SHOWED SIGNIFICANT CRANIAL MALFORMATION.
AND SOME OF THE BULGES ON THEIR HEADS APPEARED TO BE... MOVING.
WHAT DID THE MRI SHOW?
TUMORS. MASSIVE BRAIN TUMORS. IN ALL OF THEM.
WE SENT THE FIRST PATIENT INTO SURGERY RIGHT AWAY. BUT WHEN DR. CONRAD ATTEMPTED HIS INITIAL INCISION, THE TUMOR, IT UH...

...IT FOUGHT BACK.

VISHANTI BE WITH HIM.

BY THAT POINT, WE'D, UH... WE'D DISCOVERED THERE WAS A *CONNECTION* BETWEEN THE PATIENTS.

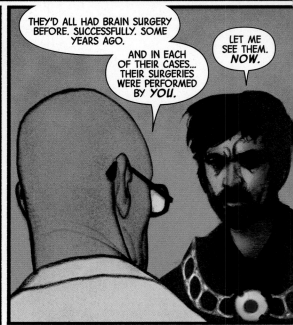

THEY'D ALL HAD BRAIN SURGERY BEFORE. SUCCESSFULLY. SOME YEARS AGO.

AND IN EACH OF THEIR CASES... THEIR SURGERIES WERE PERFORMED BY *YOU.*

LET ME SEE THEM. *NOW.*

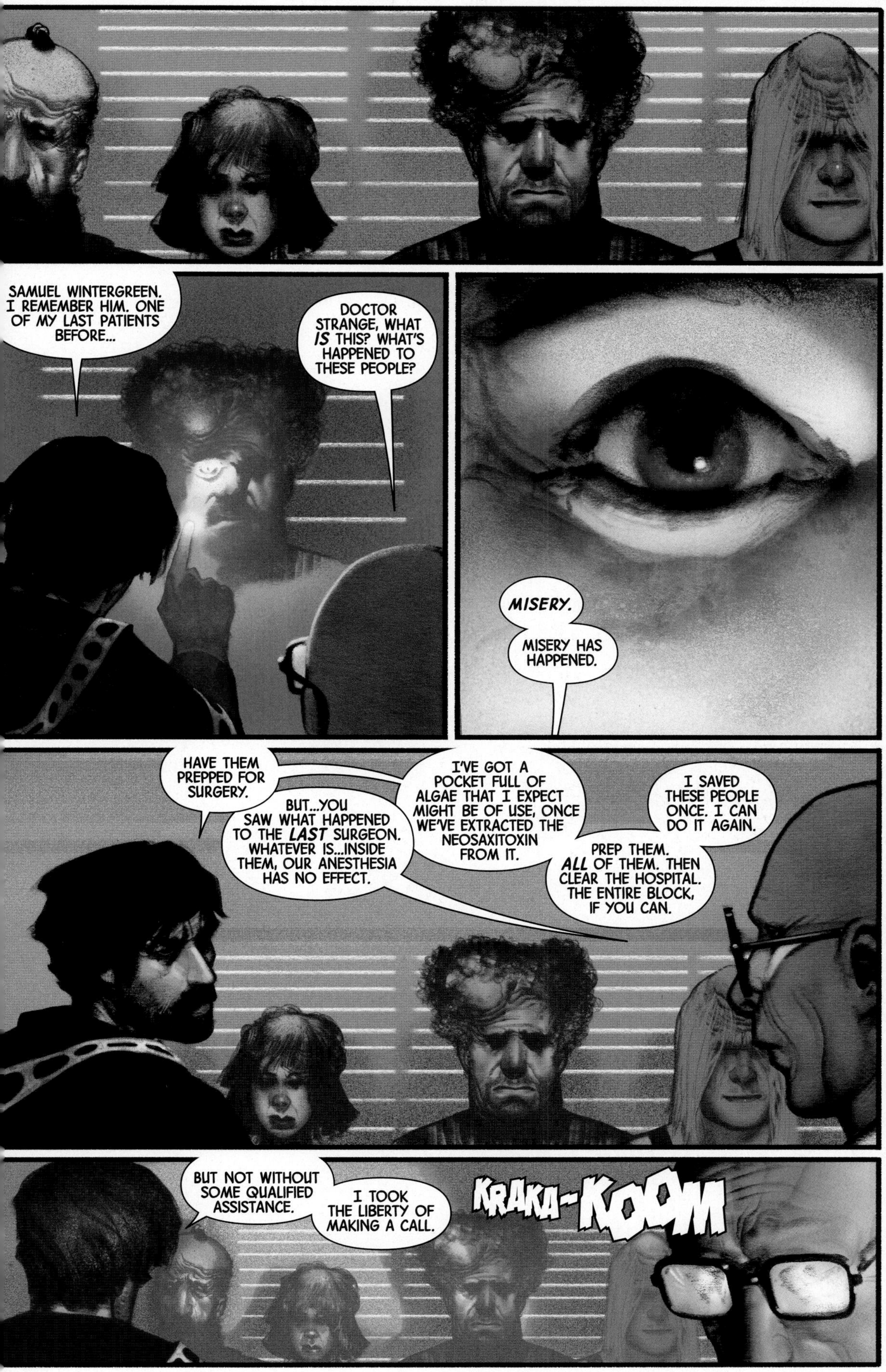
SAMUEL WINTERGREEN. I REMEMBER HIM. ONE OF MY LAST PATIENTS BEFORE...
DOCTOR STRANGE, WHAT *IS* THIS? WHAT'S HAPPENED TO THESE PEOPLE?
MISERY.
MISERY HAS HAPPENED.
HAVE THEM PREPPED FOR SURGERY.
BUT...YOU SAW WHAT HAPPENED TO THE *LAST* SURGEON. WHATEVER IS...INSIDE THEM, OUR ANESTHESIA HAS NO EFFECT.
I'VE GOT A POCKET FULL OF ALGAE THAT I EXPECT MIGHT BE OF USE, ONCE WE'VE EXTRACTED THE NEOSAXITOXIN FROM IT.
I SAVED THESE PEOPLE ONCE. I CAN DO IT AGAIN.
PREP THEM. *ALL* OF THEM. THEN CLEAR THE HOSPITAL. THE ENTIRE BLOCK, IF YOU CAN.
BUT NOT WITHOUT SOME QUALIFIED ASSISTANCE.
I TOOK THE LIBERTY OF MAKING A CALL.
KRAKA-KOOM

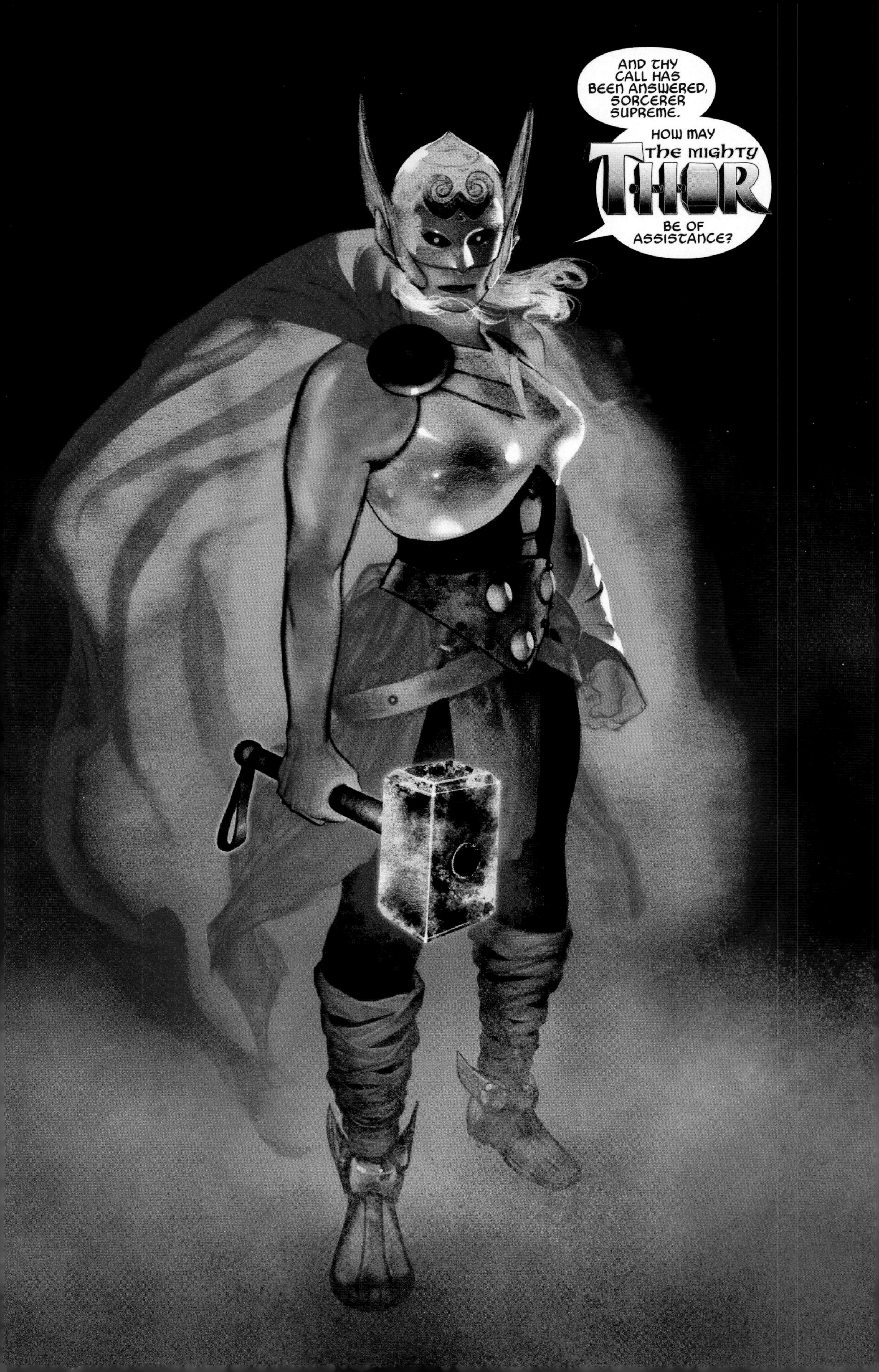
AND THY CALL HAS BEEN ANSWERED, SORCERER SUPREME.
HOW MAY THE MIGHTY THOR BE OF ASSISTANCE?

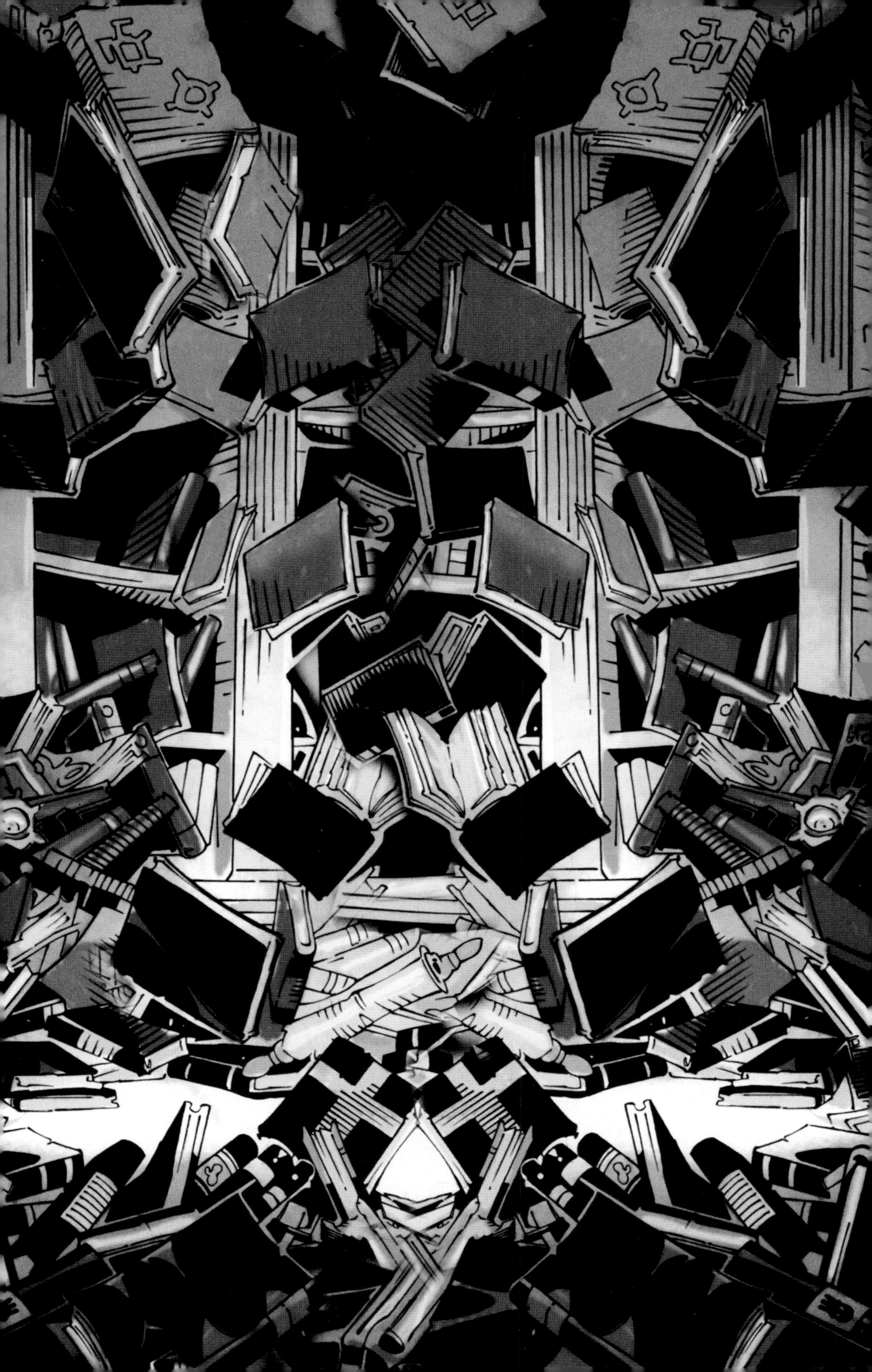

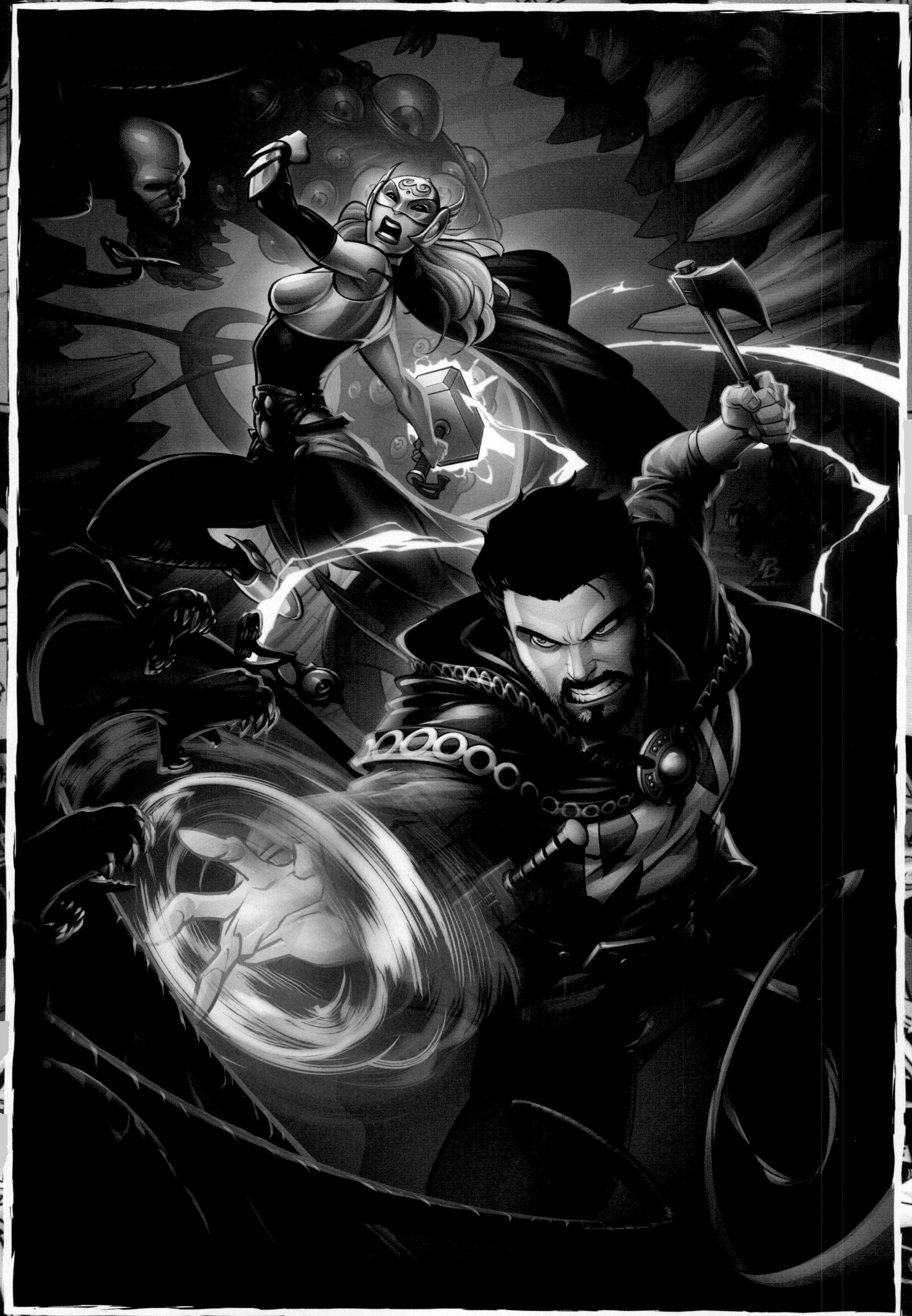

DOCTOR STRANGE THE WORLD'S FINEST SUPER-SURGEONS

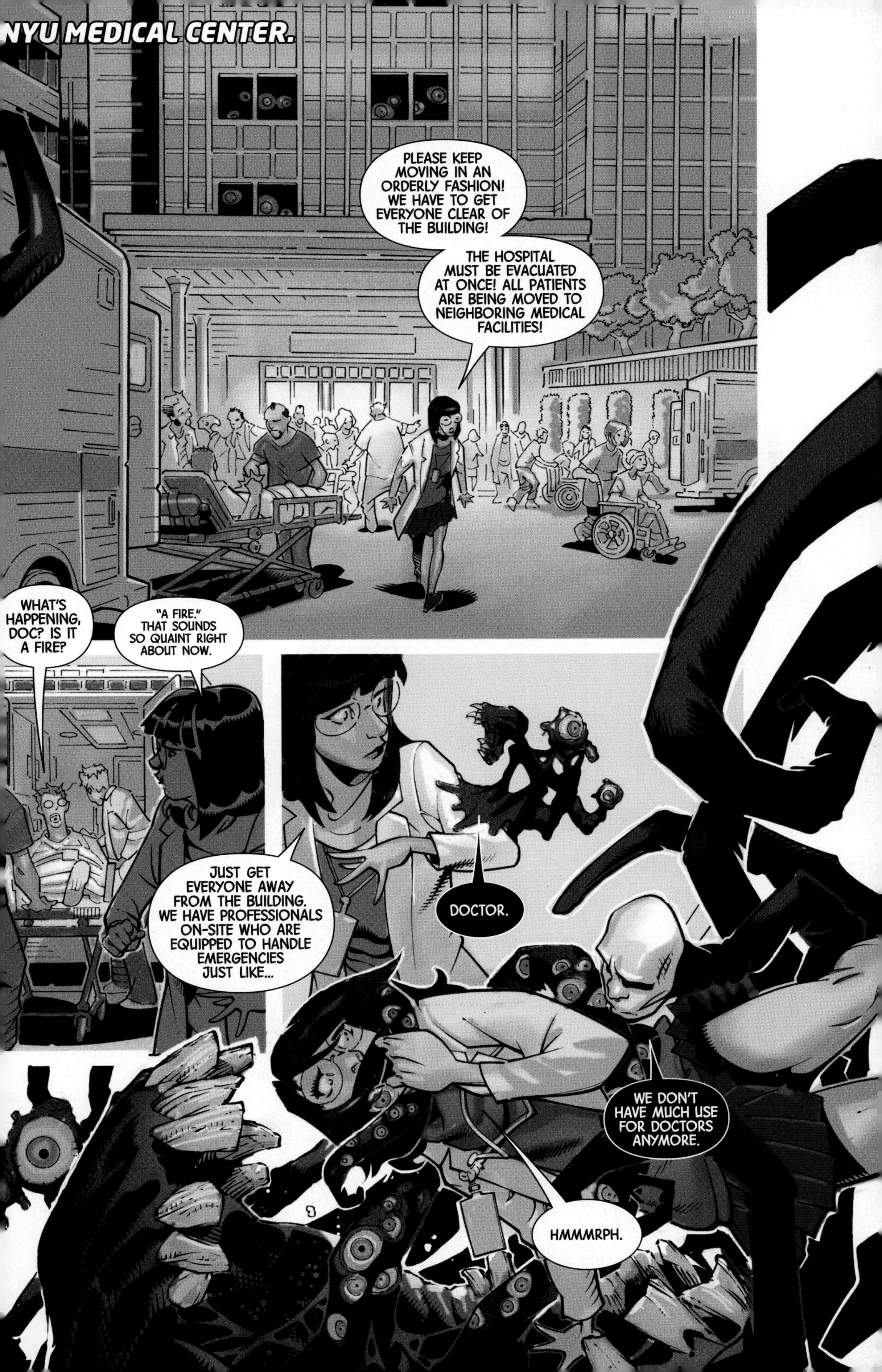
NYU MEDICAL CENTER.
PLEASE KEEP MOVING IN AN ORDERLY FASHION! WE HAVE TO GET EVERYONE CLEAR OF THE BUILDING!
THE HOSPITAL MUST BE EVACUATED AT ONCE! ALL PATIENTS ARE BEING MOVED TO NEIGHBORING MEDICAL FACILITIES!
WHAT'S HAPPENING, DOC? IS IT A FIRE?
"A FIRE." THAT SOUNDS SO QUAINT RIGHT ABOUT NOW.
JUST GET EVERYONE AWAY FROM THE BUILDING. WE HAVE PROFESSIONALS ON-SITE WHO ARE EQUIPPED TO HANDLE EMERGENCIES JUST LIKE...
DOCTOR.
WE DON'T HAVE MUCH USE FOR DOCTORS ANYMORE.
HMMMRPH.

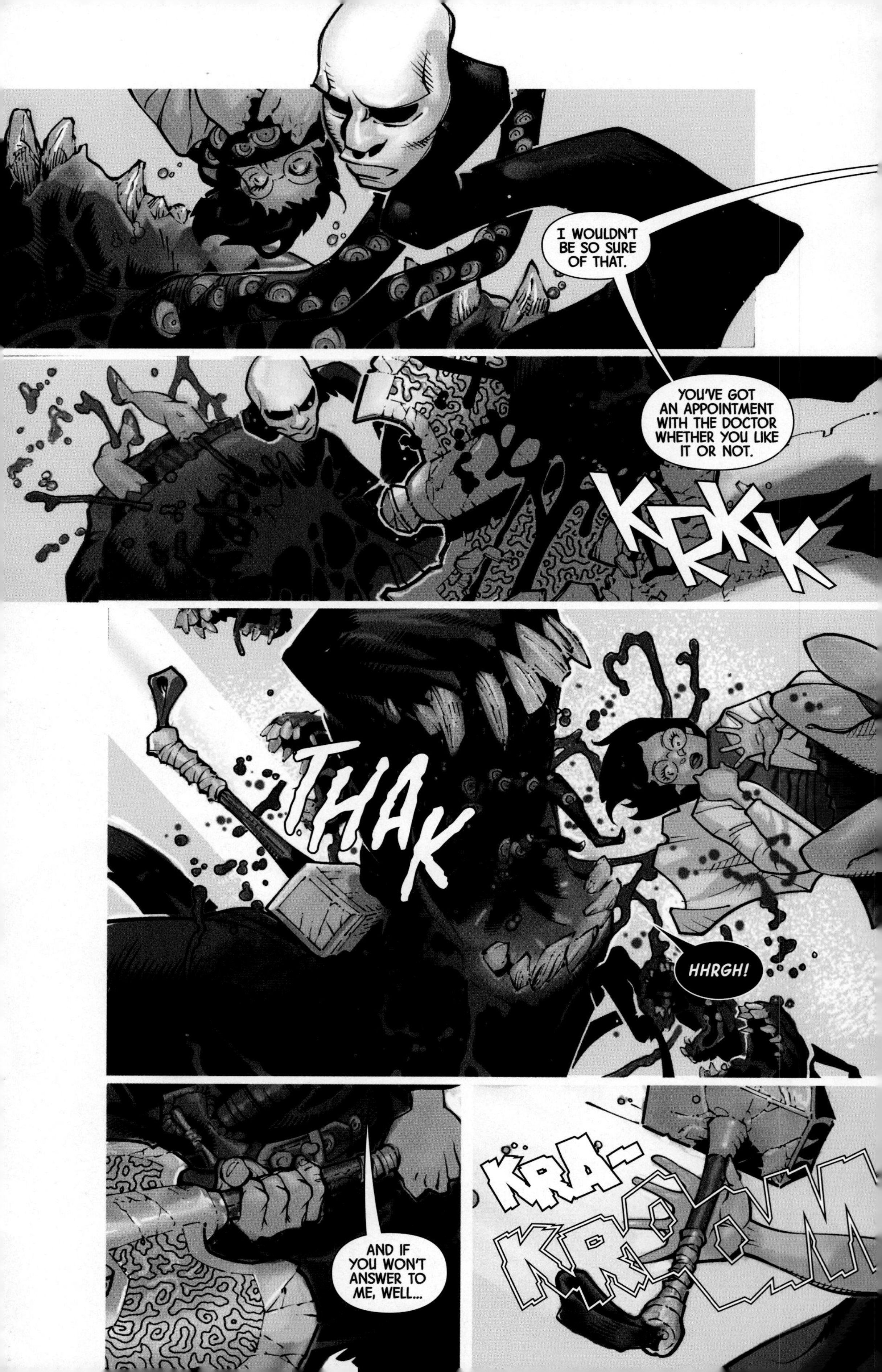
I WOULDN'T BE SO SURE OF THAT.
YOU'VE GOT AN APPOINTMENT WITH THE DOCTOR WHETHER YOU LIKE IT OR NOT.
KRKK
THAK
HHRGH!
AND IF YOU WON'T ANSWER TO ME, WELL...
KRA-KROOM

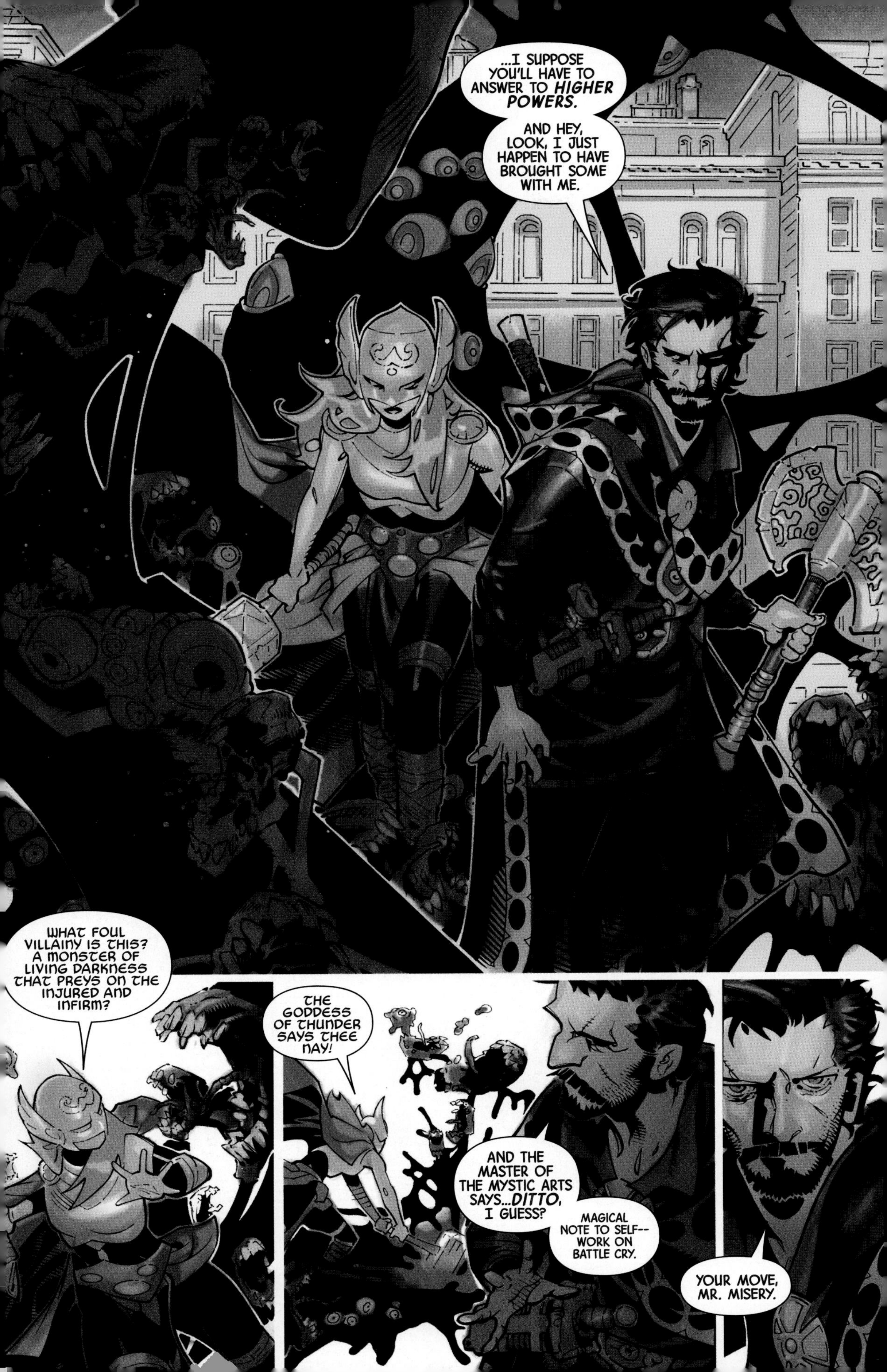
...I SUPPOSE YOU'LL HAVE TO ANSWER TO *HIGHER POWERS.*
AND HEY, LOOK, I JUST HAPPEN TO HAVE BROUGHT SOME WITH ME.
WHAT FOUL VILLAINY IS THIS? A MONSTER OF LIVING DARKNESS THAT PREYS ON THE INJURED AND INFIRM?
THE GODDESS OF THUNDER SAYS THEE NAY!
AND THE MASTER OF THE MYSTIC ARTS SAYS...*DITTO,* I GUESS?
MAGICAL NOTE TO SELF-- WORK ON BATTLE CRY.
YOUR MOVE, MR. MISERY.

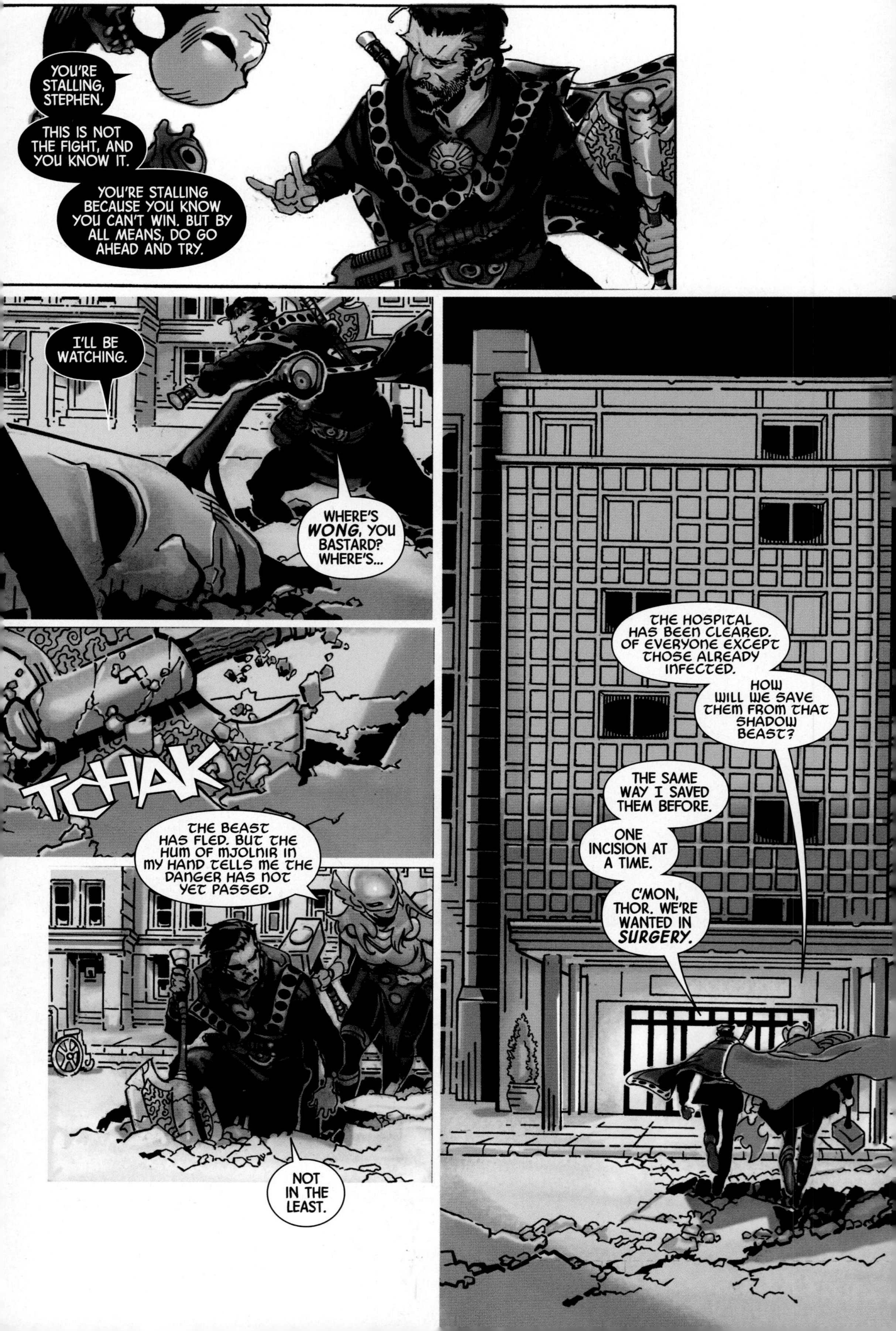
YOU'RE STALLING, STEPHEN.
THIS IS NOT THE FIGHT, AND YOU KNOW IT.
YOU'RE STALLING BECAUSE YOU KNOW YOU CAN'T WIN. BUT BY ALL MEANS, DO GO AHEAD AND TRY.
I'LL BE WATCHING.
WHERE'S WONG, YOU BASTARD? WHERE'S...
TCHAK
THE BEAST HAS FLED. BUT THE HUM OF MJOLNIR IN MY HAND TELLS ME THE DANGER HAS NOT YET PASSED.
NOT IN THE LEAST.
THE HOSPITAL HAS BEEN CLEARED OF EVERYONE EXCEPT THOSE ALREADY INFECTED.
HOW WILL WE SAVE THEM FROM THAT SHADOW BEAST?
THE SAME WAY I SAVED THEM BEFORE.
ONE INCISION AT A TIME.
C'MON, THOR. WE'RE WANTED IN SURGERY.

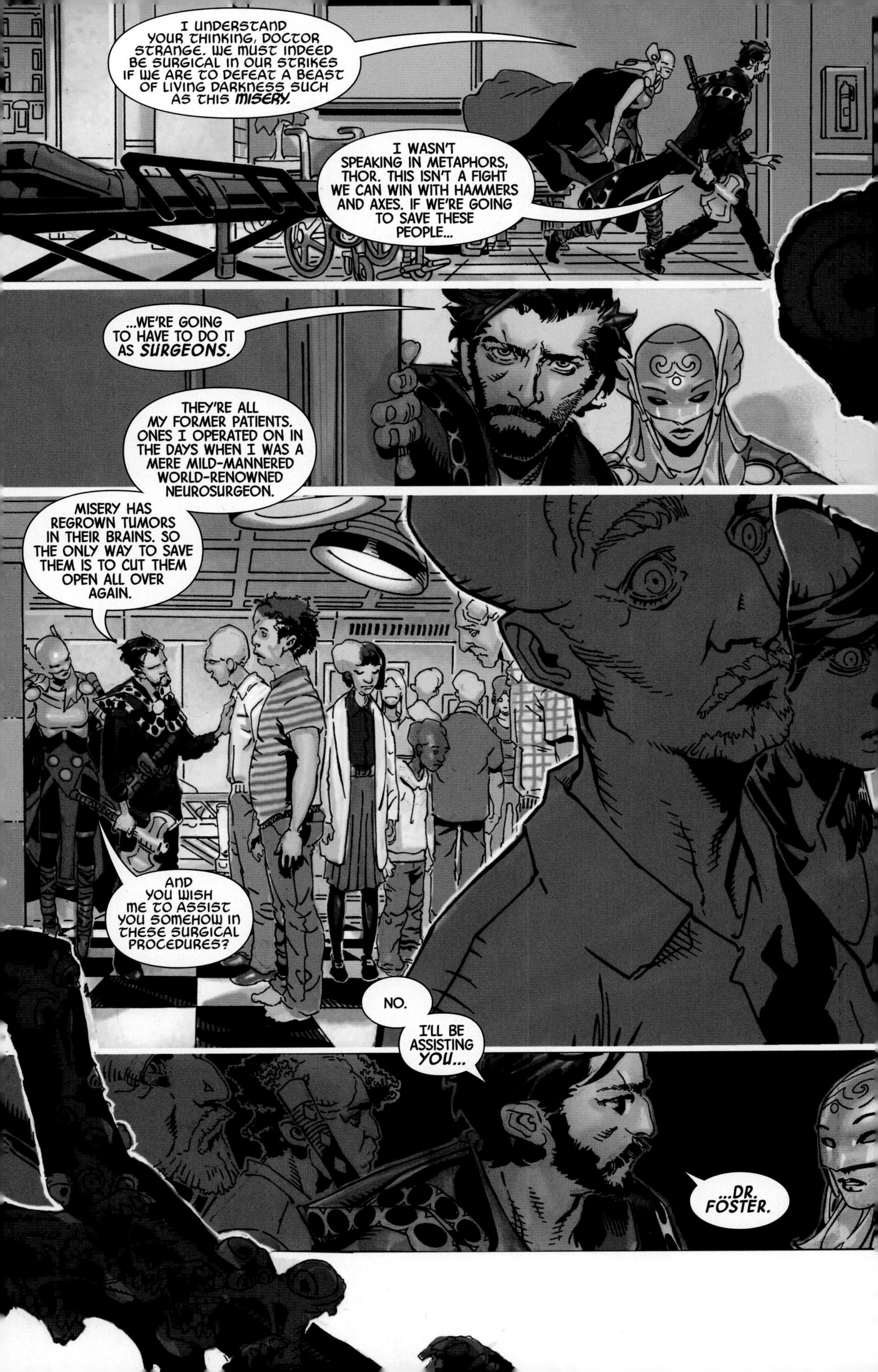
I UNDERSTAND YOUR THINKING, DOCTOR STRANGE. WE MUST INDEED BE SURGICAL IN OUR STRIKES IF WE ARE TO DEFEAT A BEAST OF LIVING DARKNESS SUCH AS THIS MISERY.
I WASN'T SPEAKING IN METAPHORS, THOR. THIS ISN'T A FIGHT WE CAN WIN WITH HAMMERS AND AXES. IF WE'RE GOING TO SAVE THESE PEOPLE...
...WE'RE GOING TO HAVE TO DO IT AS SURGEONS.
THEY'RE ALL MY FORMER PATIENTS. ONES I OPERATED ON IN THE DAYS WHEN I WAS A MERE MILD-MANNERED WORLD-RENOWNED NEUROSURGEON.
MISERY HAS REGROWN TUMORS IN THEIR BRAINS. SO THE ONLY WAY TO SAVE THEM IS TO CUT THEM OPEN ALL OVER AGAIN.
AND YOU WISH ME TO ASSIST YOU SOMEHOW IN THESE SURGICAL PROCEDURES?
NO.
I'LL BE ASSISTING YOU...
...DR. FOSTER.

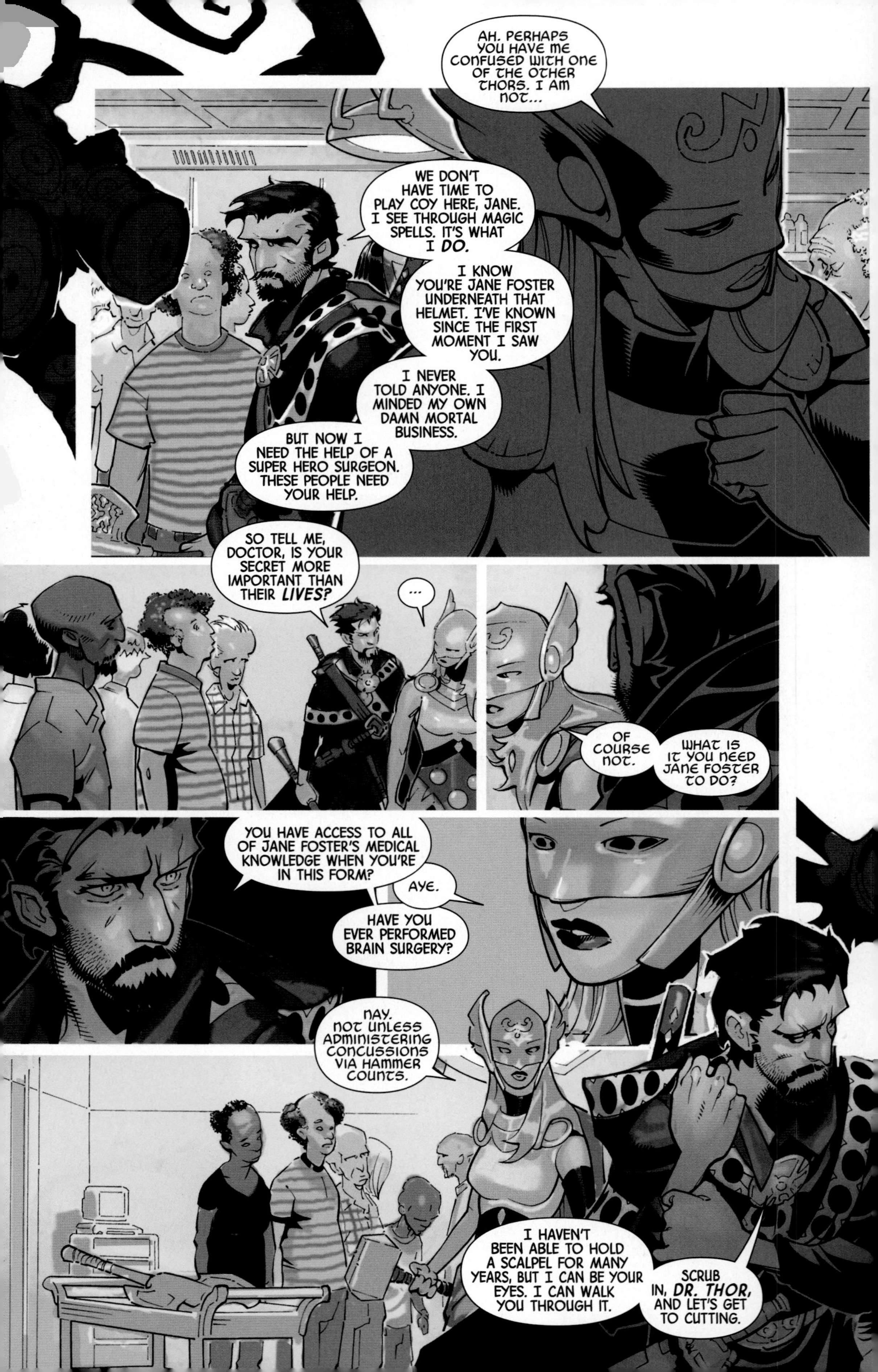
AH. PERHAPS YOU HAVE ME CONFUSED WITH ONE OF THE OTHER THORS. I AM NOT...
WE DON'T HAVE TIME TO PLAY COY HERE, JANE. I SEE THROUGH MAGIC SPELLS. IT'S WHAT I DO.
I KNOW YOU'RE JANE FOSTER UNDERNEATH THAT HELMET. I'VE KNOWN SINCE THE FIRST MOMENT I SAW YOU.
I NEVER TOLD ANYONE. I MINDED MY OWN DAMN MORTAL BUSINESS.
BUT NOW I NEED THE HELP OF A SUPER HERO SURGEON. THESE PEOPLE NEED YOUR HELP.
SO TELL ME, DOCTOR, IS YOUR SECRET MORE IMPORTANT THAN THEIR LIVES?
...
OF COURSE NOT.
WHAT IS IT YOU NEED JANE FOSTER TO DO?
YOU HAVE ACCESS TO ALL OF JANE FOSTER'S MEDICAL KNOWLEDGE WHEN YOU'RE IN THIS FORM?
AYE.
HAVE YOU EVER PERFORMED BRAIN SURGERY?
NAY. NOT UNLESS ADMINISTERING CONCUSSIONS VIA HAMMER COUNTS.
I HAVEN'T BEEN ABLE TO HOLD A SCALPEL FOR MANY YEARS, BUT I CAN BE YOUR EYES. I CAN WALK YOU THROUGH IT.
SCRUB IN, DR. THOR, AND LET'S GET TO CUTTING.

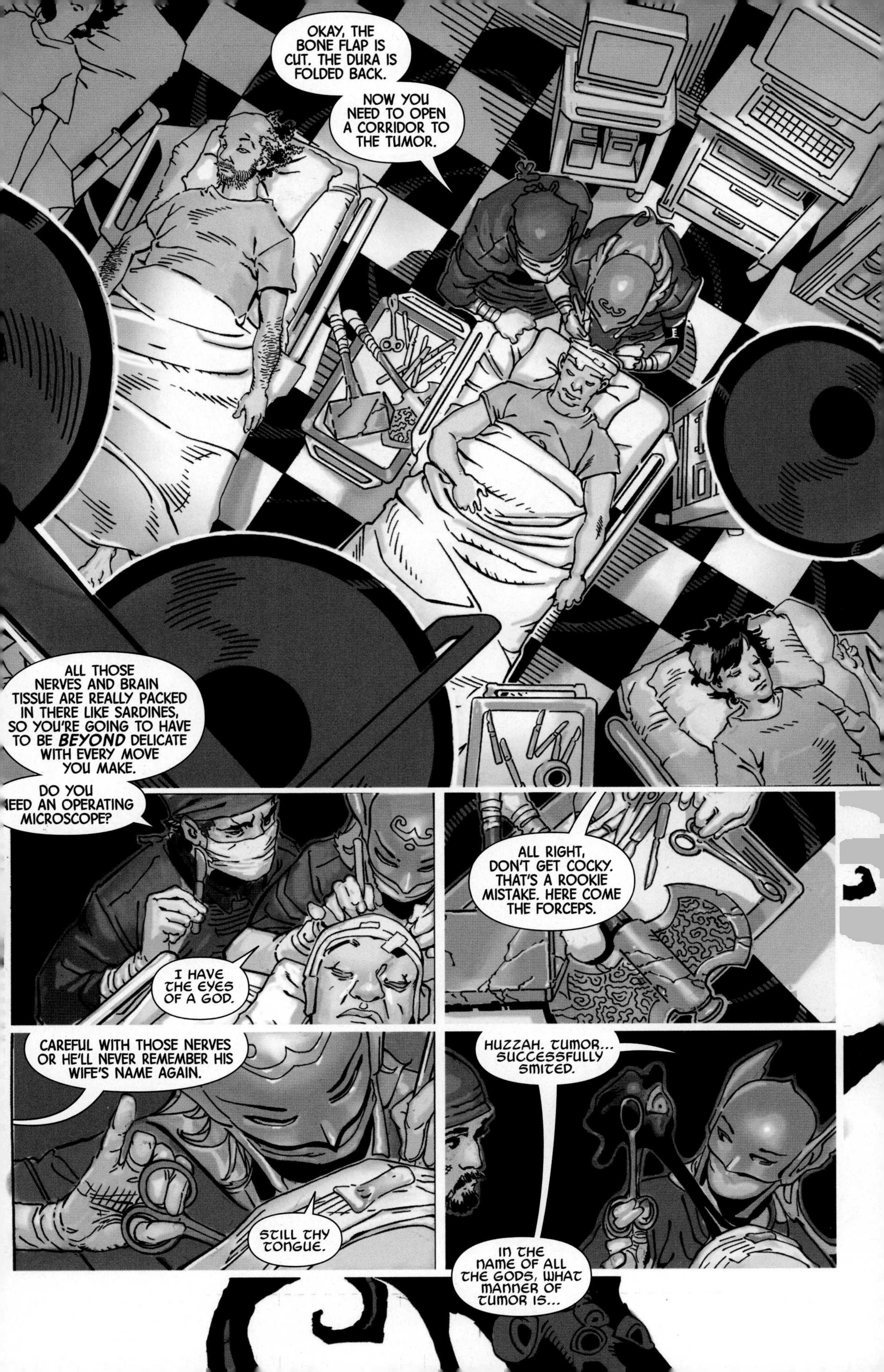
OKAY, THE BONE FLAP IS CUT. THE DURA IS FOLDED BACK.
NOW YOU NEED TO OPEN A CORRIDOR TO THE TUMOR.
ALL THOSE NERVES AND BRAIN TISSUE ARE REALLY PACKED IN THERE LIKE SARDINES, SO YOU'RE GOING TO HAVE TO BE *BEYOND* DELICATE WITH EVERY MOVE YOU MAKE.
DO YOU NEED AN OPERATING MICROSCOPE?
I HAVE THE EYES OF A GOD.
ALL RIGHT, DON'T GET COCKY. THAT'S A ROOKIE MISTAKE. HERE COME THE FORCEPS.
CAREFUL WITH THOSE NERVES OR HE'LL NEVER REMEMBER HIS WIFE'S NAME AGAIN.
STILL THY TONGUE.
HUZZAH. TUMOR... SUCCESSFULLY SMITED.
IN THE NAME OF ALL THE GODS, WHAT MANNER OF TUMOR IS...

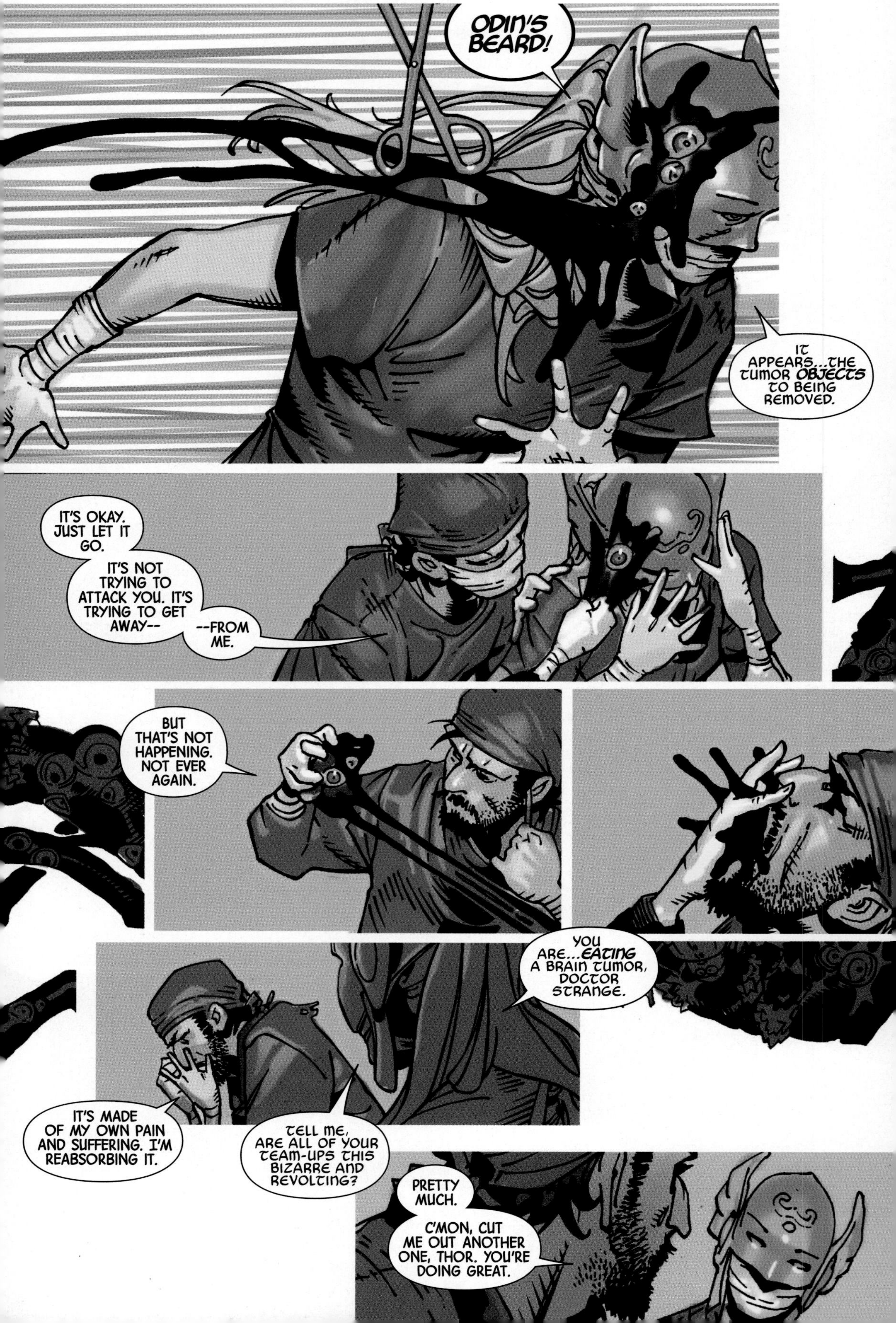
ODIN'S BEARD!
IT APPEARS...THE TUMOR OBJECTS TO BEING REMOVED.
IT'S OKAY. JUST LET IT GO.
IT'S NOT TRYING TO ATTACK YOU. IT'S TRYING TO GET AWAY--
--FROM ME.
BUT THAT'S NOT HAPPENING. NOT EVER AGAIN.
YOU ARE...EATING A BRAIN TUMOR, DOCTOR STRANGE.
IT'S MADE OF MY OWN PAIN AND SUFFERING. I'M REABSORBING IT.
TELL ME, ARE ALL OF YOUR TEAM-UPS THIS BIZARRE AND REVOLTING?
PRETTY MUCH.
C'MON, CUT ME OUT ANOTHER ONE, THOR. YOU'RE DOING GREAT.

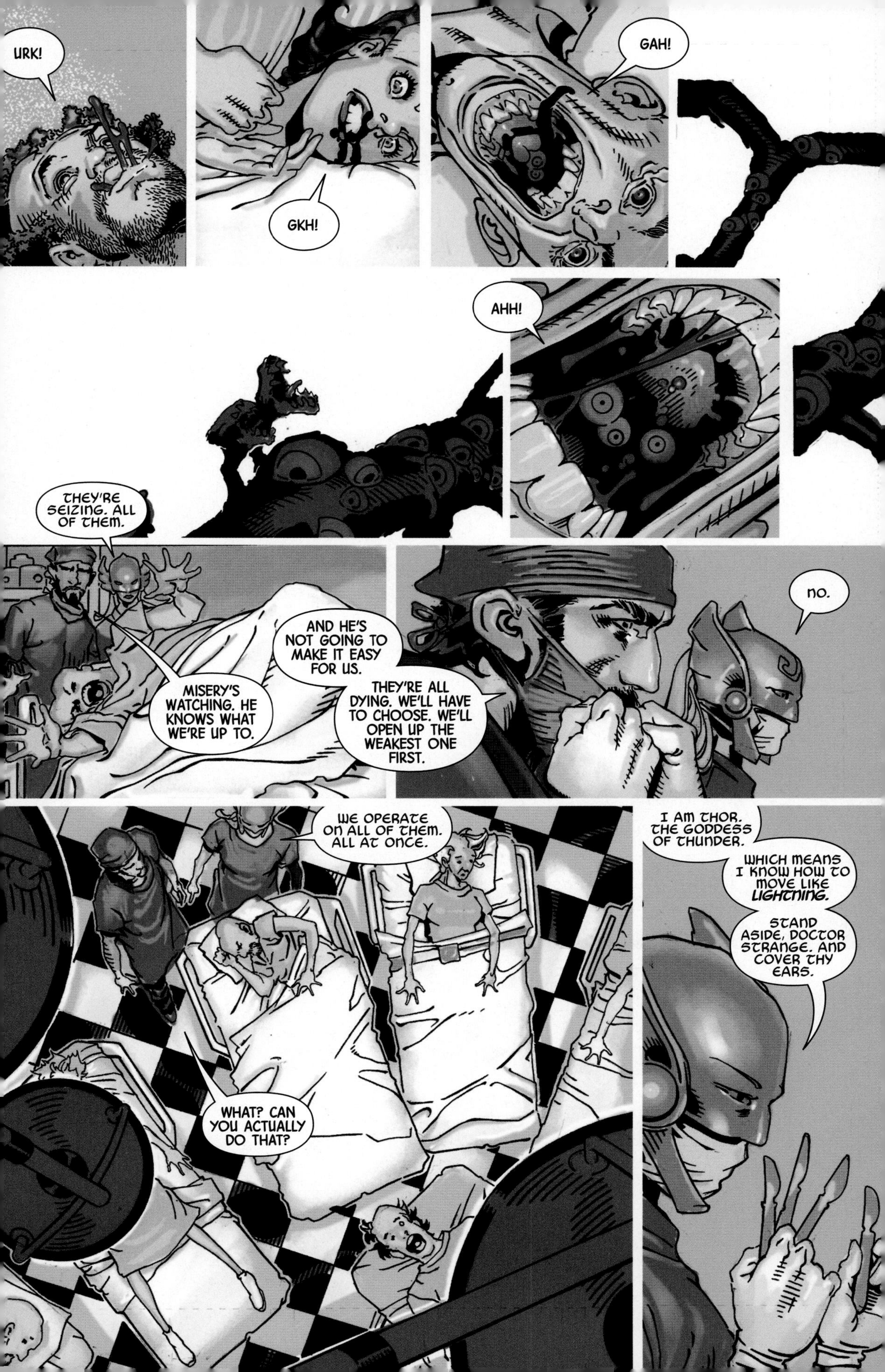
URK!
GKH!
GAH!
AHH!
THEY'RE SEIZING. ALL OF THEM.
MISERY'S WATCHING. HE KNOWS WHAT WE'RE UP TO.
AND HE'S NOT GOING TO MAKE IT EASY FOR US.
THEY'RE ALL DYING. WE'LL HAVE TO CHOOSE. WE'LL OPEN UP THE WEAKEST ONE FIRST.
NO.
WE OPERATE ON ALL OF THEM. ALL AT ONCE.
WHAT? CAN YOU ACTUALLY DO THAT?
I AM THOR. THE GODDESS OF THUNDER.
WHICH MEANS I KNOW HOW TO MOVE LIKE LIGHTNING.
STAND ASIDE, DOCTOR STRANGE. AND COVER THY EARS.

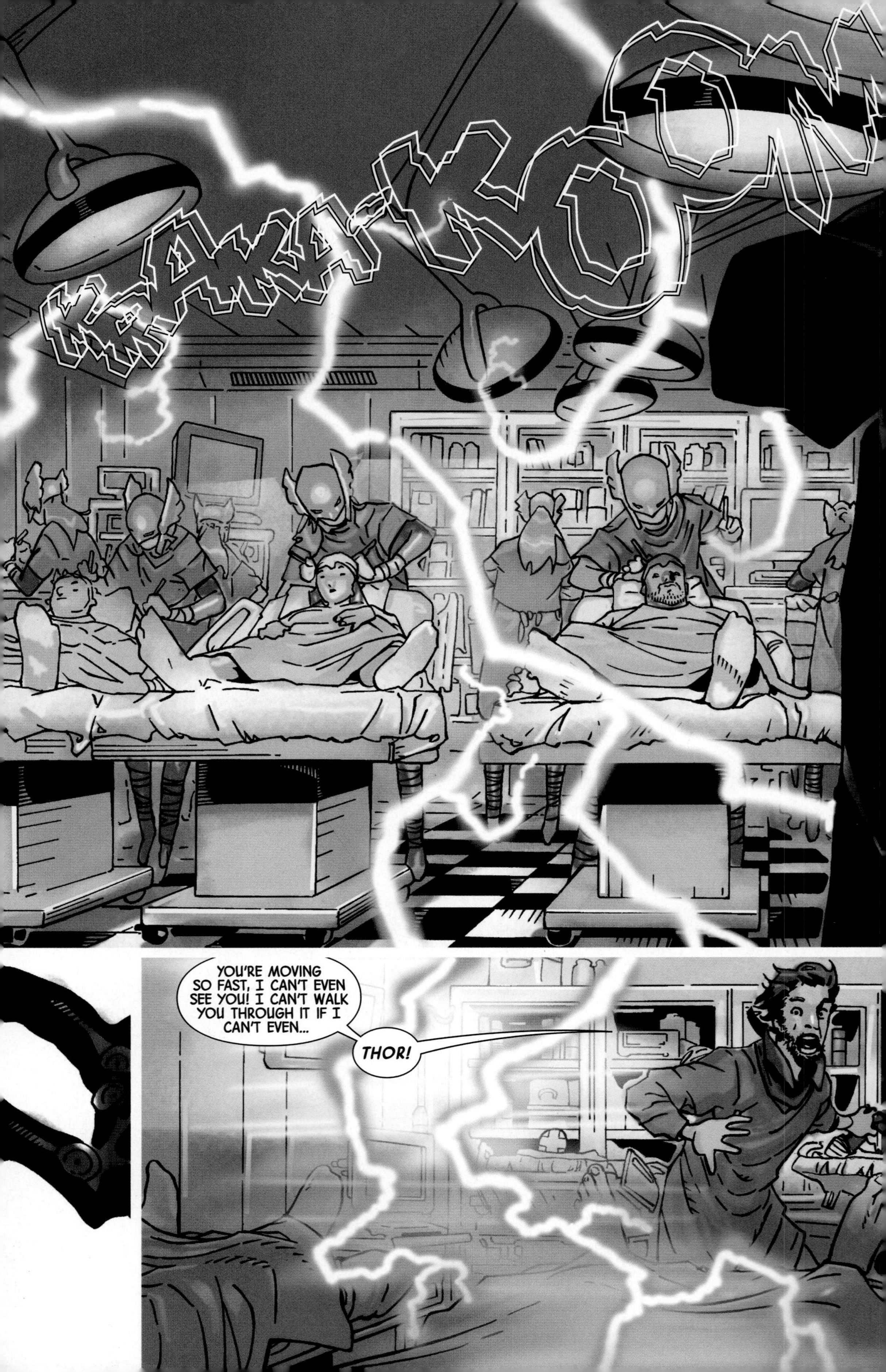
KRAKA-KOOM
YOU'RE MOVING SO FAST, I CAN'T EVEN SEE YOU! I CAN'T WALK YOU THROUGH IT IF I CAN'T EVEN...
THOR!

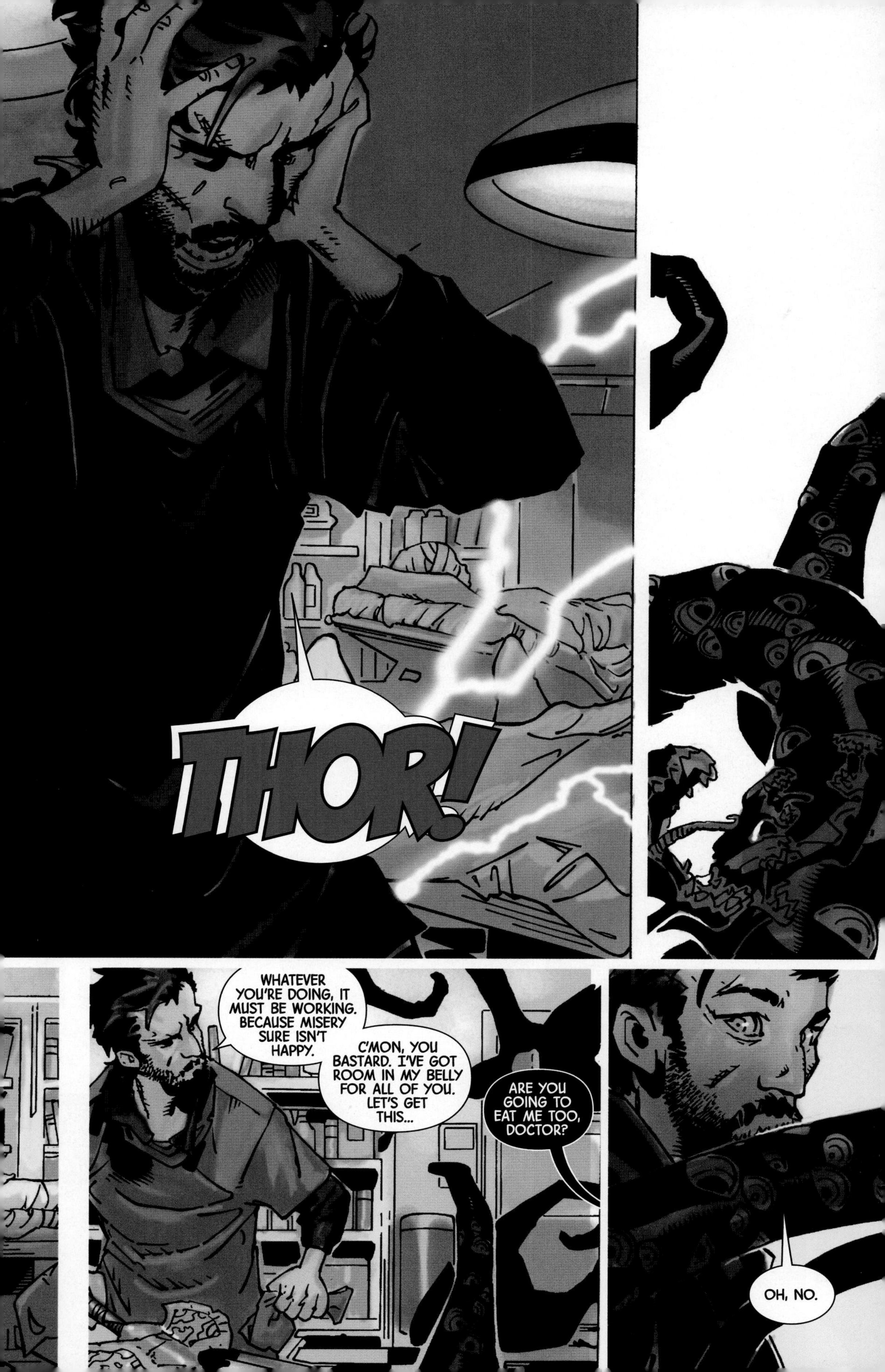
THOR!
WHATEVER YOU'RE DOING, IT MUST BE WORKING. BECAUSE MISERY SURE ISN'T HAPPY.
C'MON, YOU BASTARD. I'VE GOT ROOM IN MY BELLY FOR ALL OF YOU. LET'S GET THIS...
ARE YOU GOING TO EAT ME TOO, DOCTOR?
OH, NO.

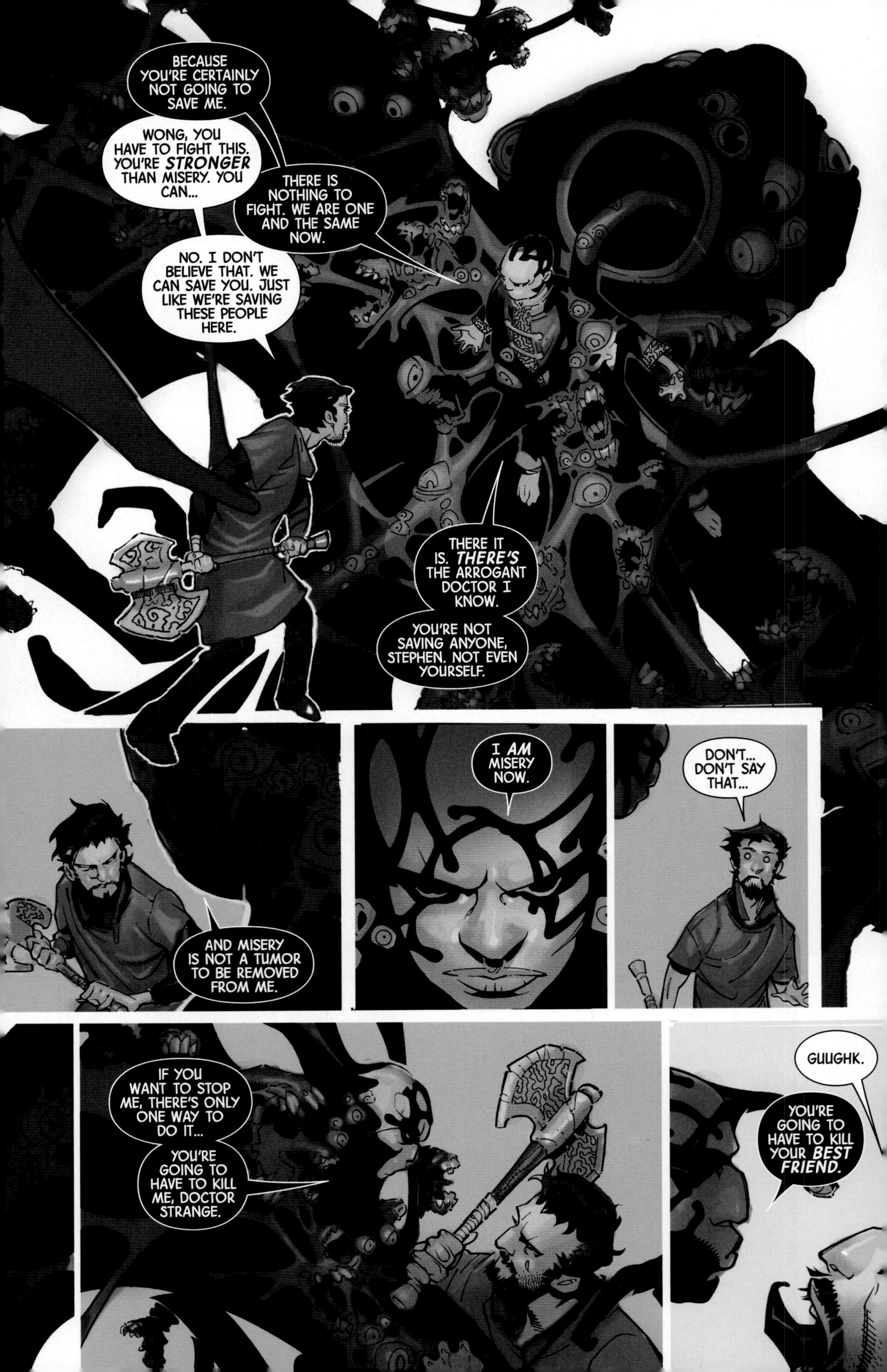
BECAUSE YOU'RE CERTAINLY NOT GOING TO SAVE ME.
WONG, YOU HAVE TO FIGHT THIS. YOU'RE STRONGER THAN MISERY. YOU CAN...
THERE IS NOTHING TO FIGHT. WE ARE ONE AND THE SAME NOW.
NO. I DON'T BELIEVE THAT. WE CAN SAVE YOU. JUST LIKE WE'RE SAVING THESE PEOPLE HERE.
THERE IT IS. THERE'S THE ARROGANT DOCTOR I KNOW.
YOU'RE NOT SAVING ANYONE, STEPHEN. NOT EVEN YOURSELF.
AND MISERY IS NOT A TUMOR TO BE REMOVED FROM ME.
I AM MISERY NOW.
DON'T... DON'T SAY THAT...
IF YOU WANT TO STOP ME, THERE'S ONLY ONE WAY TO DO IT...
YOU'RE GOING TO HAVE TO KILL ME, DOCTOR STRANGE.
GUUGHK.
YOU'RE GOING TO HAVE TO KILL YOUR BEST FRIEND.

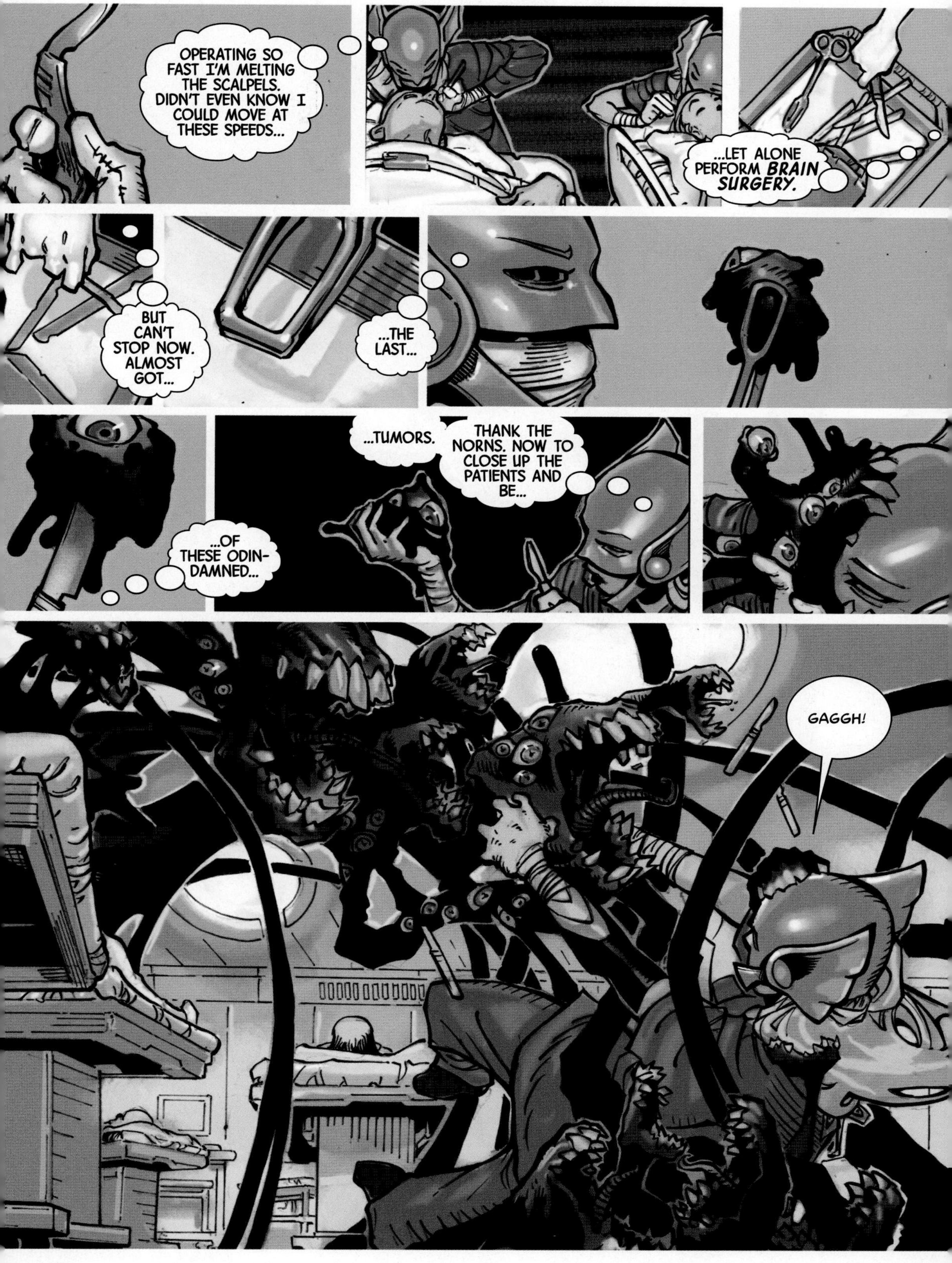
OPERATING SO FAST I'M MELTING THE SCALPELS. DIDN'T EVEN KNOW I COULD MOVE AT THESE SPEEDS...
...LET ALONE PERFORM BRAIN SURGERY.
BUT CAN'T STOP NOW. ALMOST GOT...
...THE LAST...
...OF THESE ODIN-DAMNED...
...TUMORS.
THANK THE NORNS. NOW TO CLOSE UP THE PATIENTS AND BE...
GAGGH!

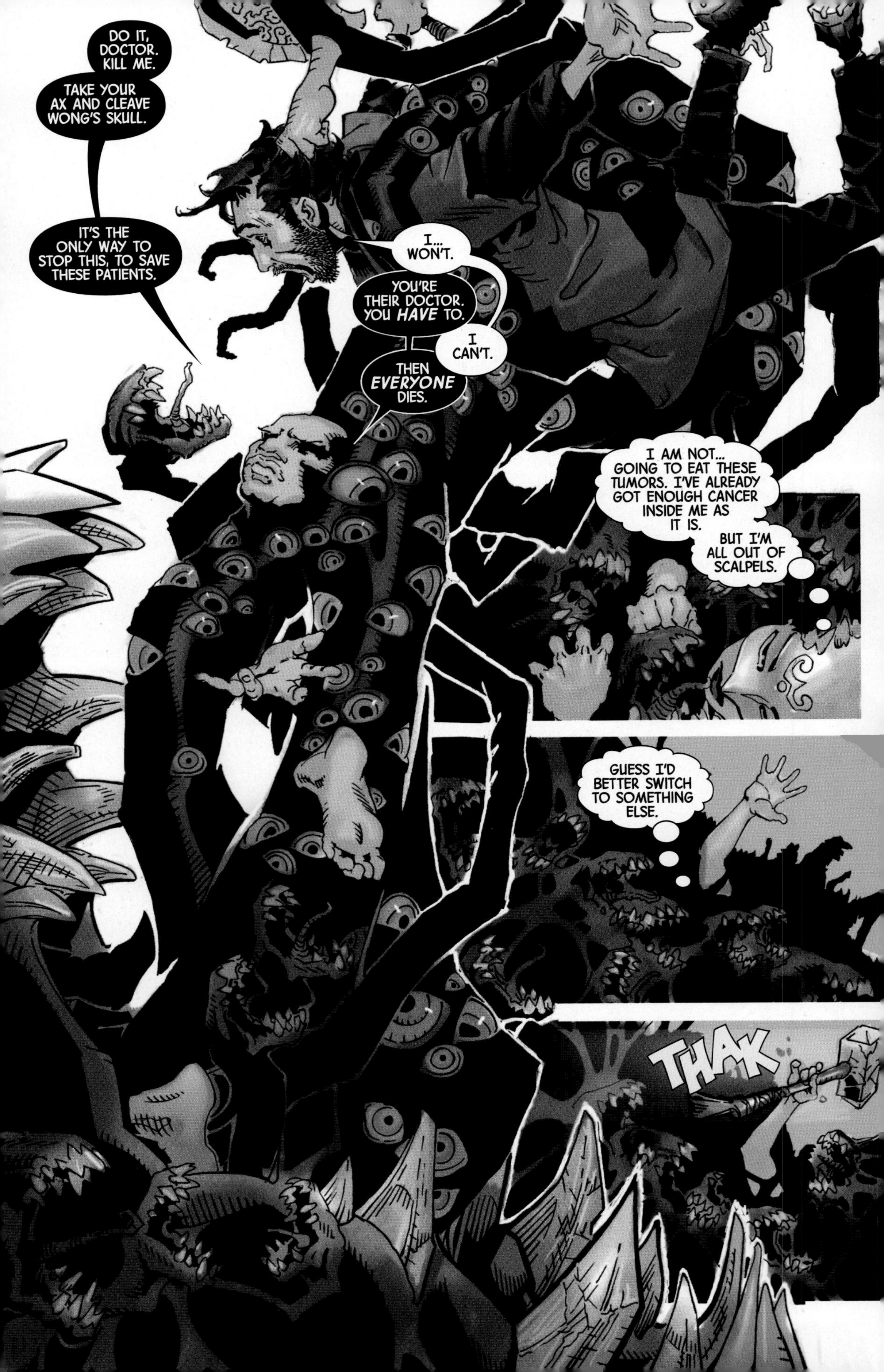
DO IT, DOCTOR. KILL ME.
TAKE YOUR AX AND CLEAVE WONG'S SKULL.
IT'S THE ONLY WAY TO STOP THIS, TO SAVE THESE PATIENTS.
I... WON'T.
YOU'RE THEIR DOCTOR. YOU HAVE TO.
I CAN'T.
THEN EVERYONE DIES.
I AM NOT... GOING TO EAT THESE TUMORS. I'VE ALREADY GOT ENOUGH CANCER INSIDE ME AS IT IS.
BUT I'M ALL OUT OF SCALPELS.
GUESS I'D BETTER SWITCH TO SOMETHING ELSE.
THAK

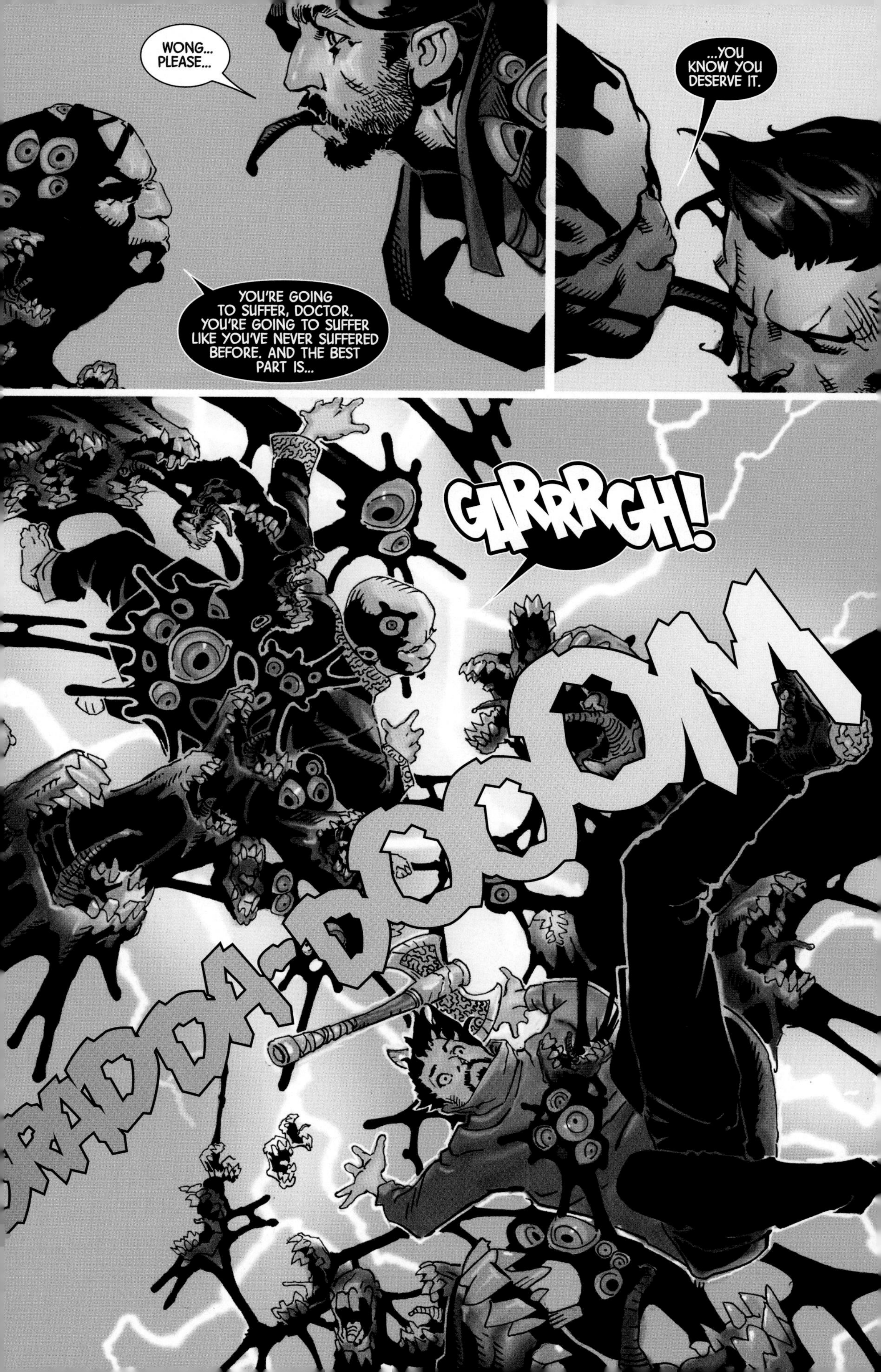
WONG... PLEASE...
YOU'RE GOING TO SUFFER, DOCTOR. YOU'RE GOING TO SUFFER LIKE YOU'VE NEVER SUFFERED BEFORE. AND THE BEST PART IS...
...YOU KNOW YOU DESERVE IT.
GARRRGH!
KRADDA-DOOOOM

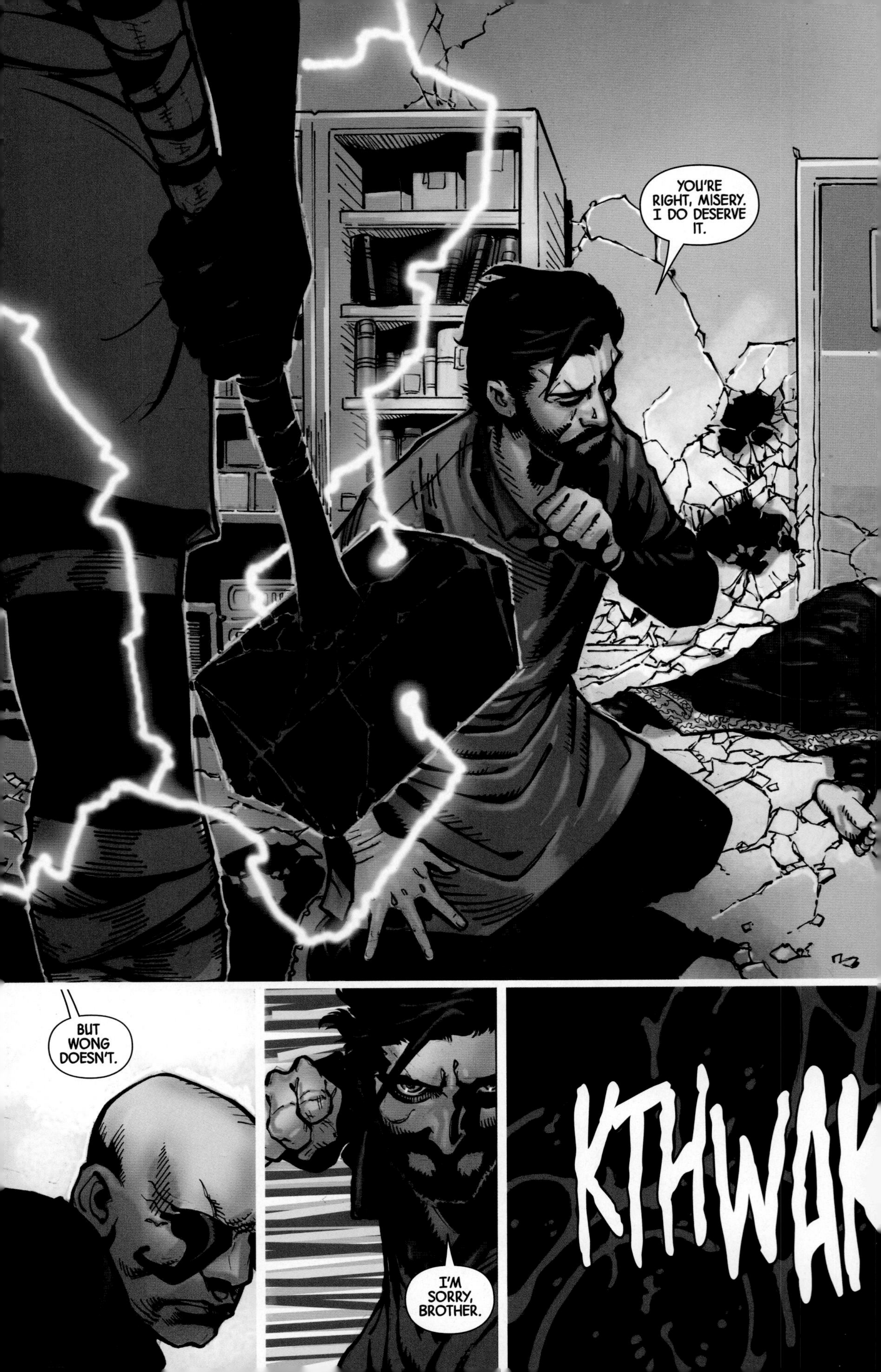
YOU'RE RIGHT, MISERY. I DO DESERVE IT.
BUT WONG DOESN'T.
I'M SORRY, BROTHER.
KTHWAK

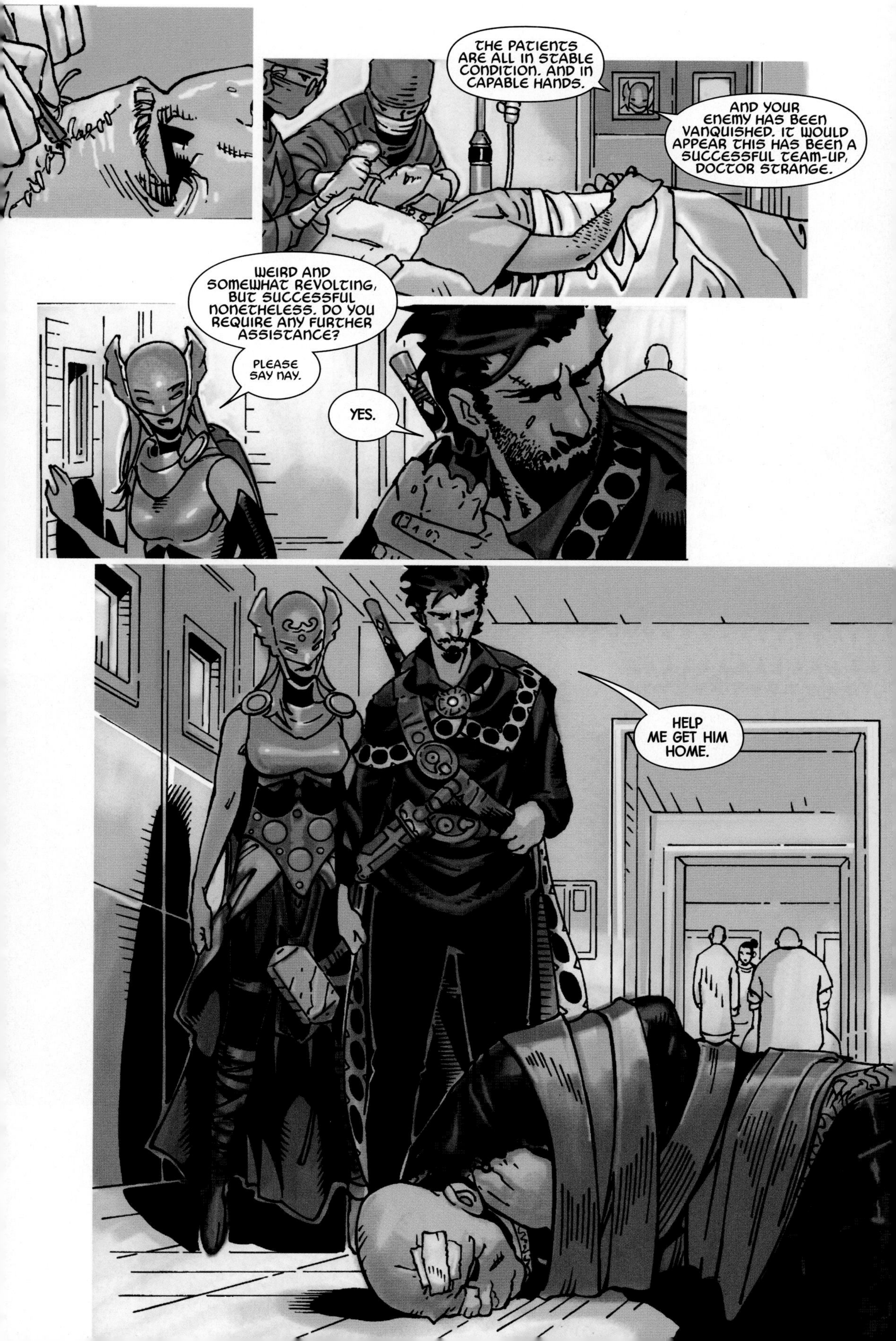
THE PATIENTS ARE ALL IN STABLE CONDITION. AND IN CAPABLE HANDS.
AND YOUR ENEMY HAS BEEN VANQUISHED. IT WOULD APPEAR THIS HAS BEEN A SUCCESSFUL TEAM-UP, DOCTOR STRANGE.
WEIRD AND SOMEWHAT REVOLTING, BUT SUCCESSFUL NONETHELESS. DO YOU REQUIRE ANY FURTHER ASSISTANCE?
PLEASE SAY NAY.
YES.
HELP ME GET HIM HOME.

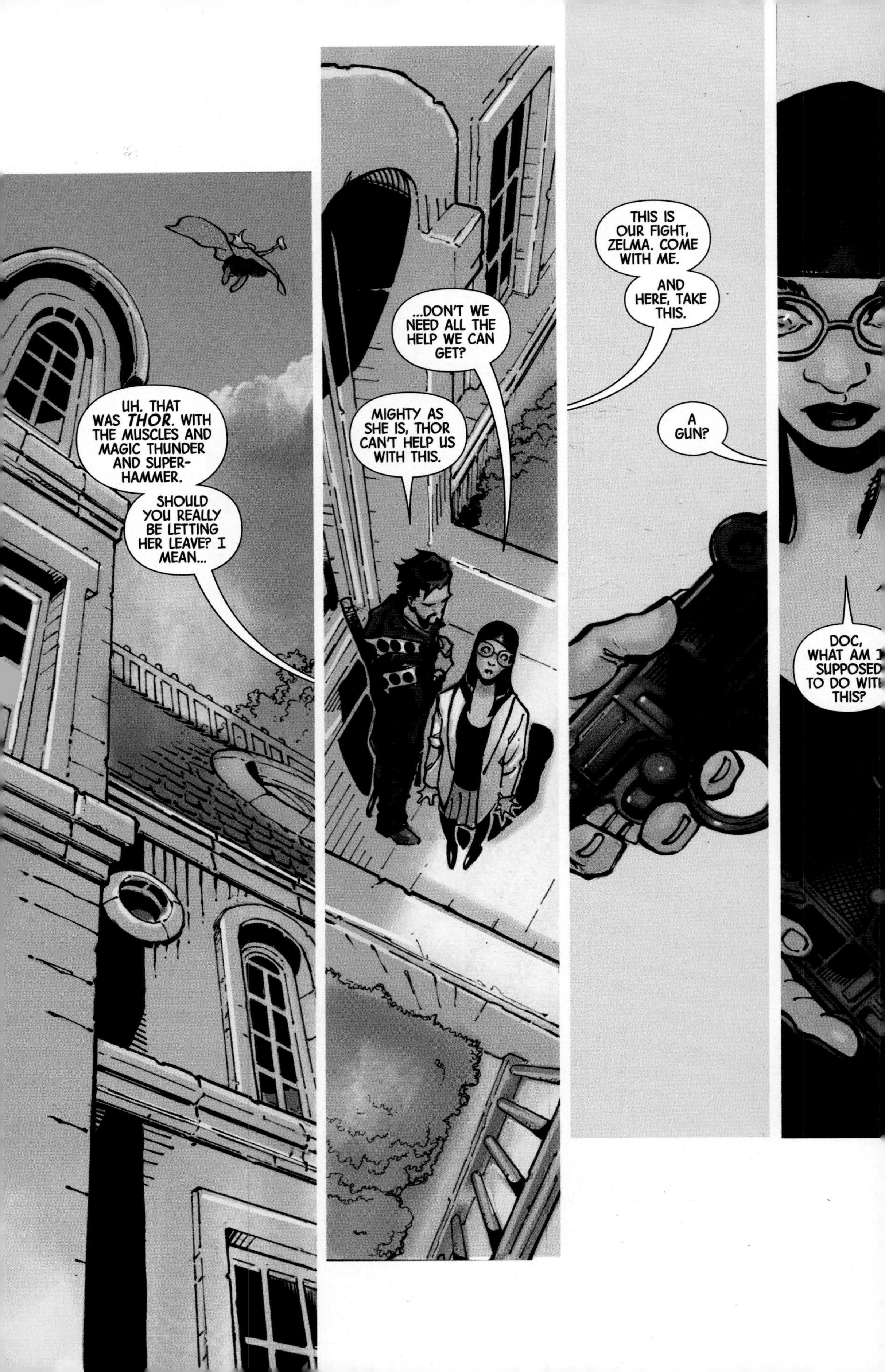
UH. THAT WAS *THOR*. WITH THE MUSCLES AND MAGIC THUNDER AND SUPER-HAMMER.
SHOULD YOU REALLY BE LETTING HER LEAVE? I MEAN...
MIGHTY AS SHE IS, THOR CAN'T HELP US WITH THIS.
...DON'T WE NEED ALL THE HELP WE CAN GET?
THIS IS OUR FIGHT, ZELMA. COME WITH ME.
AND HERE, TAKE THIS.
A GUN?
DOC, WHAT AM I SUPPOSED TO DO WITH THIS?

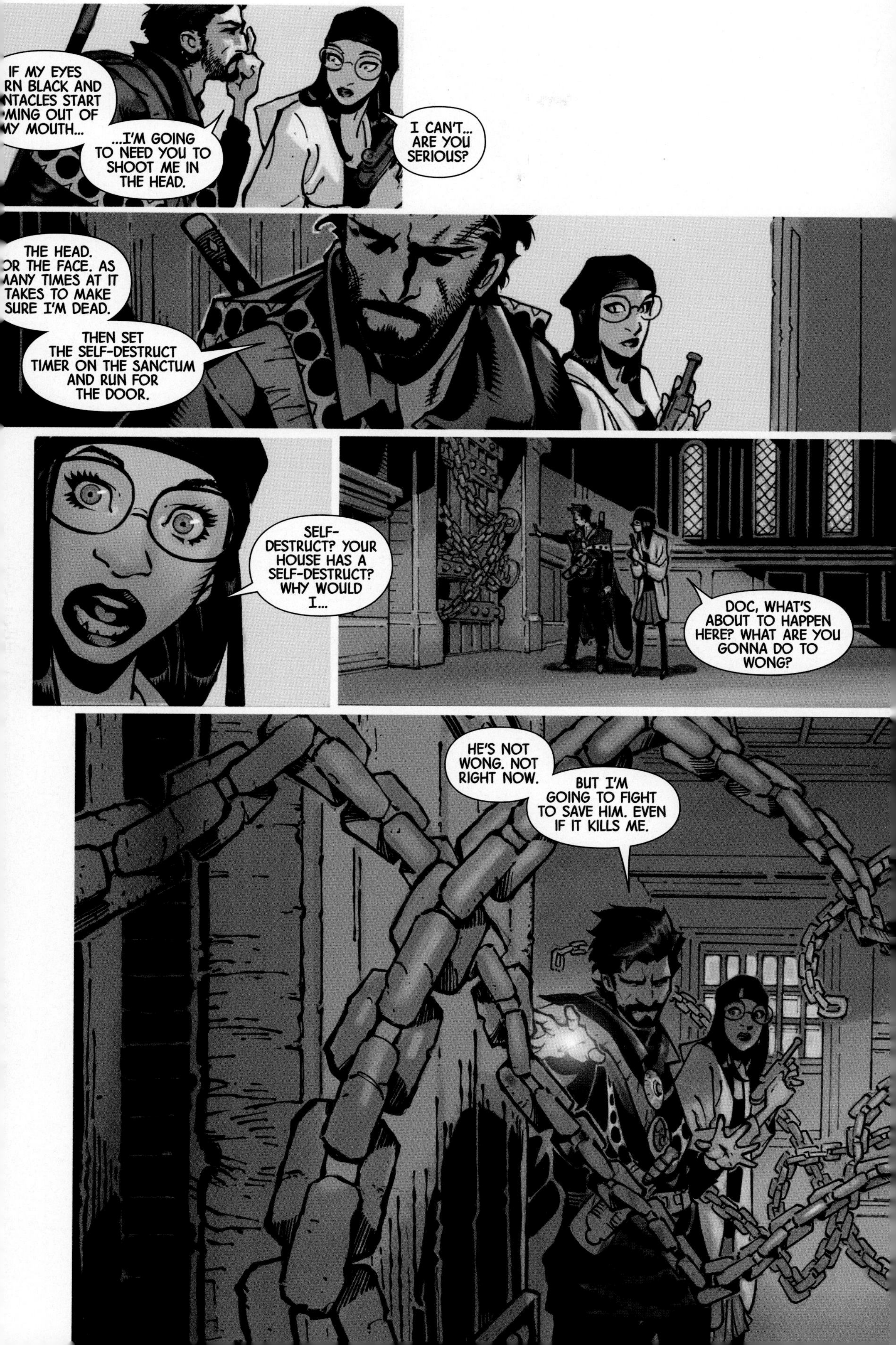
IF MY EYES
RN BLACK AND
NTACLES START
OMING OUT OF
MY MOUTH...
...I'M GOING TO NEED YOU TO SHOOT ME IN THE HEAD.
I CAN'T... ARE YOU SERIOUS?
THE HEAD.
OR THE FACE. AS
MANY TIMES AT IT
TAKES TO MAKE
SURE I'M DEAD.
THEN SET THE SELF-DESTRUCT TIMER ON THE SANCTUM AND RUN FOR THE DOOR.
SELF-DESTRUCT? YOUR HOUSE HAS A SELF-DESTRUCT? WHY WOULD I...
DOC, WHAT'S ABOUT TO HAPPEN HERE? WHAT ARE YOU GONNA DO TO WONG?
HE'S NOT WONG. NOT RIGHT NOW.
BUT I'M GOING TO FIGHT TO SAVE HIM. EVEN IF IT KILLS ME.

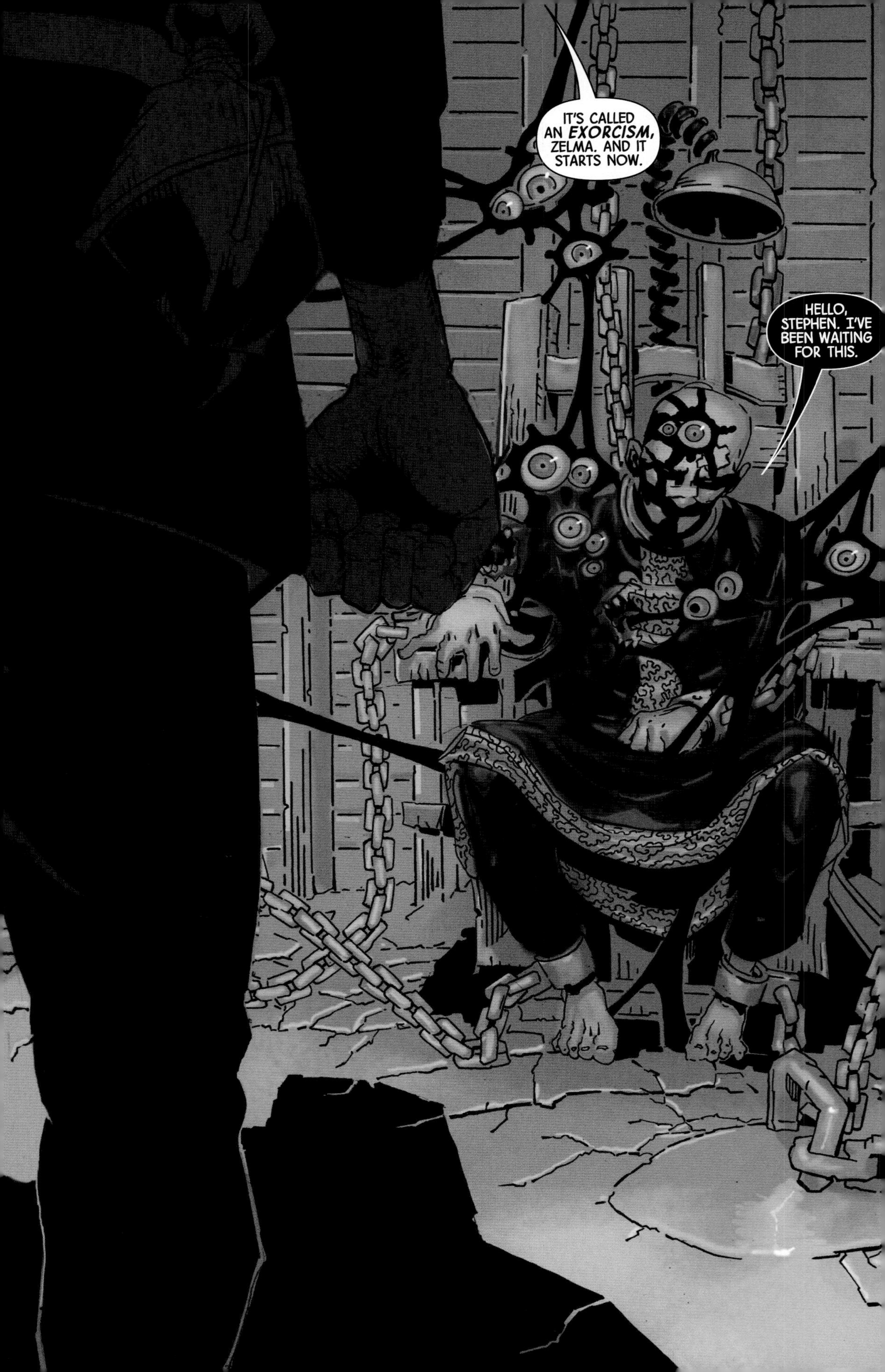
IT'S CALLED AN EXORCISM, ZELMA. AND IT STARTS NOW.
HELLO, STEPHEN. I'VE BEEN WAITING FOR THIS.

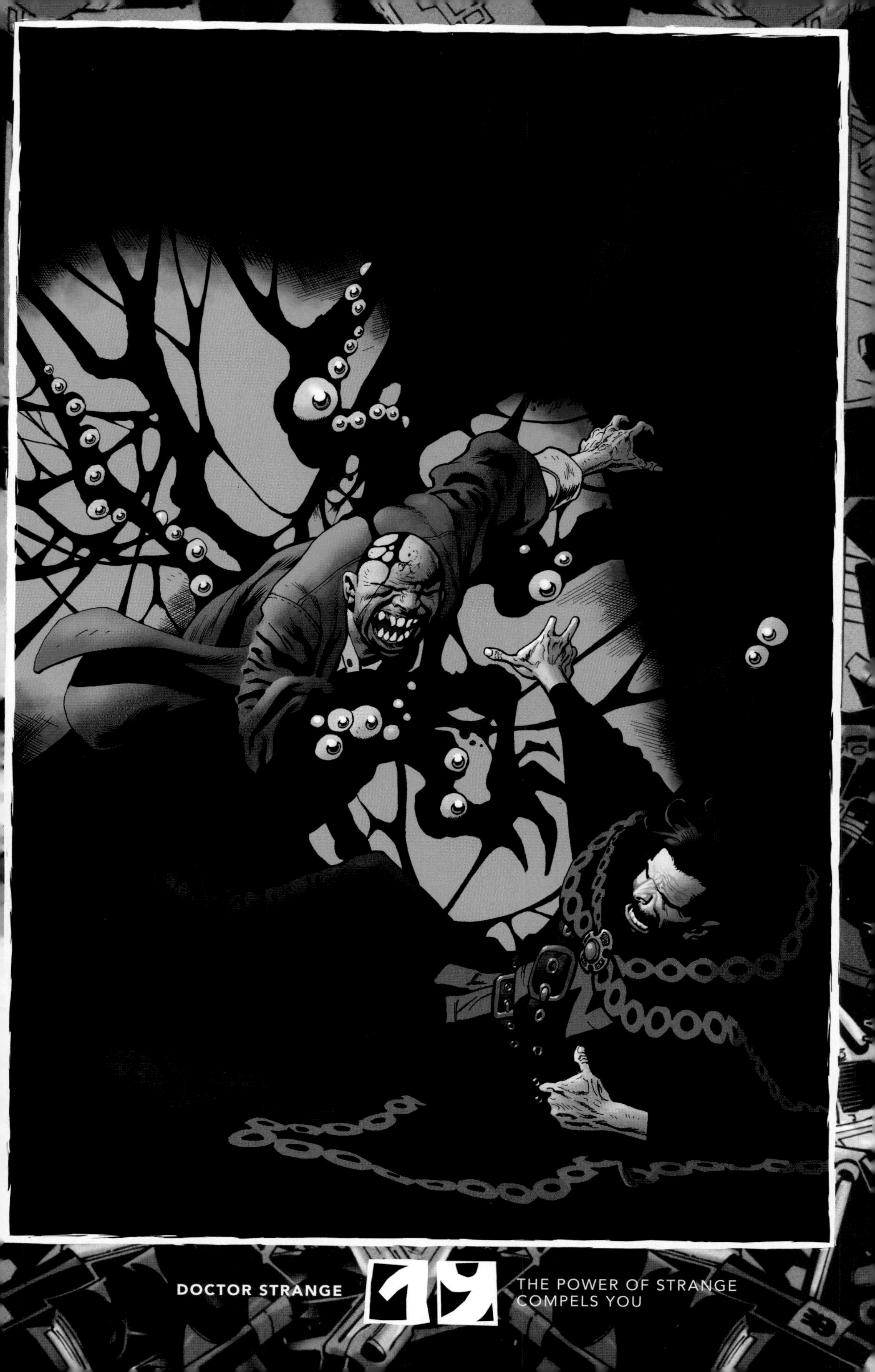
DOCTOR STRANGE
THE POWER OF STRANGE
COMPELS YOU

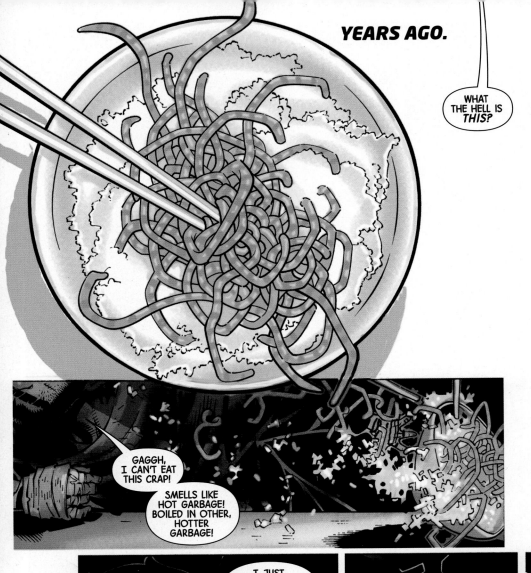

YEARS AGO.

WHAT THE HELL IS *THIS*?

GAGGH, I CAN'T EAT THIS CRAP!

SMELLS LIKE HOT GARBAGE! BOILED IN OTHER, HOTTER GARBAGE!

I JUST CLIMBED A STUPID MOUNTAIN IN TIBET WITH TWO RUINED HANDS! I NEED *REAL* FOOD!

SOMEBODY GET ME A STEAK! I DON'T CARE IF IT COMES OFF A *YAK*, BUT I DEMAND A--

THERE IS NO STEAK HERE.

NO RED MEAT AT ALL.

THERE ARE ALSO NO *DEMANDS*.

WHAT? WHO THE CRAP ARE *YOU*?

I AM THE ONE WHO MADE THIS..."HOT GARBAGE," A YOU CALL IT.

I AM A DISCIPLE OF ANCIENT O JUST AS Y WISH TO B

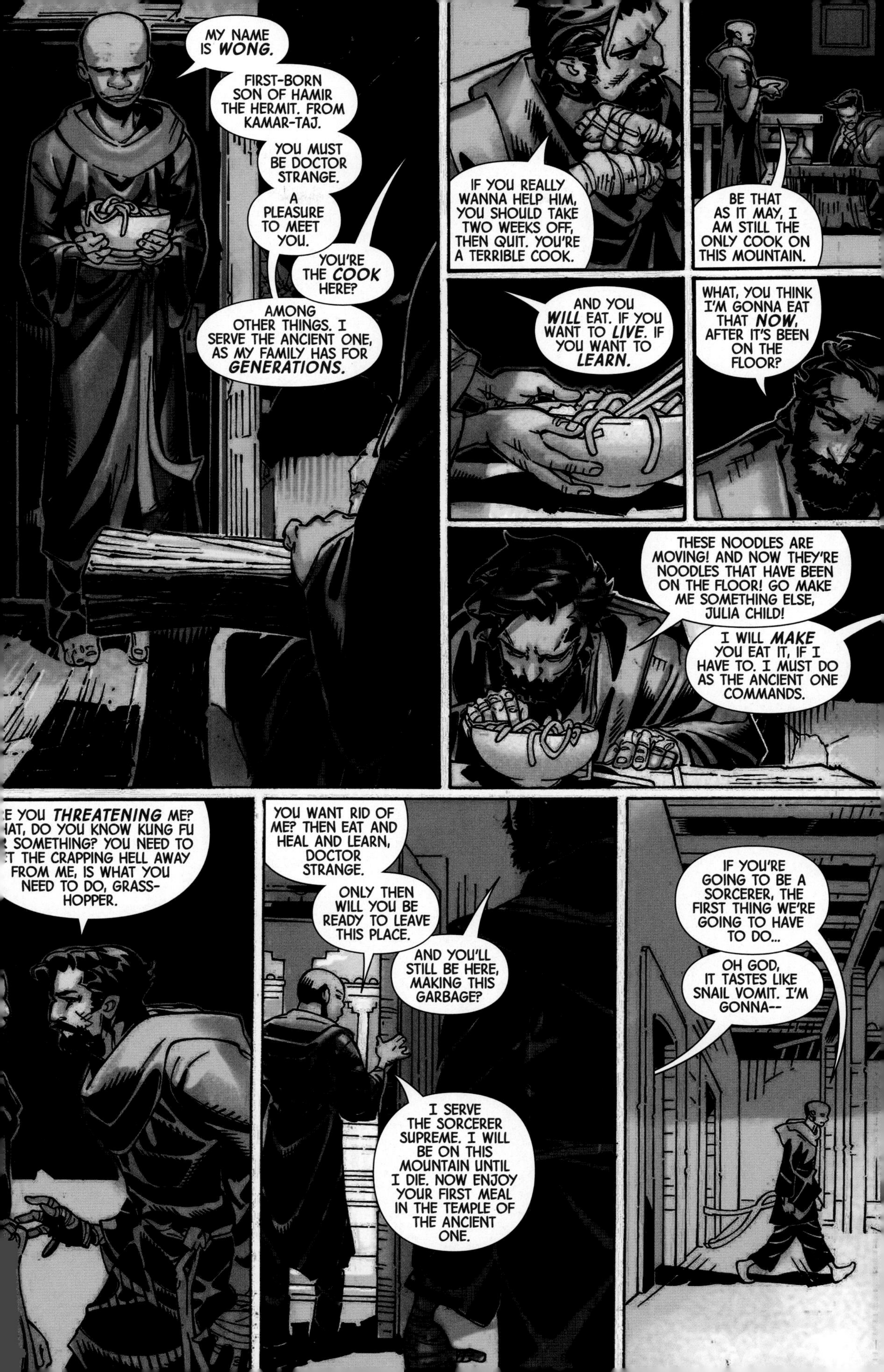
MY NAME IS WONG.
FIRST-BORN SON OF HAMIR THE HERMIT. FROM KAMAR-TAJ.
YOU MUST BE DOCTOR STRANGE.
A PLEASURE TO MEET YOU.
YOU'RE THE COOK HERE?
AMONG OTHER THINGS. I SERVE THE ANCIENT ONE, AS MY FAMILY HAS FOR GENERATIONS.
IF YOU REALLY WANNA HELP HIM, YOU SHOULD TAKE TWO WEEKS OFF, THEN QUIT. YOU'RE A TERRIBLE COOK.
BE THAT AS IT MAY, I AM STILL THE ONLY COOK ON THIS MOUNTAIN.
AND YOU WILL EAT. IF YOU WANT TO LIVE. IF YOU WANT TO LEARN.
WHAT, YOU THINK I'M GONNA EAT THAT NOW, AFTER IT'S BEEN ON THE FLOOR?
THESE NOODLES ARE MOVING! AND NOW THEY'RE NOODLES THAT HAVE BEEN ON THE FLOOR! GO MAKE ME SOMETHING ELSE, JULIA CHILD!
I WILL MAKE YOU EAT IT, IF I HAVE TO. I MUST DO AS THE ANCIENT ONE COMMANDS.
E YOU THREATENING ME? HAT, DO YOU KNOW KUNG FU SOMETHING? YOU NEED TO T THE CRAPPING HELL AWAY FROM ME, IS WHAT YOU NEED TO DO, GRASS-HOPPER.
YOU WANT RID OF ME? THEN EAT AND HEAL AND LEARN, DOCTOR STRANGE.
ONLY THEN WILL YOU BE READY TO LEAVE THIS PLACE.
AND YOU'LL STILL BE HERE, MAKING THIS GARBAGE?
I SERVE THE SORCERER SUPREME. I WILL BE ON THIS MOUNTAIN UNTIL I DIE. NOW ENJOY YOUR FIRST MEAL IN THE TEMPLE OF THE ANCIENT ONE.
IF YOU'RE GOING TO BE A SORCERER, THE FIRST THING WE'RE GOING TO HAVE TO DO...
OH GOD, IT TASTES LIKE SNAIL VOMIT. I'M GONNA--

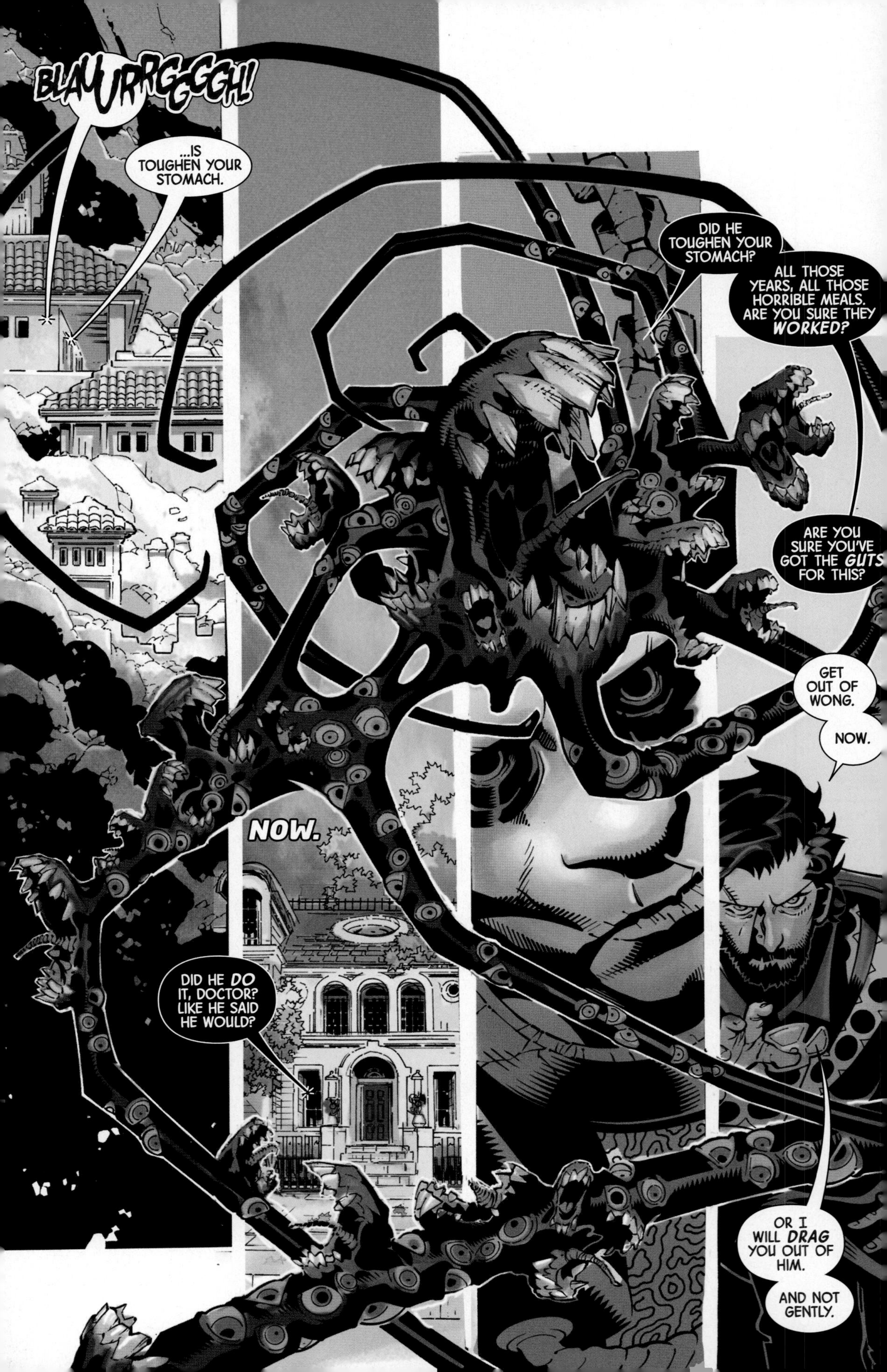
BLAUURRGGGGH!
...IS TOUGHEN YOUR STOMACH.
DID HE TOUGHEN YOUR STOMACH?
ALL THOSE YEARS, ALL THOSE HORRIBLE MEALS. ARE YOU SURE THEY WORKED?
ARE YOU SURE YOU'VE GOT THE GUTS FOR THIS?
GET OUT OF WONG.
NOW.
NOW.
DID HE DO IT, DOCTOR? LIKE HE SAID HE WOULD?
OR I WILL DRAG YOU OUT OF HIM.
AND NOT GENTLY.

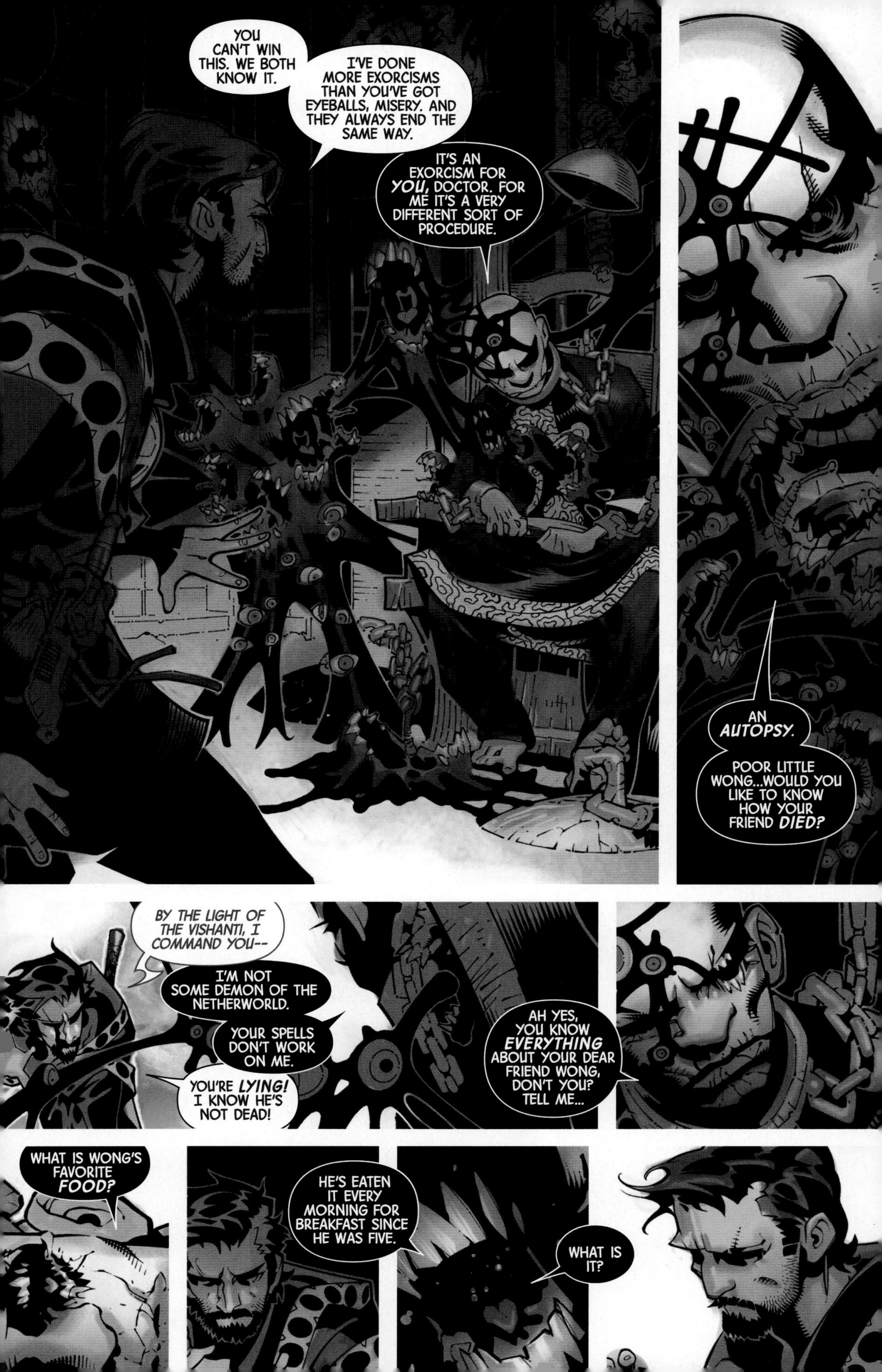
YOU CAN'T WIN THIS. WE BOTH KNOW IT.
I'VE DONE MORE EXORCISMS THAN YOU'VE GOT EYEBALLS, MISERY. AND THEY ALWAYS END THE SAME WAY.
IT'S AN EXORCISM FOR YOU, DOCTOR. FOR ME IT'S A VERY DIFFERENT SORT OF PROCEDURE.
AN AUTOPSY.
POOR LITTLE WONG...WOULD YOU LIKE TO KNOW HOW YOUR FRIEND DIED?
BY THE LIGHT OF THE VISHANTI, I COMMAND YOU--
I'M NOT SOME DEMON OF THE NETHERWORLD.
YOUR SPELLS DON'T WORK ON ME.
YOU'RE LYING! I KNOW HE'S NOT DEAD!
AH YES, YOU KNOW EVERYTHING ABOUT YOUR DEAR FRIEND WONG, DON'T YOU? TELL ME...
WHAT IS WONG'S FAVORITE FOOD?
HE'S EATEN IT EVERY MORNING FOR BREAKFAST SINCE HE WAS FIVE.
WHAT IS IT?

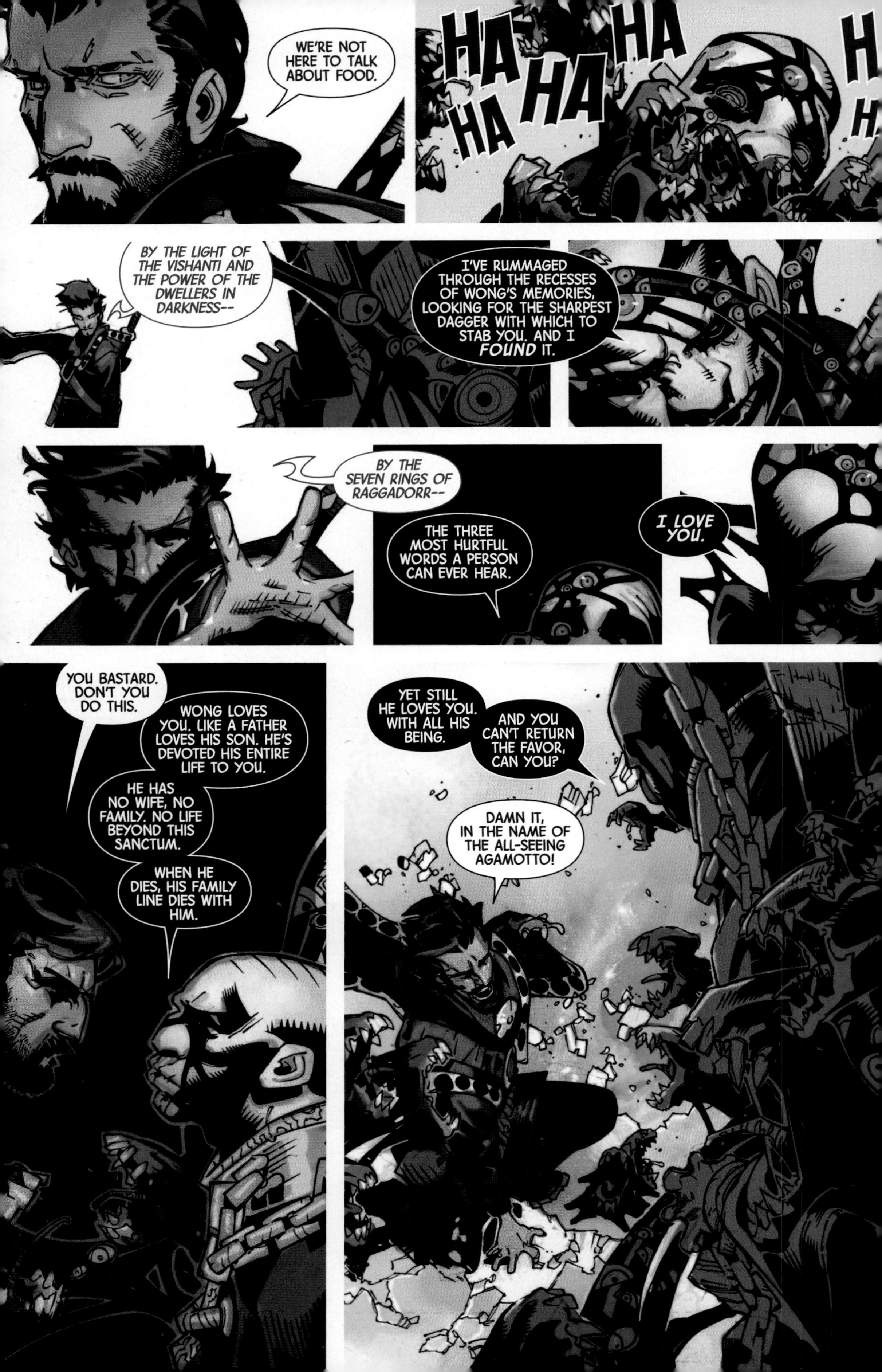
WE'RE NOT HERE TO TALK ABOUT FOOD.
HA HA HA HA HA
BY THE LIGHT OF THE VISHANTI AND THE POWER OF THE DWELLERS IN DARKNESS--
I'VE RUMMAGED THROUGH THE RECESSES OF WONG'S MEMORIES, LOOKING FOR THE SHARPEST DAGGER WITH WHICH TO STAB YOU. AND I FOUND IT.
BY THE SEVEN RINGS OF RAGGADORR--
THE THREE MOST HURTFUL WORDS A PERSON CAN EVER HEAR.
I LOVE YOU.
YOU BASTARD. DON'T YOU DO THIS.
WONG LOVES YOU. LIKE A FATHER LOVES HIS SON. HE'S DEVOTED HIS ENTIRE LIFE TO YOU.
HE HAS NO WIFE, NO FAMILY. NO LIFE BEYOND THIS SANCTUM.
WHEN HE DIES, HIS FAMILY LINE DIES WITH HIM.
YET STILL HE LOVES YOU. WITH ALL HIS BEING.
AND YOU CAN'T RETURN THE FAVOR, CAN YOU?
DAMN IT, IN THE NAME OF THE ALL-SEEING AGAMOTTO!

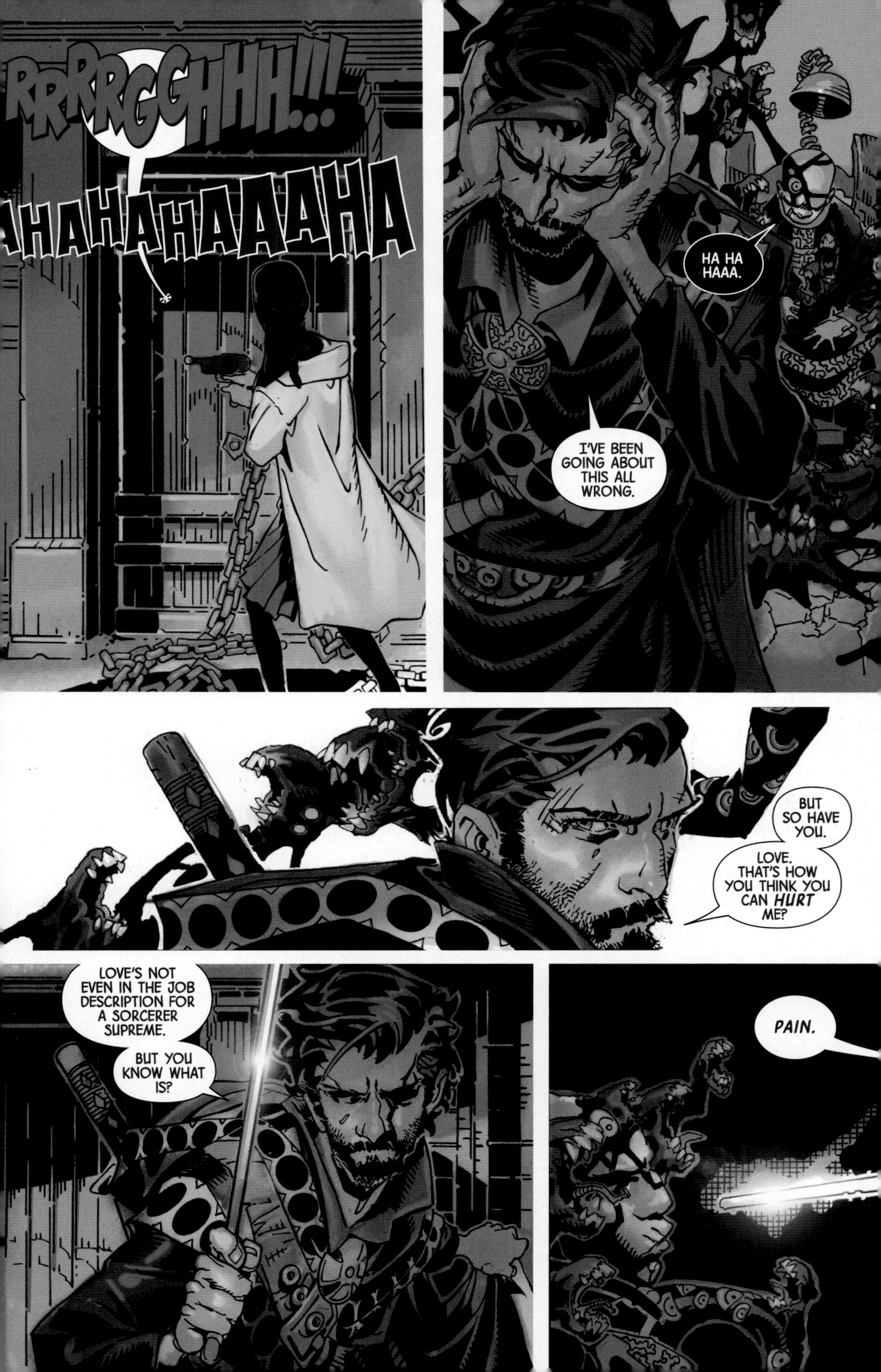
RRRRGGHHH!!!
HAHAHAHAAAAHA
HA HA HAAA.
I'VE BEEN GOING ABOUT THIS ALL WRONG.
BUT SO HAVE YOU.
LOVE. THAT'S HOW YOU THINK YOU CAN *HURT* ME?
LOVE'S NOT EVEN IN THE JOB DESCRIPTION FOR A SORCERER SUPREME.
BUT YOU KNOW WHAT IS?
PAIN.

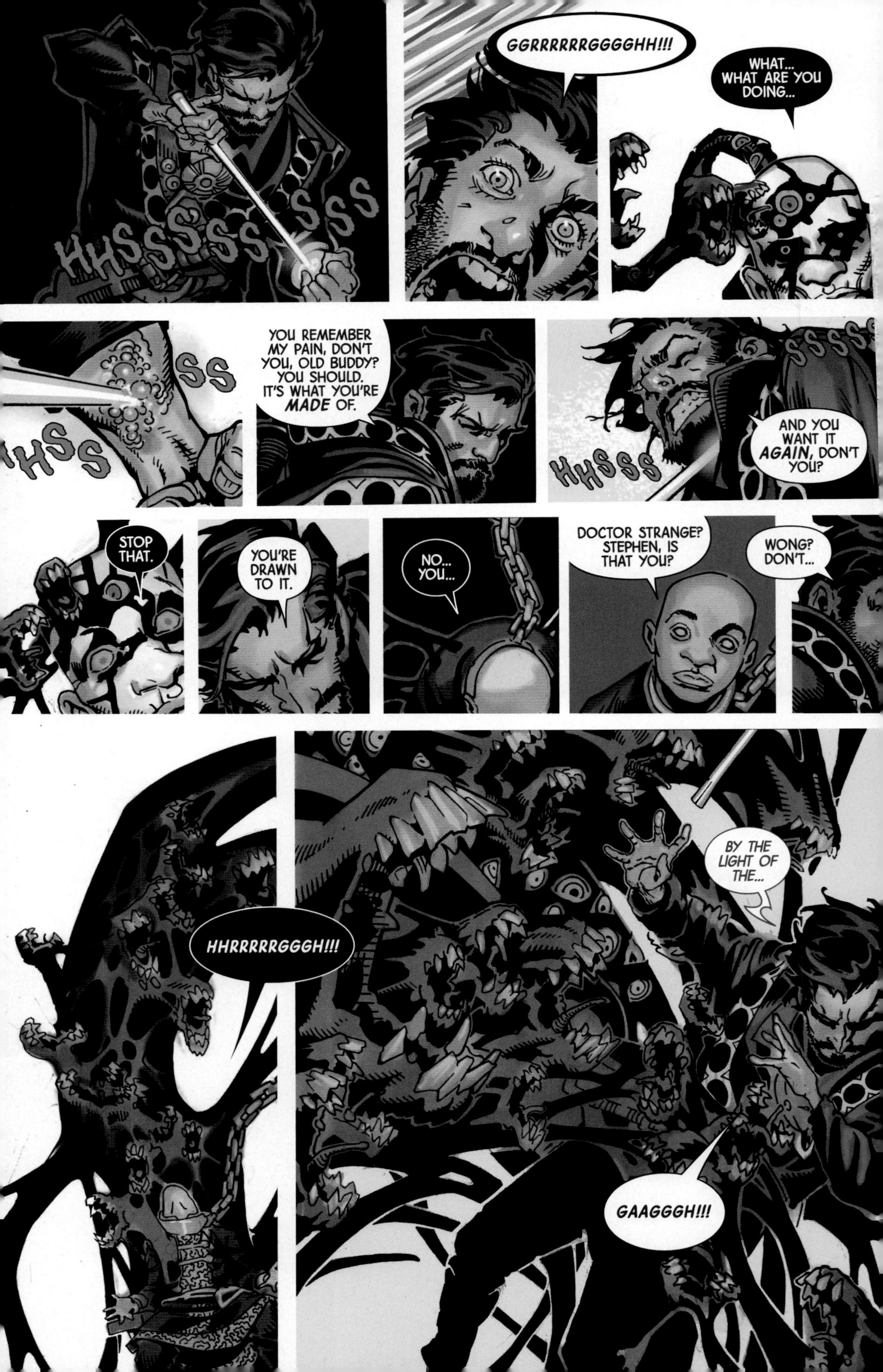
HHSSSSSSSSSSSS
GGRRRRRRGGGGHH!!!
WHAT... WHAT ARE YOU DOING...
SS
HHSSS
YOU REMEMBER MY PAIN, DON'T YOU, OLD BUDDY? YOU SHOULD. IT'S WHAT YOU'RE MADE OF.
SSSSS
HHSSSS
AND YOU WANT IT AGAIN, DON'T YOU?
STOP THAT.
YOU'RE DRAWN TO IT.
NO... YOU...
DOCTOR STRANGE? STEPHEN, IS THAT YOU?
WONG? DON'T...
HHRRRRRRGGGH!!!
BY THE LIGHT OF THE...
GAAGGGH!!!

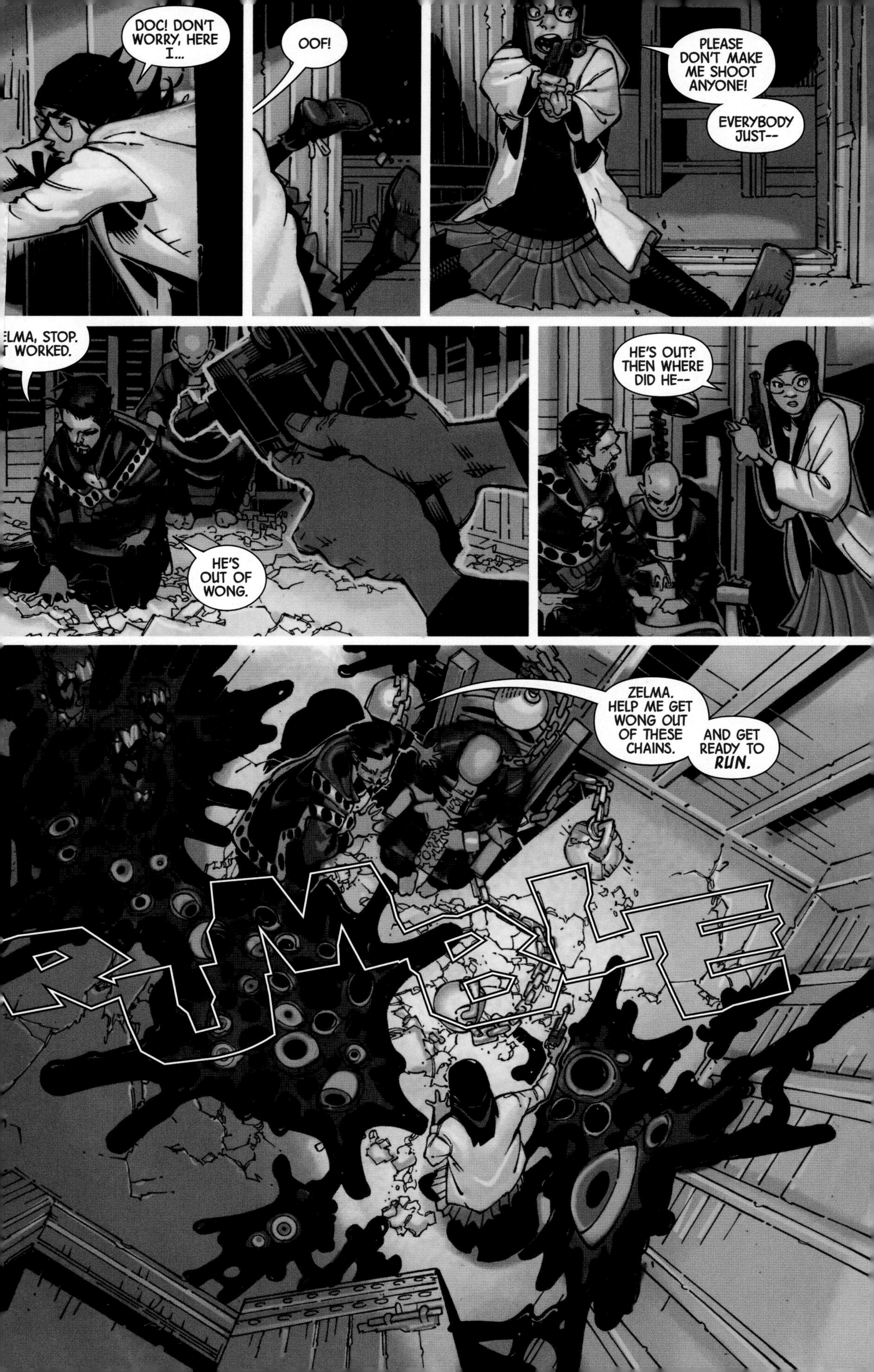
DOC! DON'T WORRY, HERE I...
OOF!
PLEASE DON'T MAKE ME SHOOT ANYONE!
EVERYBODY JUST--
ELMA, STOP. T WORKED.
HE'S OUT OF WONG.
HE'S OUT? THEN WHERE DID HE--
ZELMA. HELP ME GET WONG OUT OF THESE CHAINS.
AND GET READY TO RUN.
RUMBLE

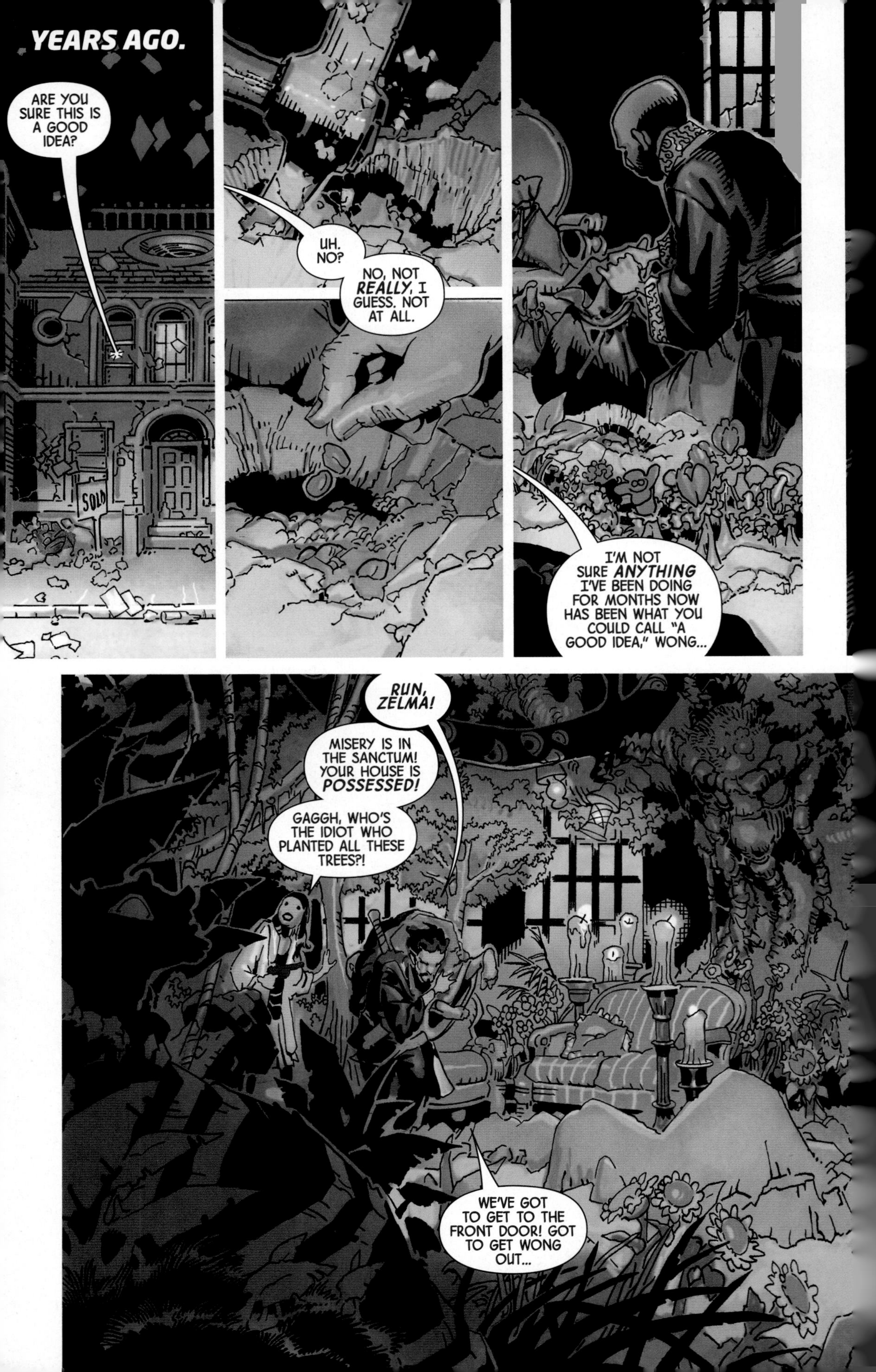
YEARS AGO.
ARE YOU SURE THIS IS A GOOD IDEA?
SOLD
UH. NO?
NO, NOT REALLY, I GUESS. NOT AT ALL.
I'M NOT SURE ANYTHING I'VE BEEN DOING FOR MONTHS NOW HAS BEEN WHAT YOU COULD CALL "A GOOD IDEA," WONG...
RUN, ZELMA!
MISERY IS IN THE SANCTUM! YOUR HOUSE IS POSSESSED!
GAGGH, WHO'S THE IDIOT WHO PLANTED ALL THESE TREES?!
WE'VE GOT TO GET TO THE FRONT DOOR! GOT TO GET WONG OUT...

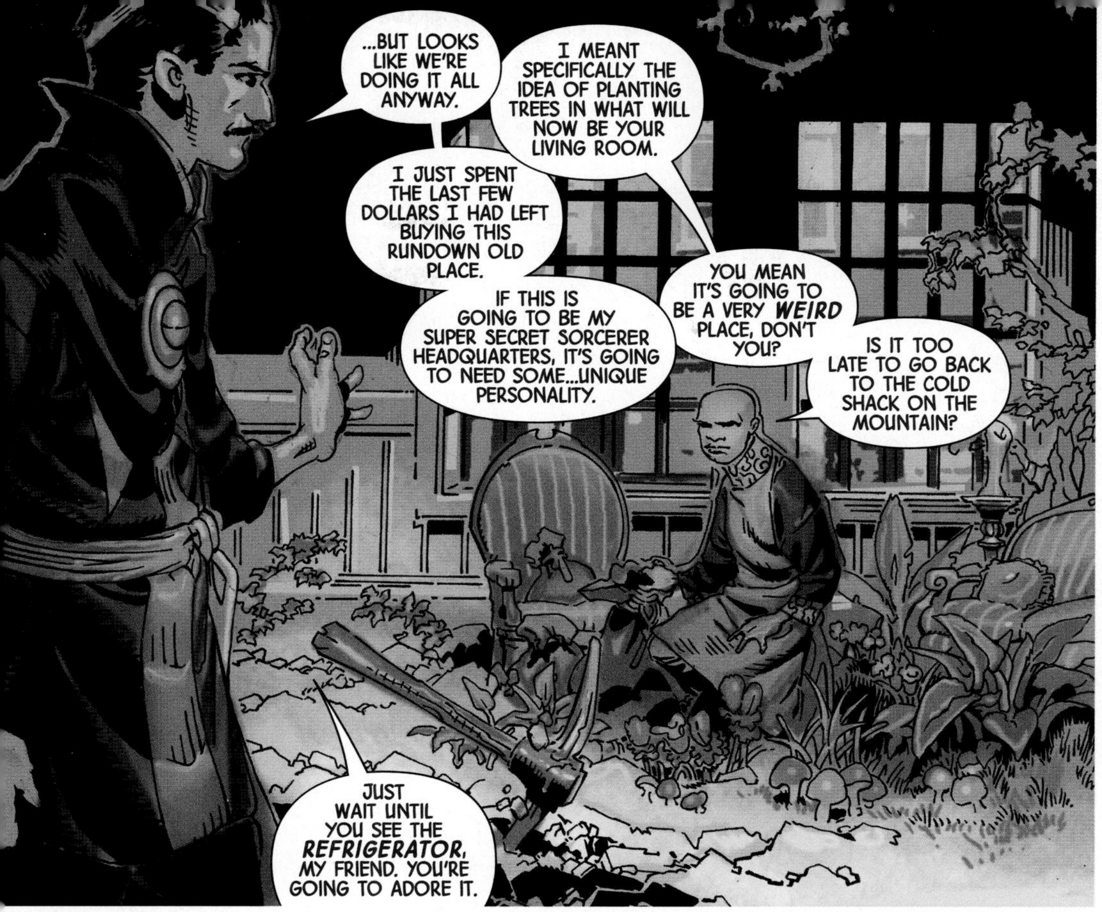
...BUT LOOKS LIKE WE'RE DOING IT ALL ANYWAY.
I JUST SPENT THE LAST FEW DOLLARS I HAD LEFT BUYING THIS RUNDOWN OLD PLACE.
I MEANT SPECIFICALLY THE IDEA OF PLANTING TREES IN WHAT WILL NOW BE YOUR LIVING ROOM.
IF THIS IS GOING TO BE MY SUPER SECRET SORCERER HEADQUARTERS, IT'S GOING TO NEED SOME...UNIQUE PERSONALITY.
YOU MEAN IT'S GOING TO BE A VERY *WEIRD* PLACE, DON'T YOU?
IS IT TOO LATE TO GO BACK TO THE COLD SHACK ON THE MOUNTAIN?
JUST WAIT UNTIL YOU SEE THE ***REFRIGERATOR***, MY FRIEND. YOU'RE GOING TO ADORE IT.

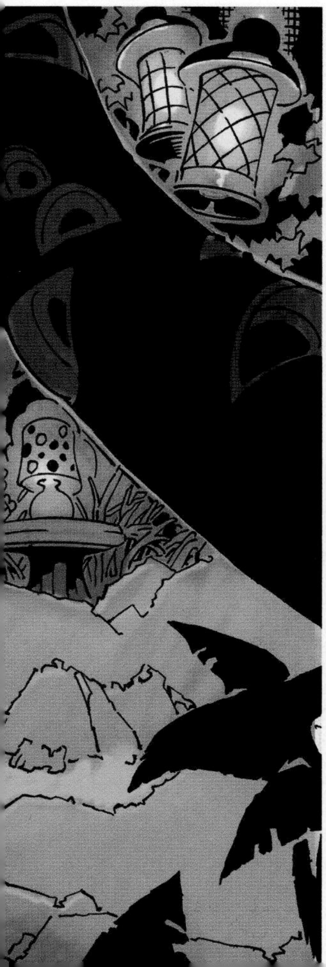

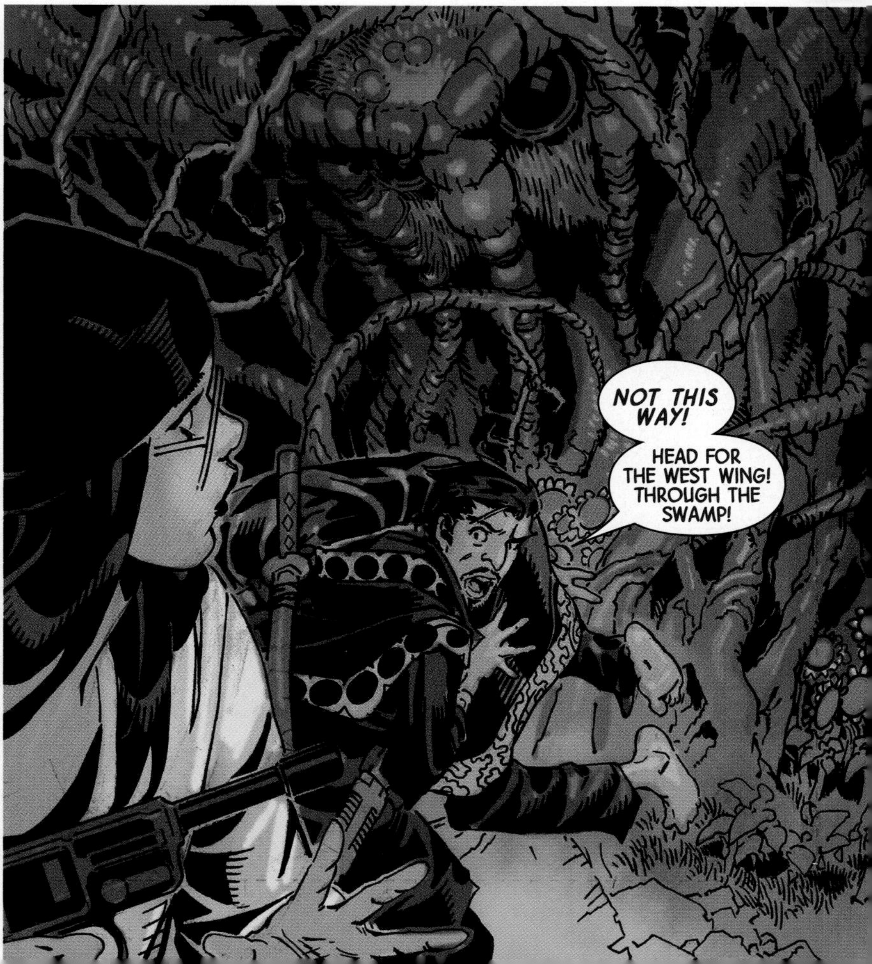
NOT THIS WAY!
HEAD FOR THE WEST WING! THROUGH THE SWAMP!

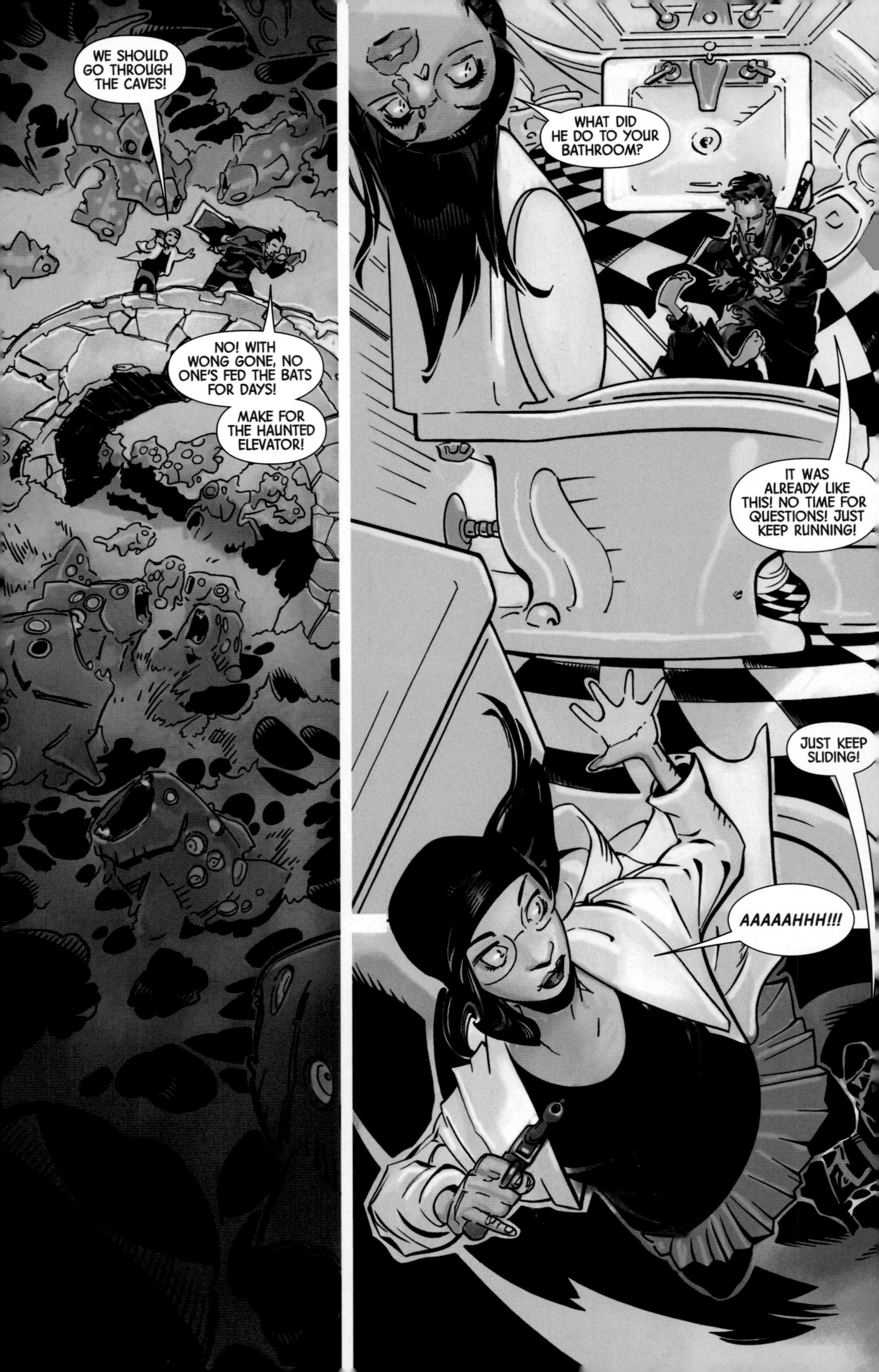

WE SHOULD GO THROUGH THE CAVES!
NO! WITH WONG GONE, NO ONE'S FED THE BATS FOR DAYS!
MAKE FOR THE HAUNTED ELEVATOR!
WHAT DID HE DO TO YOUR BATHROOM?
IT WAS ALREADY LIKE THIS! NO TIME FOR QUESTIONS! JUST KEEP RUNNING!
JUST KEEP SLIDING!
AAAAAHHH!!!

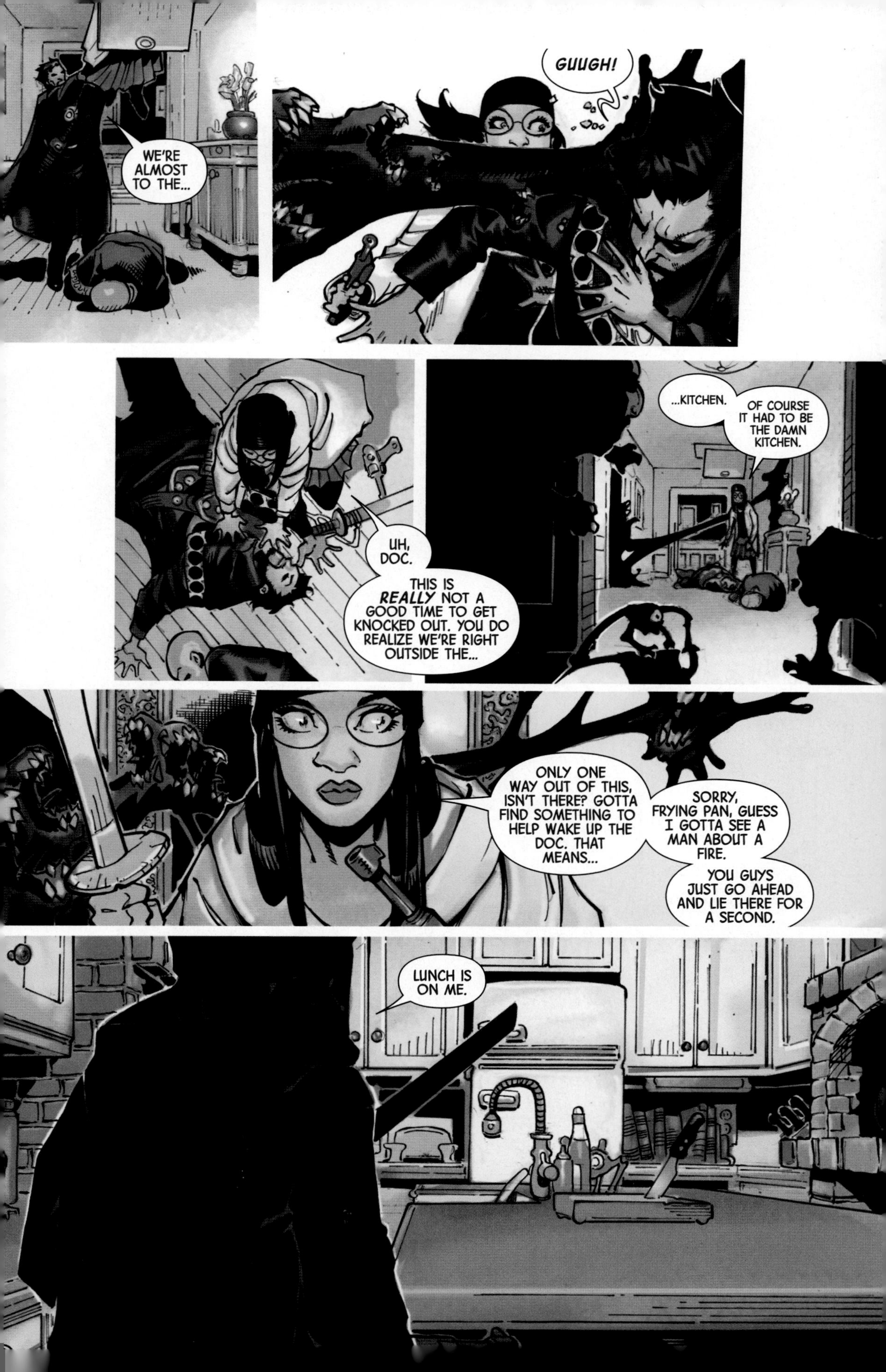
WE'RE ALMOST TO THE...
GUUGH!
UH, DOC.
THIS IS REALLY NOT A GOOD TIME TO GET KNOCKED OUT. YOU DO REALIZE WE'RE RIGHT OUTSIDE THE...
...KITCHEN.
OF COURSE IT HAD TO BE THE DAMN KITCHEN.
ONLY ONE WAY OUT OF THIS, ISN'T THERE? GOTTA FIND SOMETHING TO HELP WAKE UP THE DOC. THAT MEANS...
SORRY, FRYING PAN, GUESS I GOTTA SEE A MAN ABOUT A FIRE.
YOU GUYS JUST GO AHEAD AND LIE THERE FOR A SECOND.
LUNCH IS ON ME.

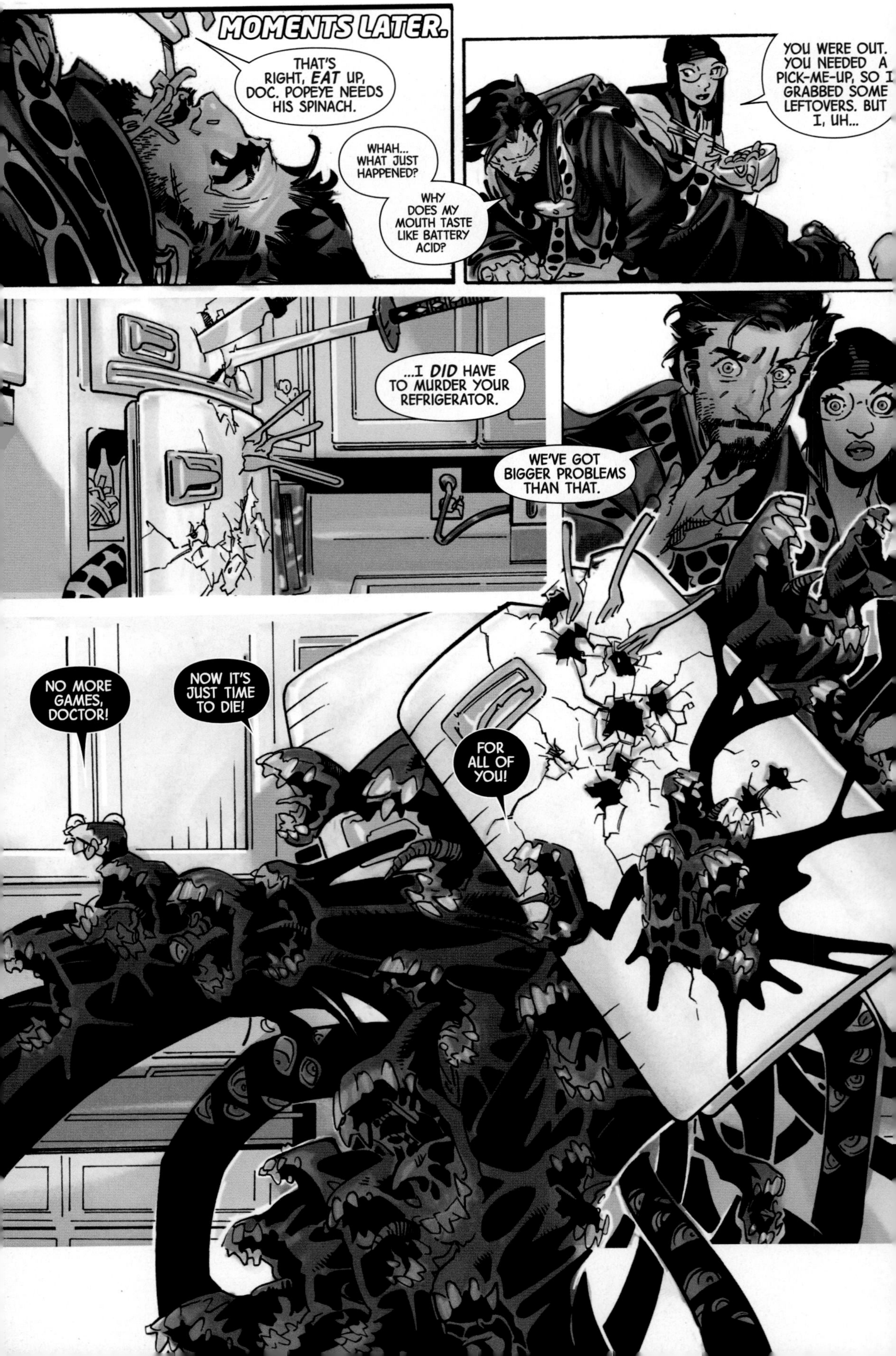
MOMENTS LATER.
THAT'S RIGHT, EAT UP, DOC. POPEYE NEEDS HIS SPINACH.
WHAH... WHAT JUST HAPPENED?
WHY DOES MY MOUTH TASTE LIKE BATTERY ACID?
YOU WERE OUT. YOU NEEDED A PICK-ME-UP, SO I GRABBED SOME LEFTOVERS. BUT I, UH...
...I DID HAVE TO MURDER YOUR REFRIGERATOR.
WE'VE GOT BIGGER PROBLEMS THAN THAT.
NO MORE GAMES, DOCTOR!
NOW IT'S JUST TIME TO DIE!
FOR ALL OF YOU!

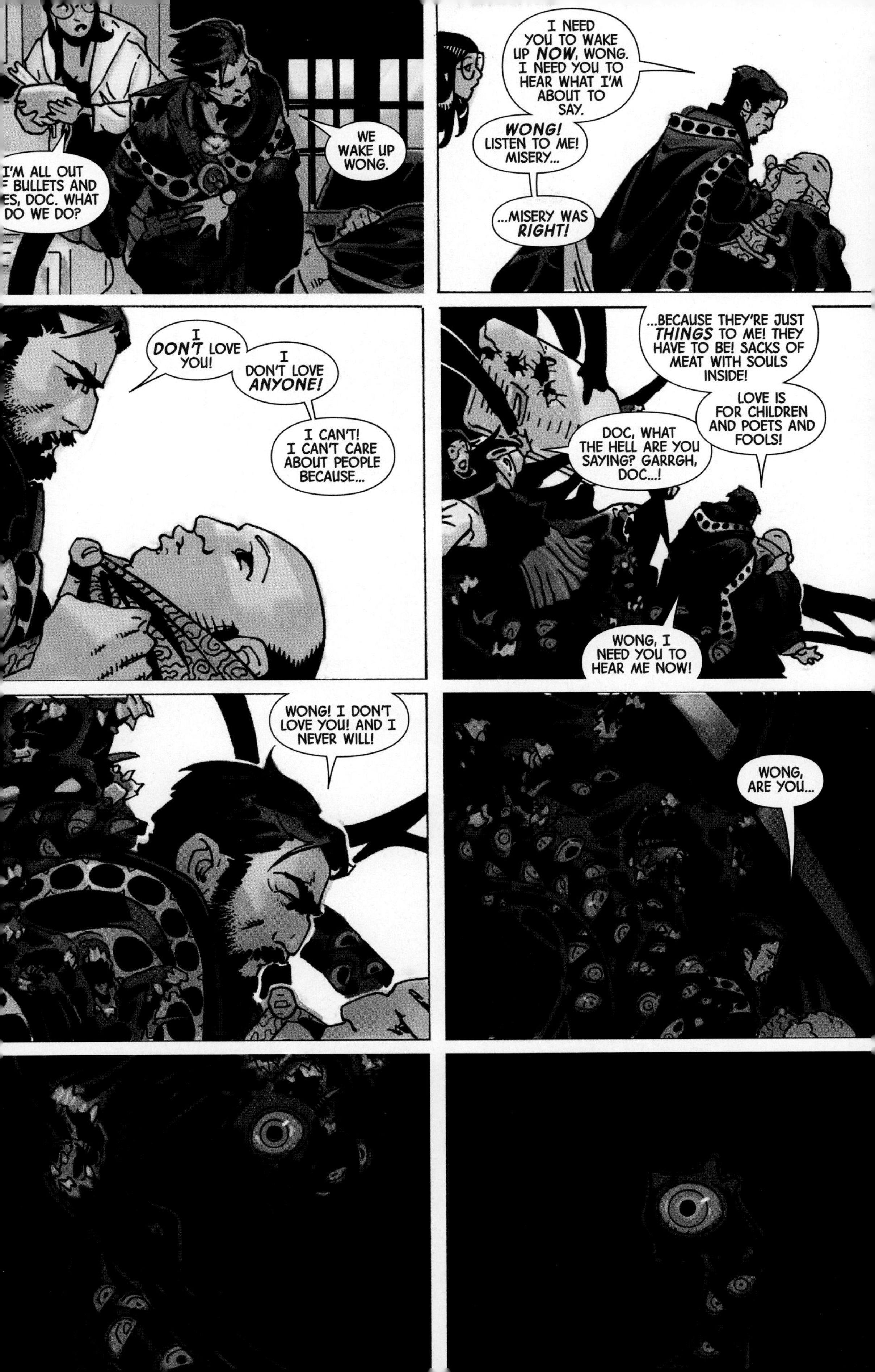
I'M ALL OUT
BULLETS AND
ES, DOC. WHAT
DO WE DO?
WE WAKE UP WONG.
I NEED YOU TO WAKE UP NOW, WONG. I NEED YOU TO HEAR WHAT I'M ABOUT TO SAY.
WONG! LISTEN TO ME! MISERY...
...MISERY WAS RIGHT!
I DON'T LOVE YOU!
I DON'T LOVE ANYONE!
I CAN'T! I CAN'T CARE ABOUT PEOPLE BECAUSE...
...BECAUSE THEY'RE JUST THINGS TO ME! THEY HAVE TO BE! SACKS OF MEAT WITH SOULS INSIDE!
LOVE IS FOR CHILDREN AND POETS AND FOOLS!
DOC, WHAT THE HELL ARE YOU SAYING? GARRGH, DOC...!
WONG, I NEED YOU TO HEAR ME NOW!
WONG! I DON'T LOVE YOU! AND I NEVER WILL!
WONG, ARE YOU...

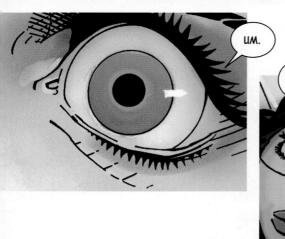

UM.

NOT DEAD YET. HOW AM I NOT...

IT'S ALL RIGHT.

I'VE GOT THINGS IN HAND.

SORT OF.

I THINK.

OH WOW. OKAY, IS NOW THE TIME I'M SUPPOSED TO USE THE--

NO.

IT'S OVER.

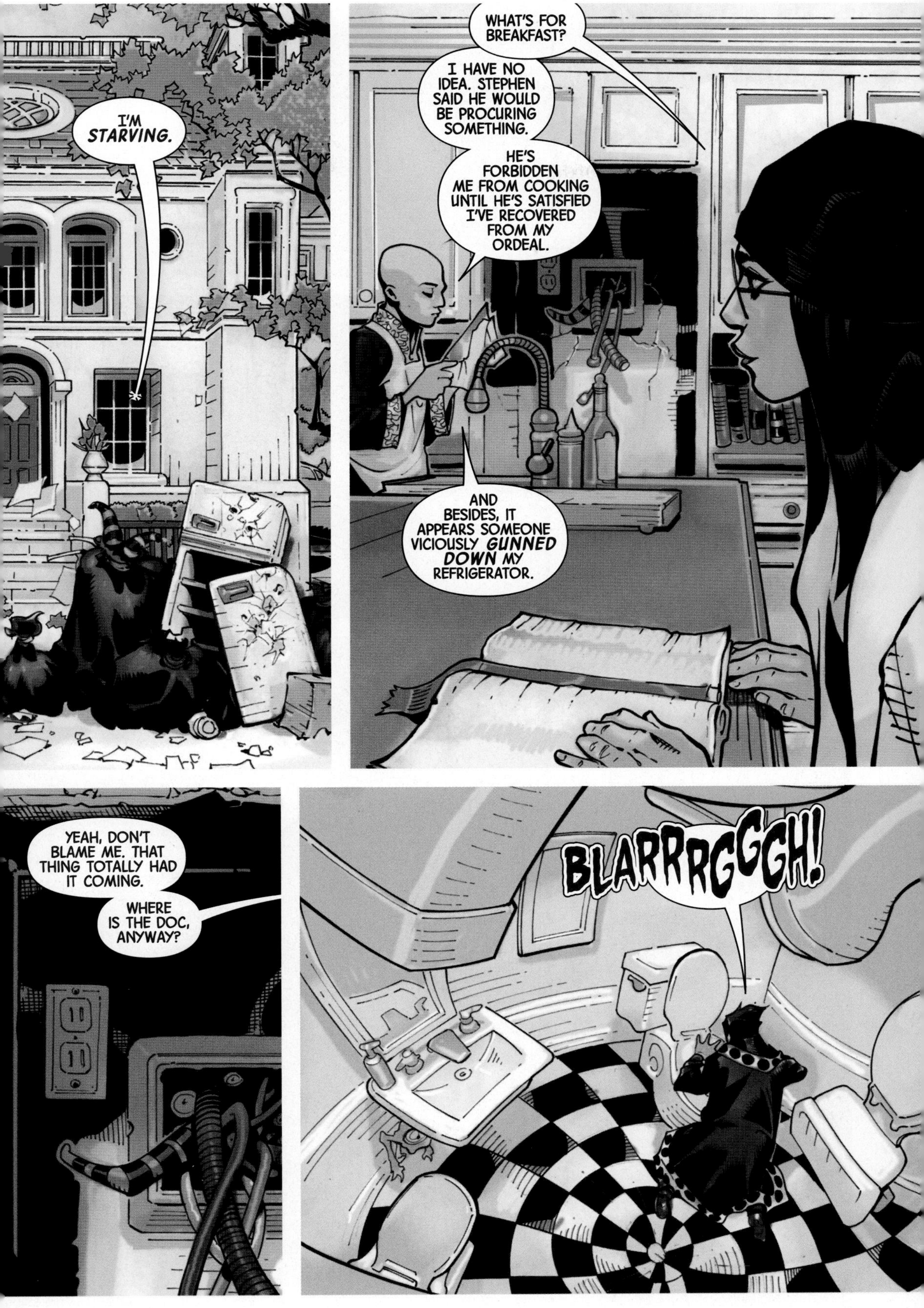
I'M STARVING.
WHAT'S FOR BREAKFAST?
I HAVE NO IDEA. STEPHEN SAID HE WOULD BE PROCURING SOMETHING.
HE'S FORBIDDEN ME FROM COOKING UNTIL HE'S SATISFIED I'VE RECOVERED FROM MY ORDEAL.
AND BESIDES, IT APPEARS SOMEONE VICIOUSLY GUNNED DOWN MY REFRIGERATOR.
YEAH, DON'T BLAME ME. THAT THING TOTALLY HAD IT COMING.
WHERE IS THE DOC, ANYWAY?
BLARRRGGGH!

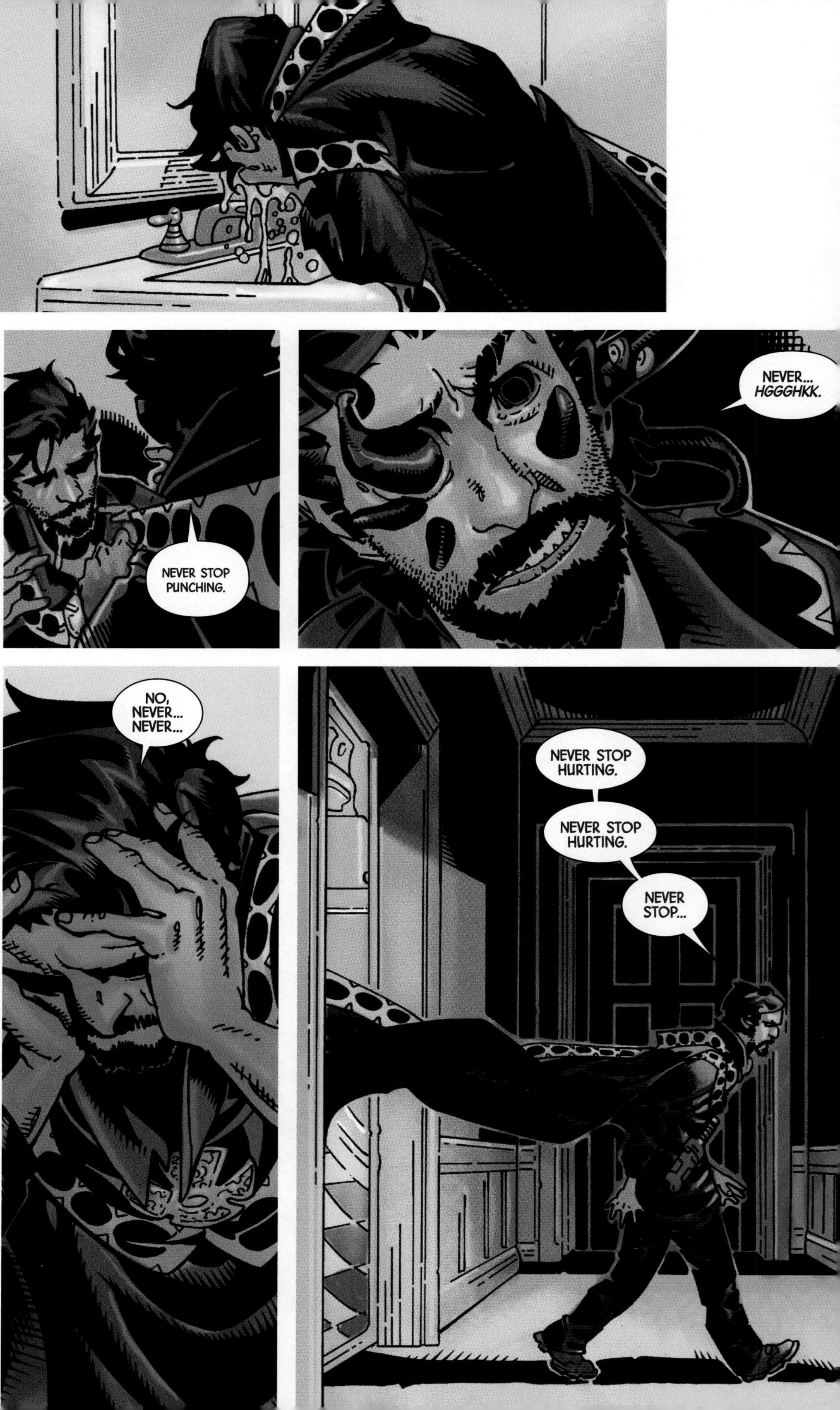
NEVER STOP PUNCHING.
NEVER... HGGGHKK.
NO, NEVER... NEVER...
NEVER STOP HURTING.
NEVER STOP HURTING.
NEVER STOP...

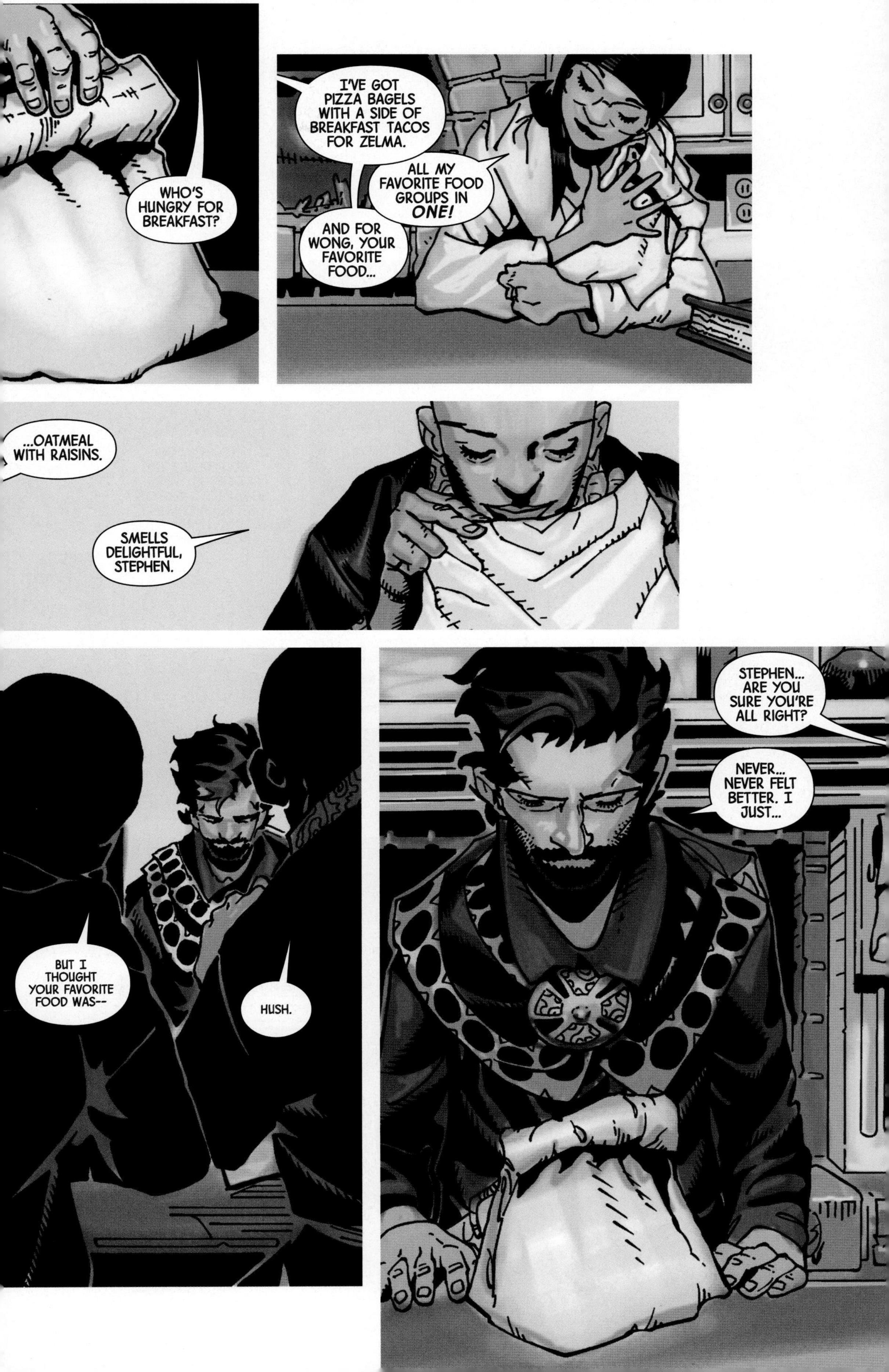
WHO'S HUNGRY FOR BREAKFAST?
I'VE GOT PIZZA BAGELS WITH A SIDE OF BREAKFAST TACOS FOR ZELMA.
ALL MY FAVORITE FOOD GROUPS IN *ONE!*
AND FOR WONG, YOUR FAVORITE FOOD...
...OATMEAL WITH RAISINS.
SMELLS DELIGHTFUL, STEPHEN.
BUT I THOUGHT YOUR FAVORITE FOOD WAS--
HUSH.
STEPHEN... ARE YOU SURE YOU'RE ALL RIGHT?
NEVER... NEVER FELT BETTER. I JUST...

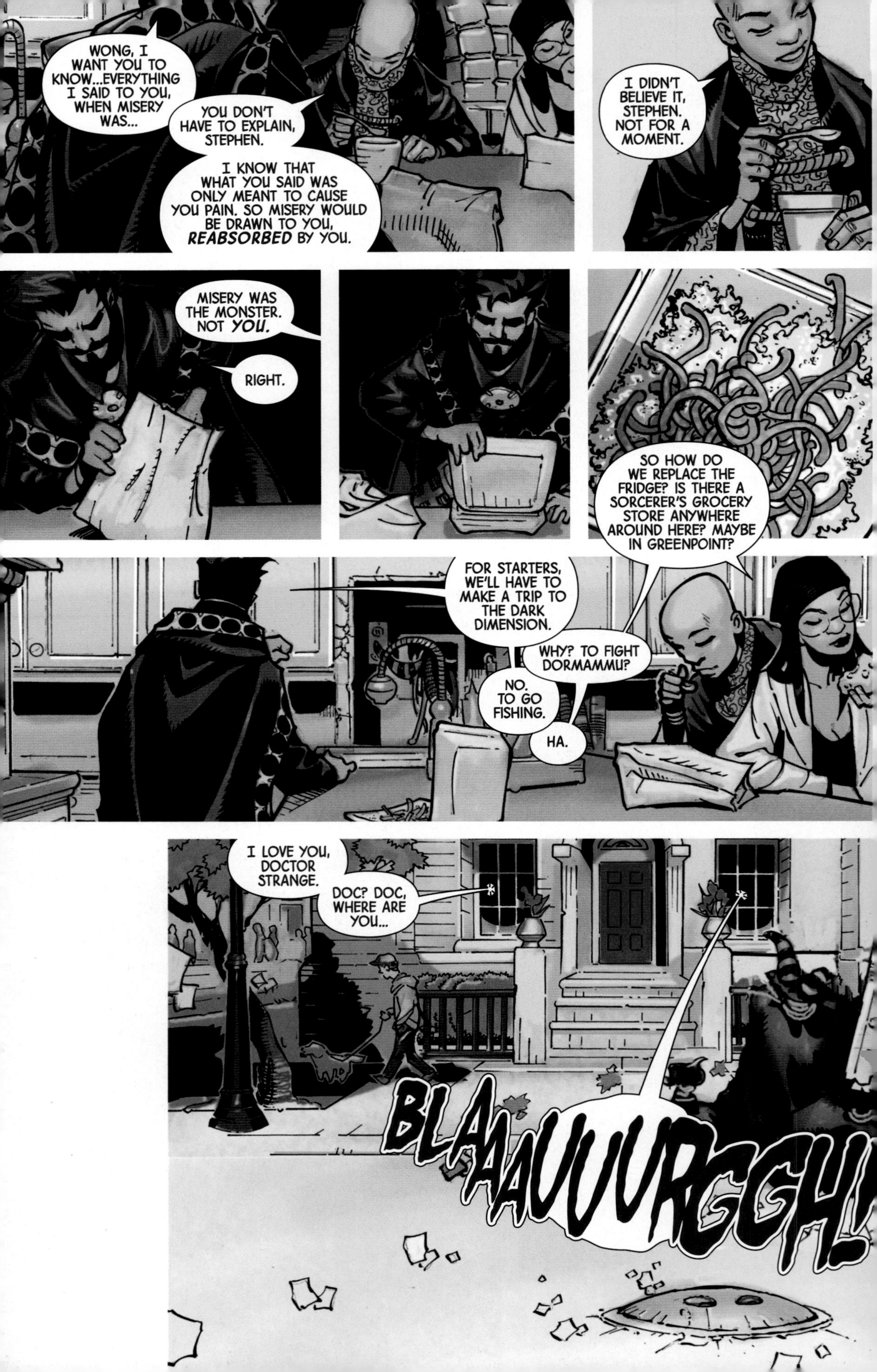
WONG, I WANT YOU TO KNOW...EVERYTHING I SAID TO YOU, WHEN MISERY WAS...
YOU DON'T HAVE TO EXPLAIN, STEPHEN.
I KNOW THAT WHAT YOU SAID WAS ONLY MEANT TO CAUSE YOU PAIN. SO MISERY WOULD BE DRAWN TO YOU, REABSORBED BY YOU.
I DIDN'T BELIEVE IT, STEPHEN. NOT FOR A MOMENT.
MISERY WAS THE MONSTER. NOT YOU.
RIGHT.
SO HOW DO WE REPLACE THE FRIDGE? IS THERE A SORCERER'S GROCERY STORE ANYWHERE AROUND HERE? MAYBE IN GREENPOINT?
FOR STARTERS, WE'LL HAVE TO MAKE A TRIP TO THE DARK DIMENSION.
WHY? TO FIGHT DORMAMMU?
NO. TO GO FISHING.
HA.
I LOVE YOU, DOCTOR STRANGE.
DOC? DOC, WHERE ARE YOU...
BLAAAUUURGGH!

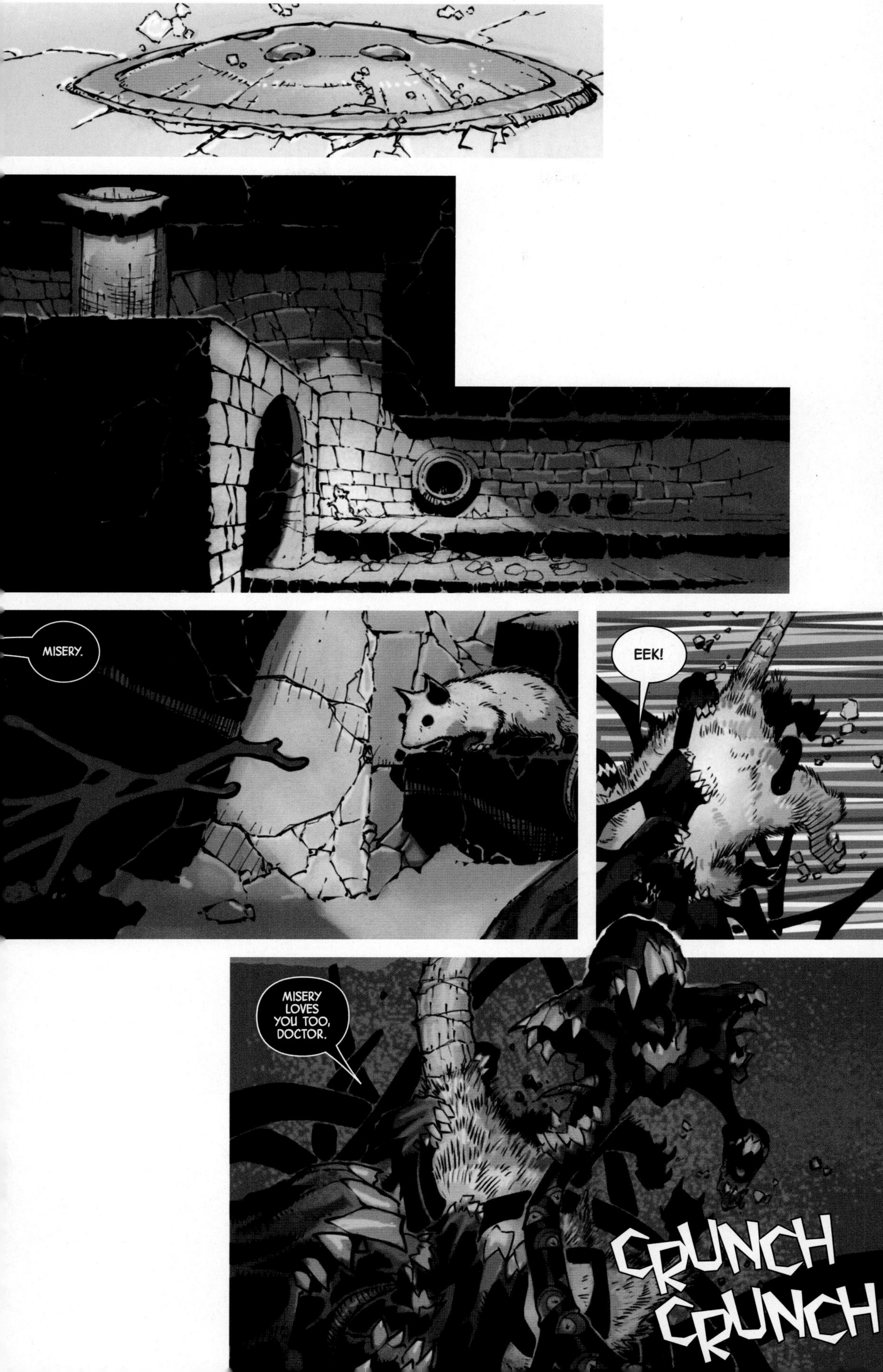
MISERY.
EEK!
MISERY LOVES YOU TOO, DOCTOR.
CRUNCH CRUNCH

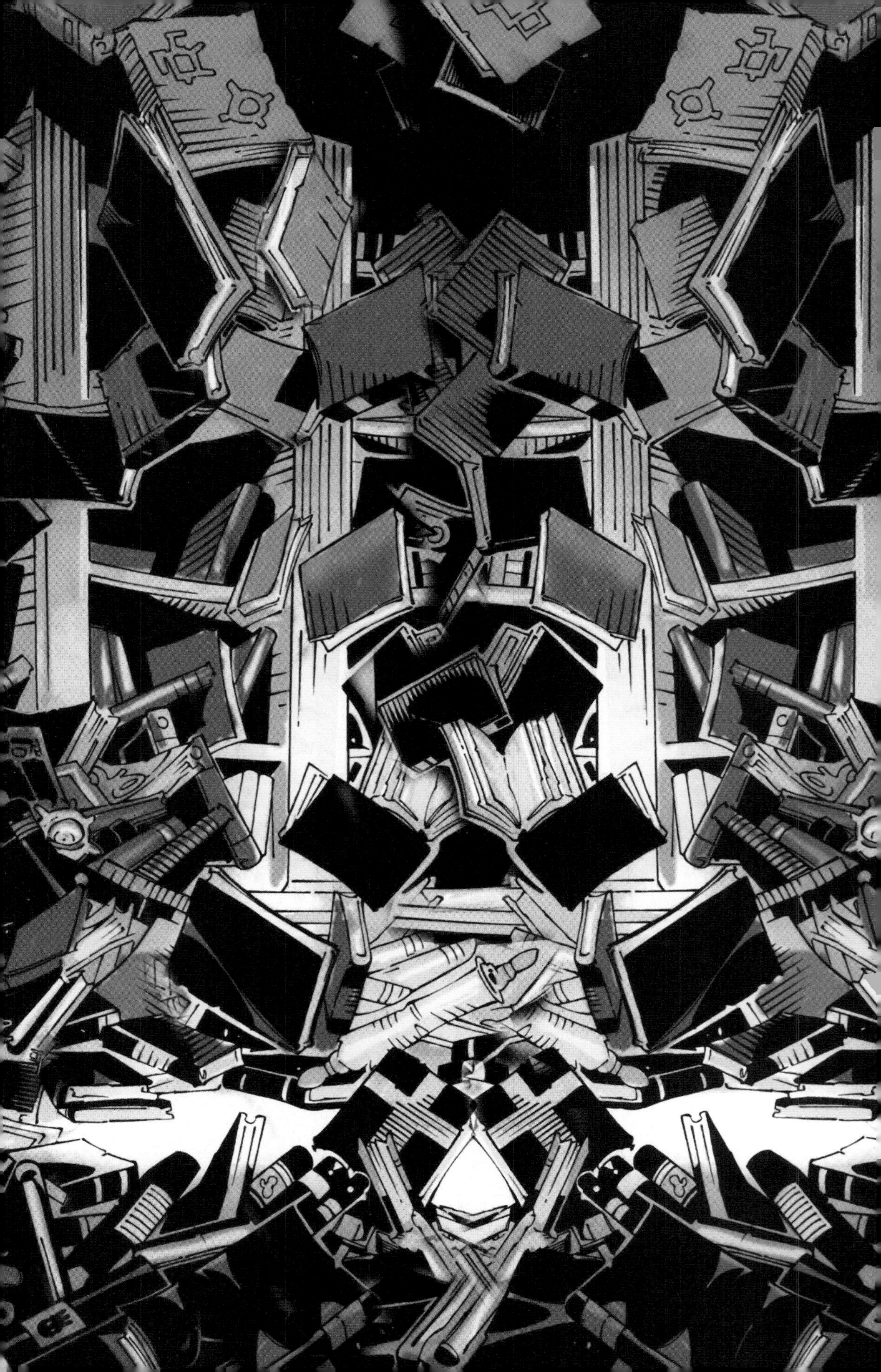

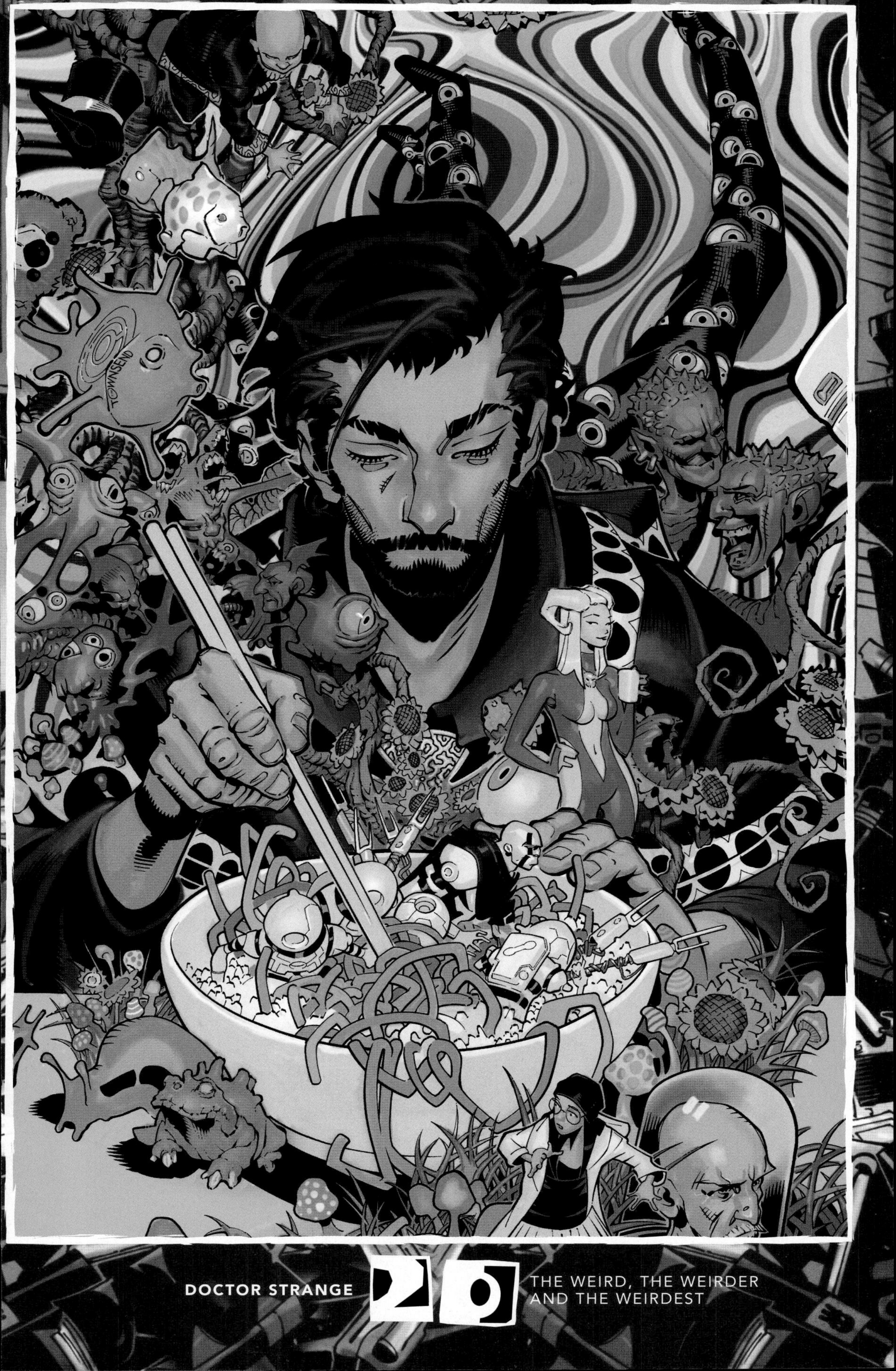
TOWNSEND

DOCTOR STRANGE 20 THE WEIRD, THE WEIRDER AND THE WEIRDEST

SOLD! TO THE GOAT IN THE BACK FOR THREE PHOENIX FEATHERS!

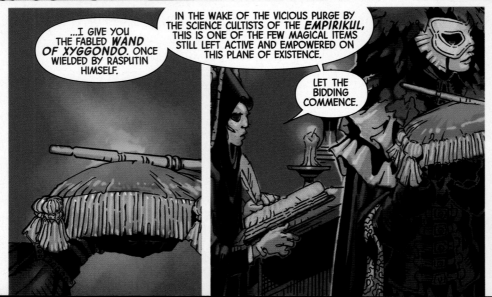

...I GIVE YOU THE FABLED *WAND OF XYGGONDO*. ONCE WIELDED BY RASPUTIN HIMSELF.

IN THE WAKE OF THE VICIOUS PURGE BY THE SCIENCE CULTISTS OF THE *EMPIRIKUL*, THIS IS ONE OF THE FEW MAGICAL ITEMS STILL LEFT ACTIVE AND EMPOWERED ON THIS PLANE OF EXISTENCE.

LET THE BIDDING COMMENCE.

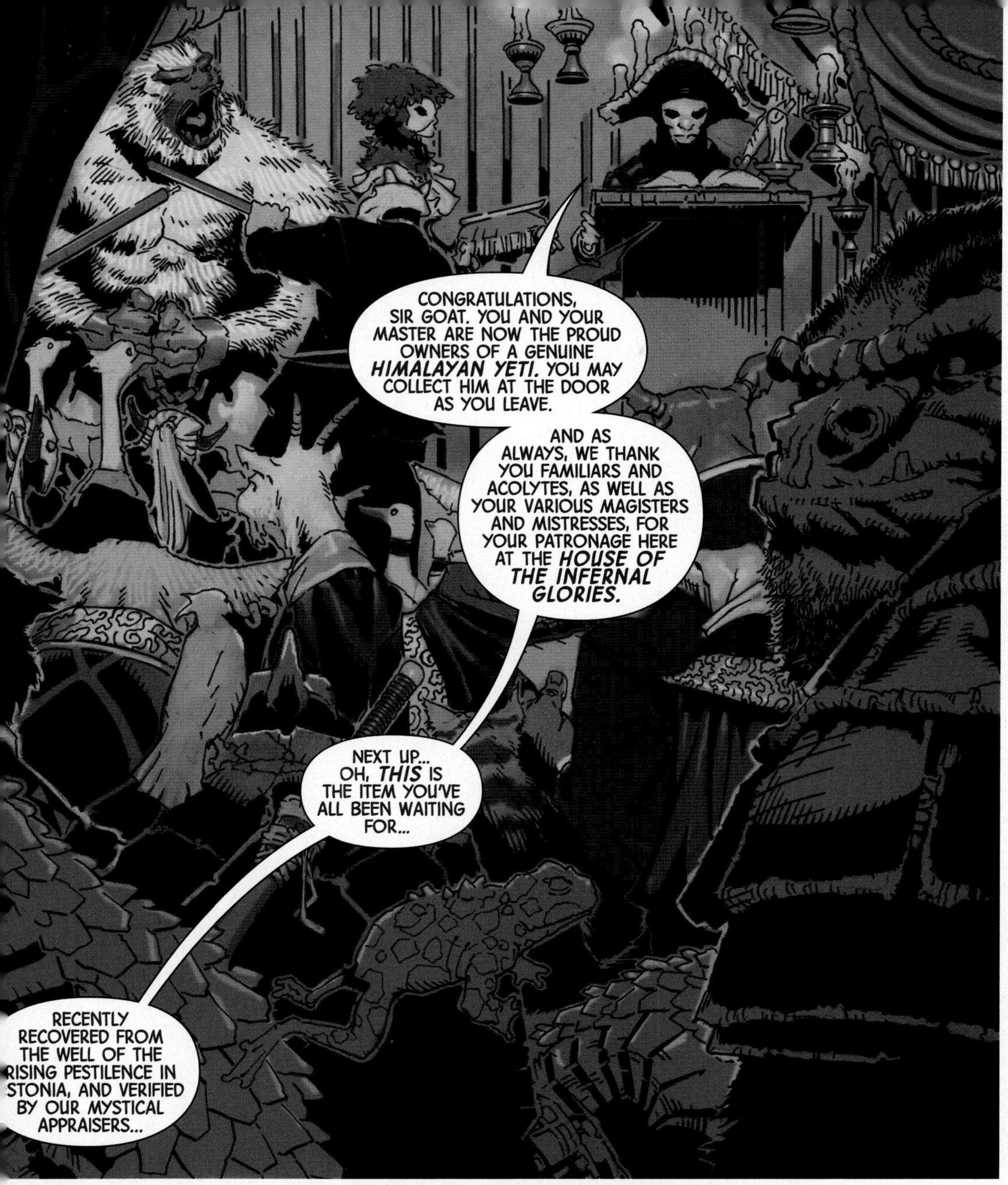
CONGRATULATIONS, SIR GOAT. YOU AND YOUR MASTER ARE NOW THE PROUD OWNERS OF A GENUINE HIMALAYAN YETI. YOU MAY COLLECT HIM AT THE DOOR AS YOU LEAVE.
AND AS ALWAYS, WE THANK YOU FAMILIARS AND ACOLYTES, AS WELL AS YOUR VARIOUS MAGISTERS AND MISTRESSES, FOR YOUR PATRONAGE HERE AT THE HOUSE OF THE INFERNAL GLORIES.
NEXT UP... OH, THIS IS THE ITEM YOU'VE ALL BEEN WAITING FOR...
RECENTLY RECOVERED FROM THE WELL OF THE RISING PESTILENCE IN ESTONIA, AND VERIFIED BY OUR MYSTICAL APPRAISERS...

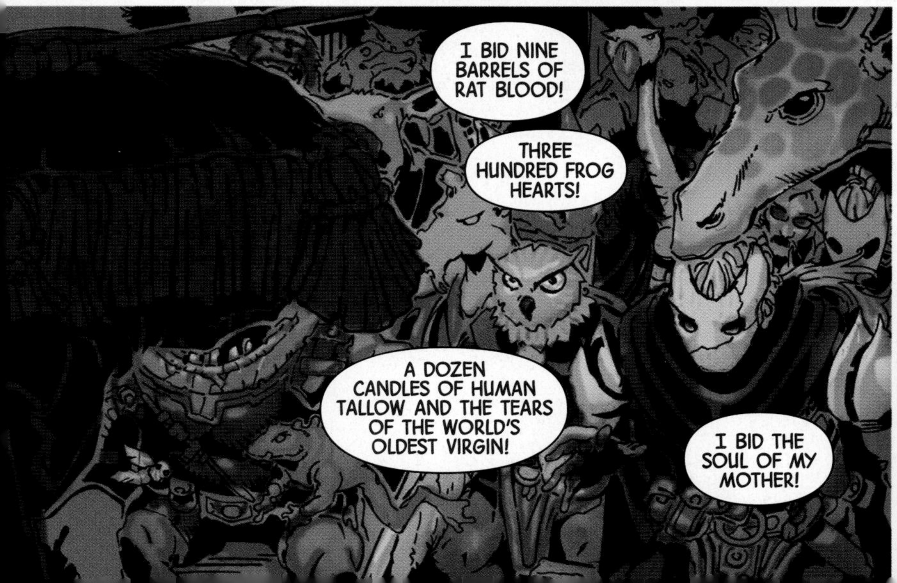
I BID NINE BARRELS OF RAT BLOOD!
THREE HUNDRED FROG HEARTS!
A DOZEN CANDLES OF HUMAN TALLOW AND THE TEARS OF THE WORLD'S OLDEST VIRGIN!
I BID THE SOUL OF MY MOTHER!

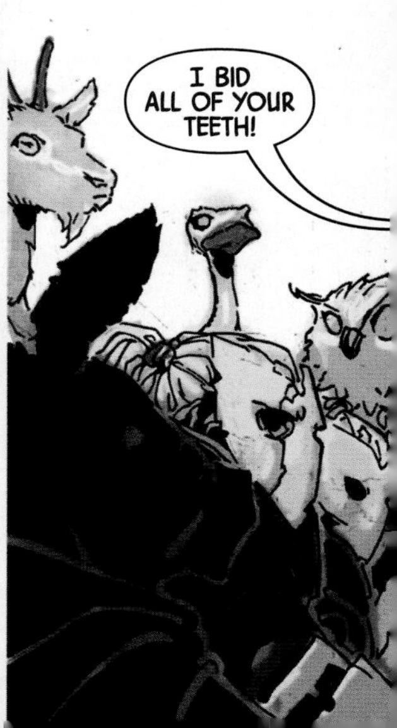
I BID ALL OF YOUR TEETH!

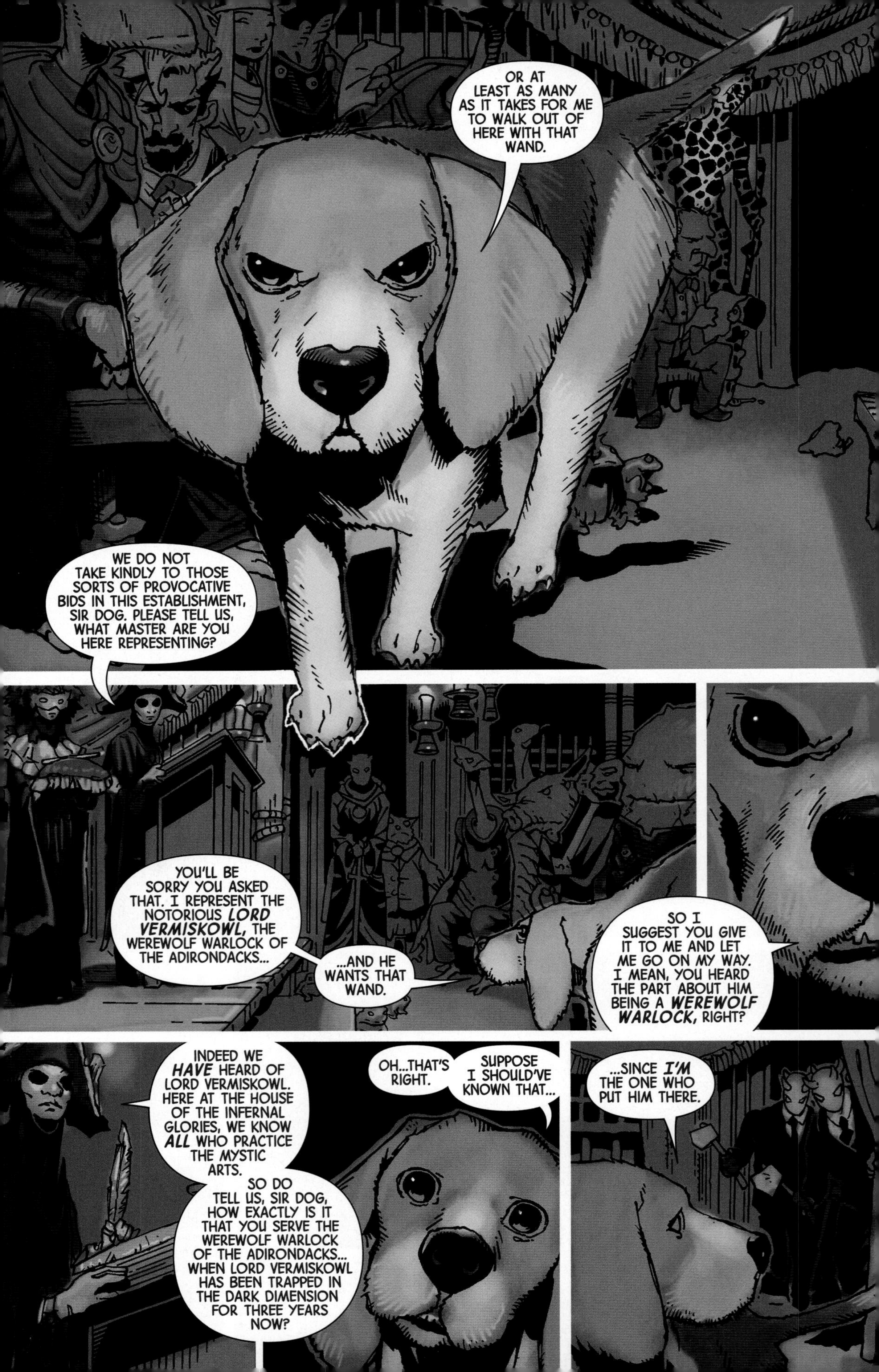
OR AT LEAST AS MANY AS IT TAKES FOR ME TO WALK OUT OF HERE WITH THAT WAND.
WE DO NOT TAKE KINDLY TO THOSE SORTS OF PROVOCATIVE BIDS IN THIS ESTABLISHMENT, SIR DOG. PLEASE TELL US, WHAT MASTER ARE YOU HERE REPRESENTING?
YOU'LL BE SORRY YOU ASKED THAT. I REPRESENT THE NOTORIOUS **LORD VERMISKOWL,** THE WEREWOLF WARLOCK OF THE ADIRONDACKS...
...AND HE WANTS THAT WAND.
SO I SUGGEST YOU GIVE IT TO ME AND LET ME GO ON MY WAY. I MEAN, YOU HEARD THE PART ABOUT HIM BEING A **WEREWOLF WARLOCK,** RIGHT?
INDEED WE **HAVE** HEARD OF LORD VERMISKOWL. HERE AT THE HOUSE OF THE INFERNAL GLORIES, WE KNOW **ALL** WHO PRACTICE THE MYSTIC ARTS.
SO DO TELL US, SIR DOG, HOW EXACTLY IS IT THAT YOU SERVE THE WEREWOLF WARLOCK OF THE ADIRONDACKS... WHEN LORD VERMISKOWL HAS BEEN TRAPPED IN THE DARK DIMENSION FOR THREE YEARS NOW?
OH...THAT'S RIGHT.
SUPPOSE I SHOULD'VE KNOWN THAT...
...SINCE **I'M** THE ONE WHO PUT HIM THERE.

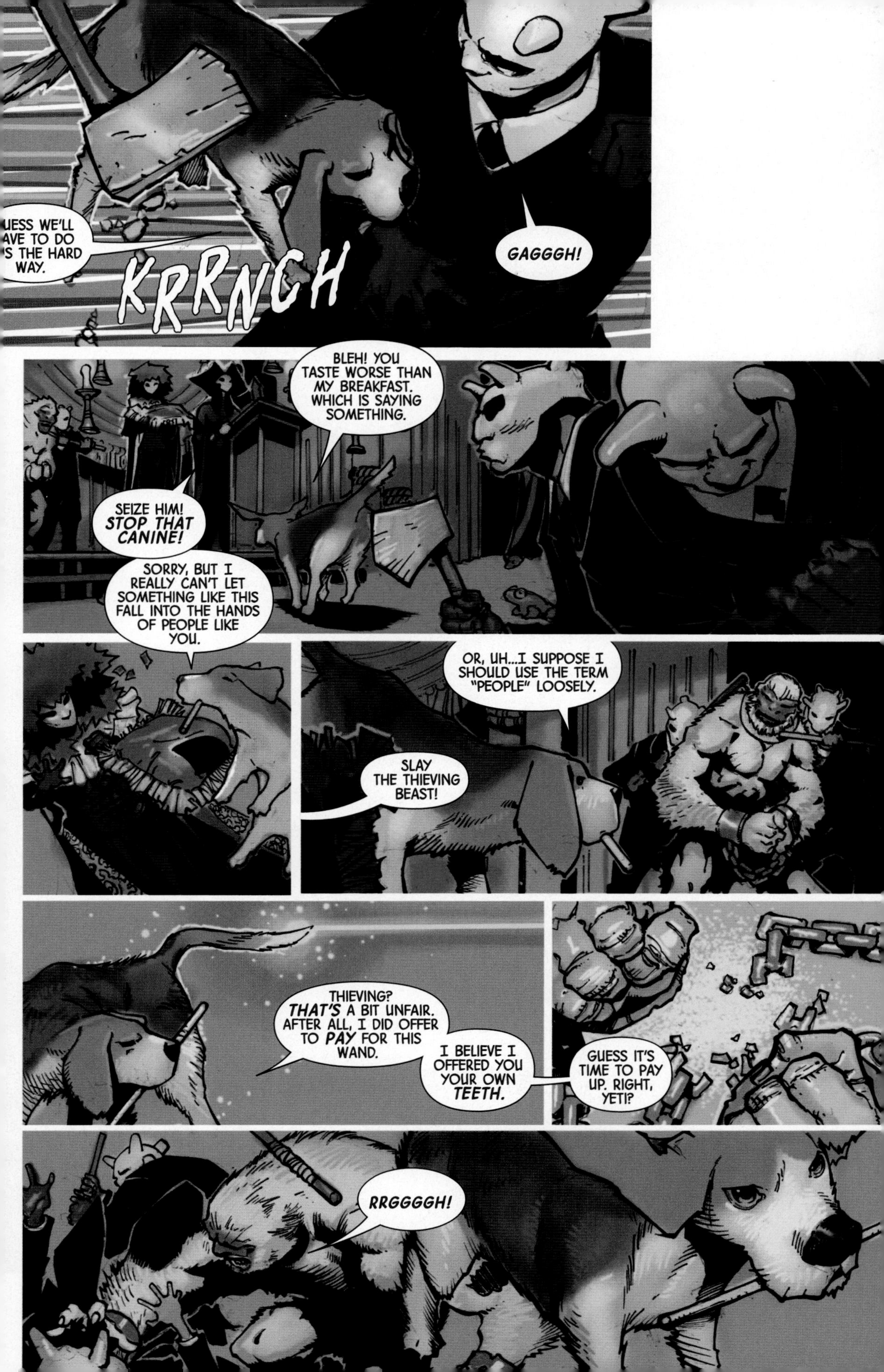

UESS WE'LL AVE TO DO 'S THE HARD WAY.
KRRNCH
GAGGGH!
BLEH! YOU TASTE WORSE THAN MY BREAKFAST. WHICH IS SAYING SOMETHING.
SEIZE HIM! STOP THAT CANINE!
SORRY, BUT I REALLY CAN'T LET SOMETHING LIKE THIS FALL INTO THE HANDS OF PEOPLE LIKE YOU.
OR, UH...I SUPPOSE I SHOULD USE THE TERM "PEOPLE" LOOSELY.
SLAY THE THIEVING BEAST!
THIEVING? THAT'S A BIT UNFAIR. AFTER ALL, I DID OFFER TO PAY FOR THIS WAND.
I BELIEVE I OFFERED YOU YOUR OWN TEETH.
GUESS IT'S TIME TO PAY UP. RIGHT, YETI?
RRGGGGH!

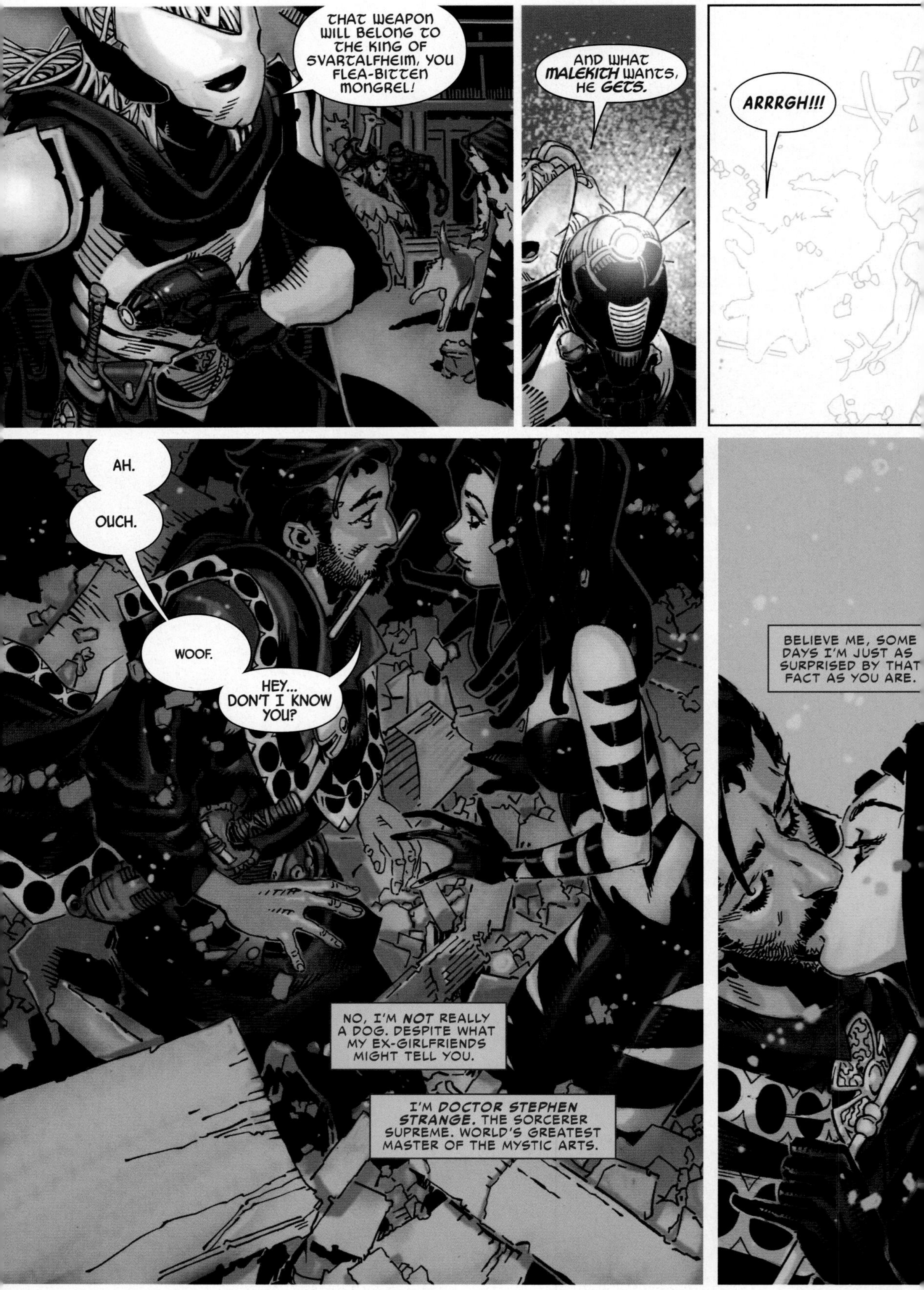
THAT WEAPON WILL BELONG TO THE KING OF SVARTALFHEIM, YOU FLEA-BITTEN MONGREL!
AND WHAT MALEKITH WANTS, HE GETS.
ARRRGH!!!
AH.
OUCH.
WOOF.
HEY... DON'T I KNOW YOU?
NO, I'M NOT REALLY A DOG. DESPITE WHAT MY EX-GIRLFRIENDS MIGHT TELL YOU.
I'M DOCTOR STEPHEN STRANGE. THE SORCERER SUPREME. WORLD'S GREATEST MASTER OF THE MYSTIC ARTS.
BELIEVE ME, SOME DAYS I'M JUST AS SURPRISED BY THAT FACT AS YOU ARE.

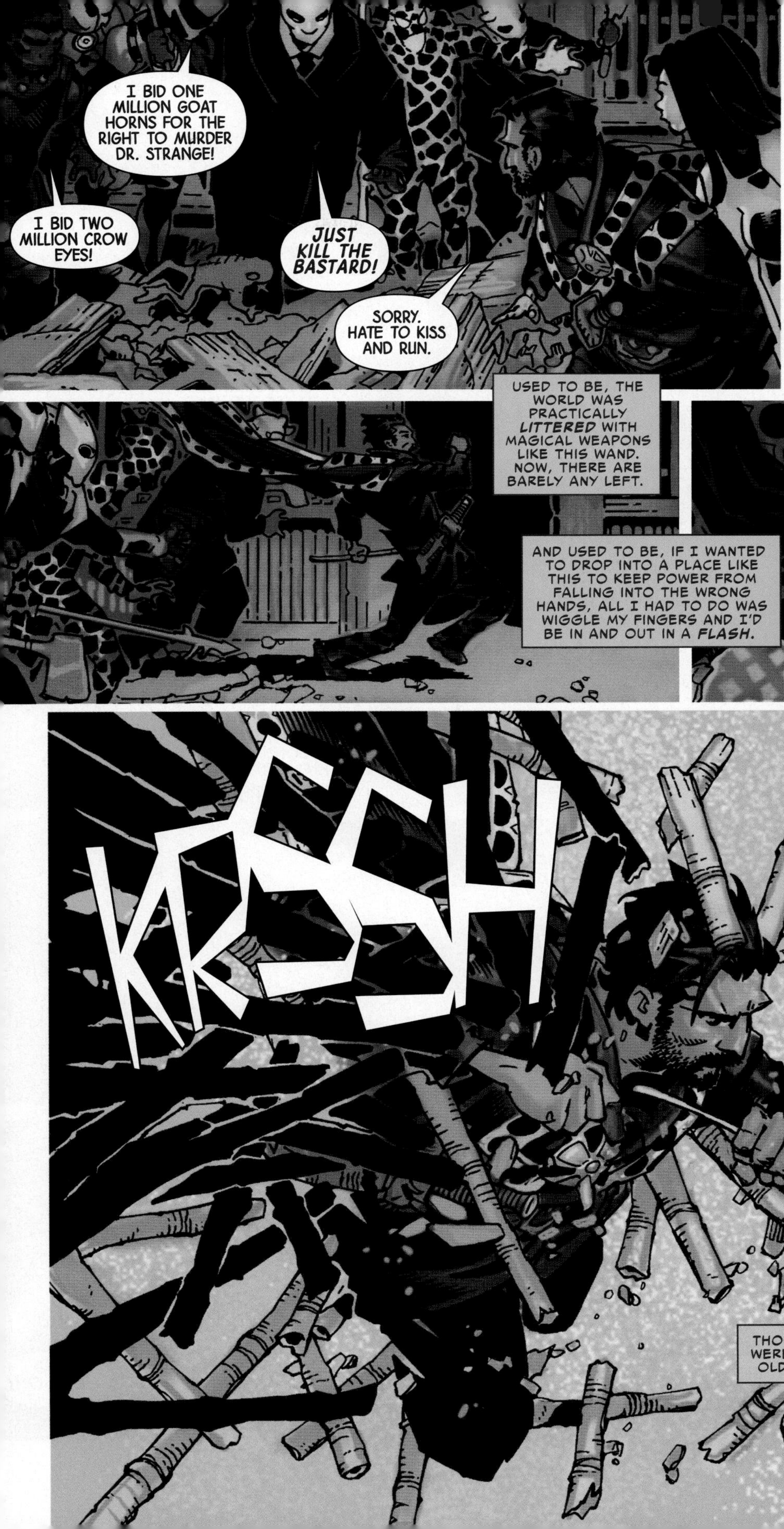
I BID ONE MILLION GOAT HORNS FOR THE RIGHT TO MURDER DR. STRANGE!
I BID TWO MILLION CROW EYES!
JUST KILL THE BASTARD!
SORRY. HATE TO KISS AND RUN.
USED TO BE, THE WORLD WAS PRACTICALLY LITTERED WITH MAGICAL WEAPONS LIKE THIS WAND. NOW, THERE ARE BARELY ANY LEFT.
AND USED TO BE, IF I WANTED TO DROP INTO A PLACE LIKE THIS TO KEEP POWER FROM FALLING INTO THE WRONG HANDS, ALL I HAD TO DO WAS WIGGLE MY FINGERS AND I'D BE IN AND OUT IN A FLASH.
KRSSH
THOSE SURE WERE GRAND OLD DAYS.

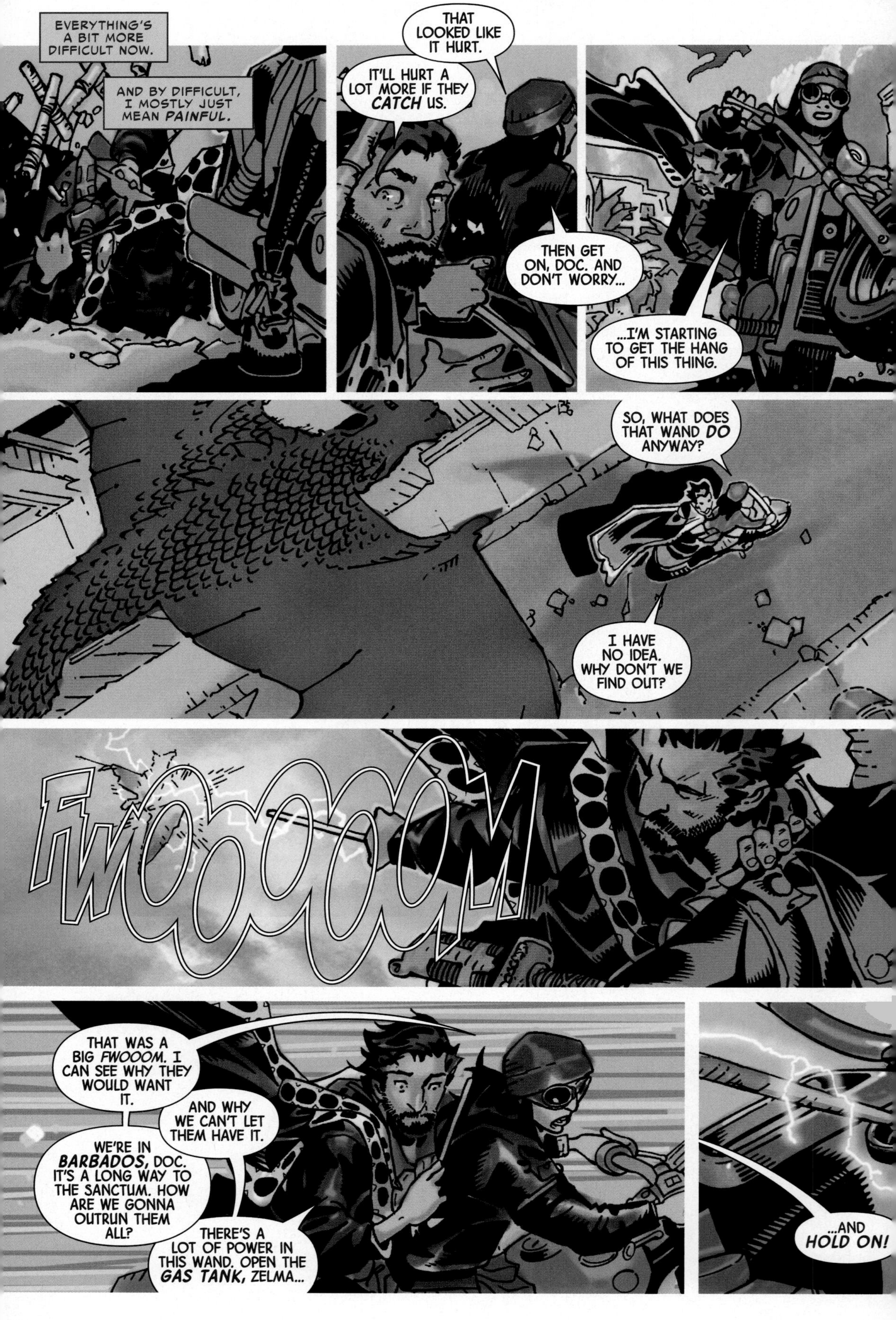
EVERYTHING'S A BIT MORE DIFFICULT NOW.
AND BY DIFFICULT, I MOSTLY JUST MEAN PAINFUL.
THAT LOOKED LIKE IT HURT.
IT'LL HURT A LOT MORE IF THEY CATCH US.
THEN GET ON, DOC. AND DON'T WORRY...
...I'M STARTING TO GET THE HANG OF THIS THING.
SO, WHAT DOES THAT WAND DO ANYWAY?
I HAVE NO IDEA. WHY DON'T WE FIND OUT?
FWOOOOOOM
THAT WAS A BIG FWOOOM. I CAN SEE WHY THEY WOULD WANT IT.
AND WHY WE CAN'T LET THEM HAVE IT.
WE'RE IN BARBADOS, DOC. IT'S A LONG WAY TO THE SANCTUM. HOW ARE WE GONNA OUTRUN THEM ALL?
THERE'S A LOT OF POWER IN THIS WAND. OPEN THE GAS TANK, ZELMA...
...AND HOLD ON!

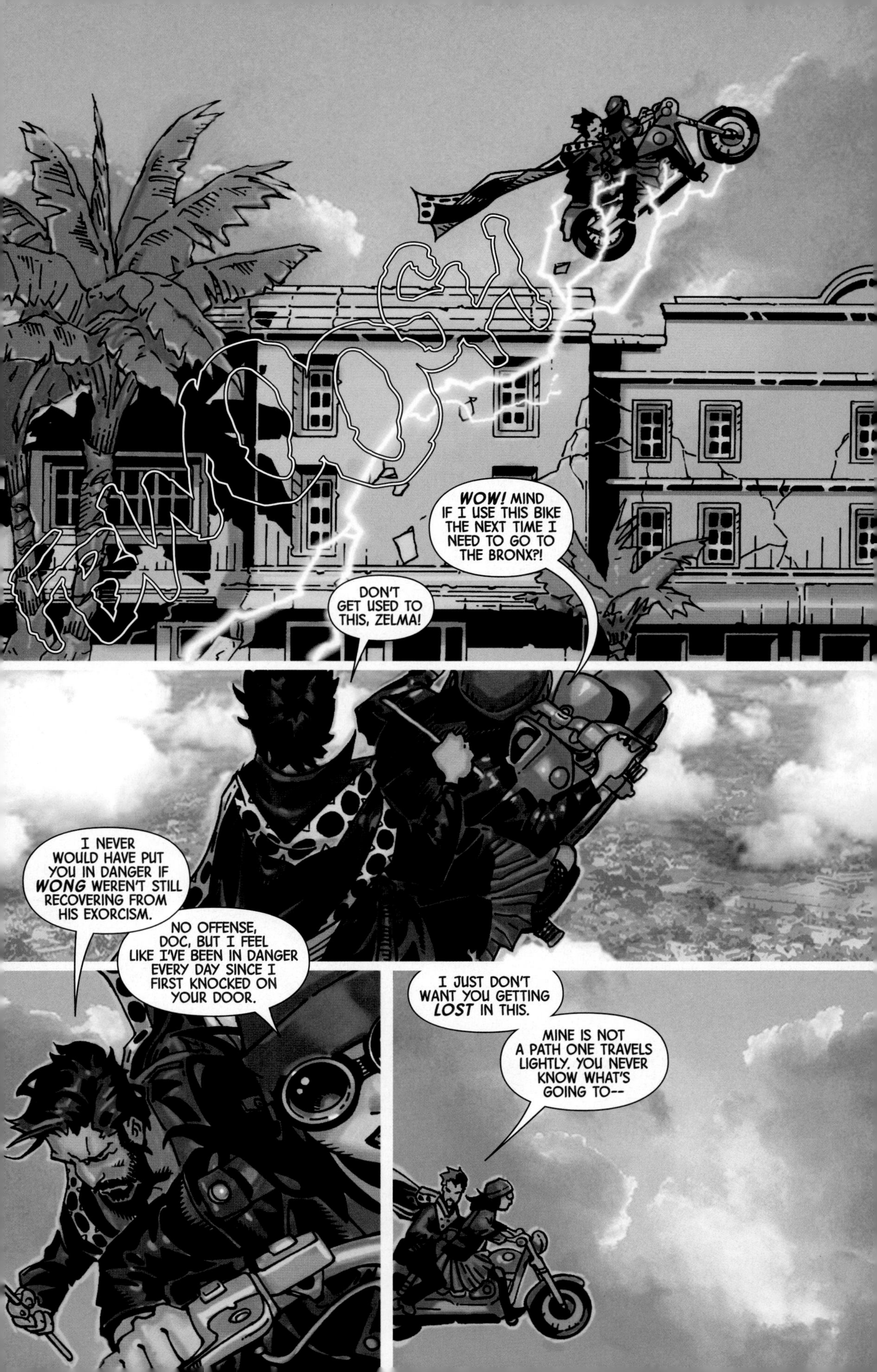
WOW! MIND IF I USE THIS BIKE THE NEXT TIME I NEED TO GO TO THE BRONX?!
DON'T GET USED TO THIS, ZELMA!
I NEVER WOULD HAVE PUT YOU IN DANGER IF WONG WEREN'T STILL RECOVERING FROM HIS EXORCISM.
NO OFFENSE, DOC, BUT I FEEL LIKE I'VE BEEN IN DANGER EVERY DAY SINCE I FIRST KNOCKED ON YOUR DOOR.
I JUST DON'T WANT YOU GETTING LOST IN THIS.
MINE IS NOT A PATH ONE TRAVELS LIGHTLY. YOU NEVER KNOW WHAT'S GOING TO--

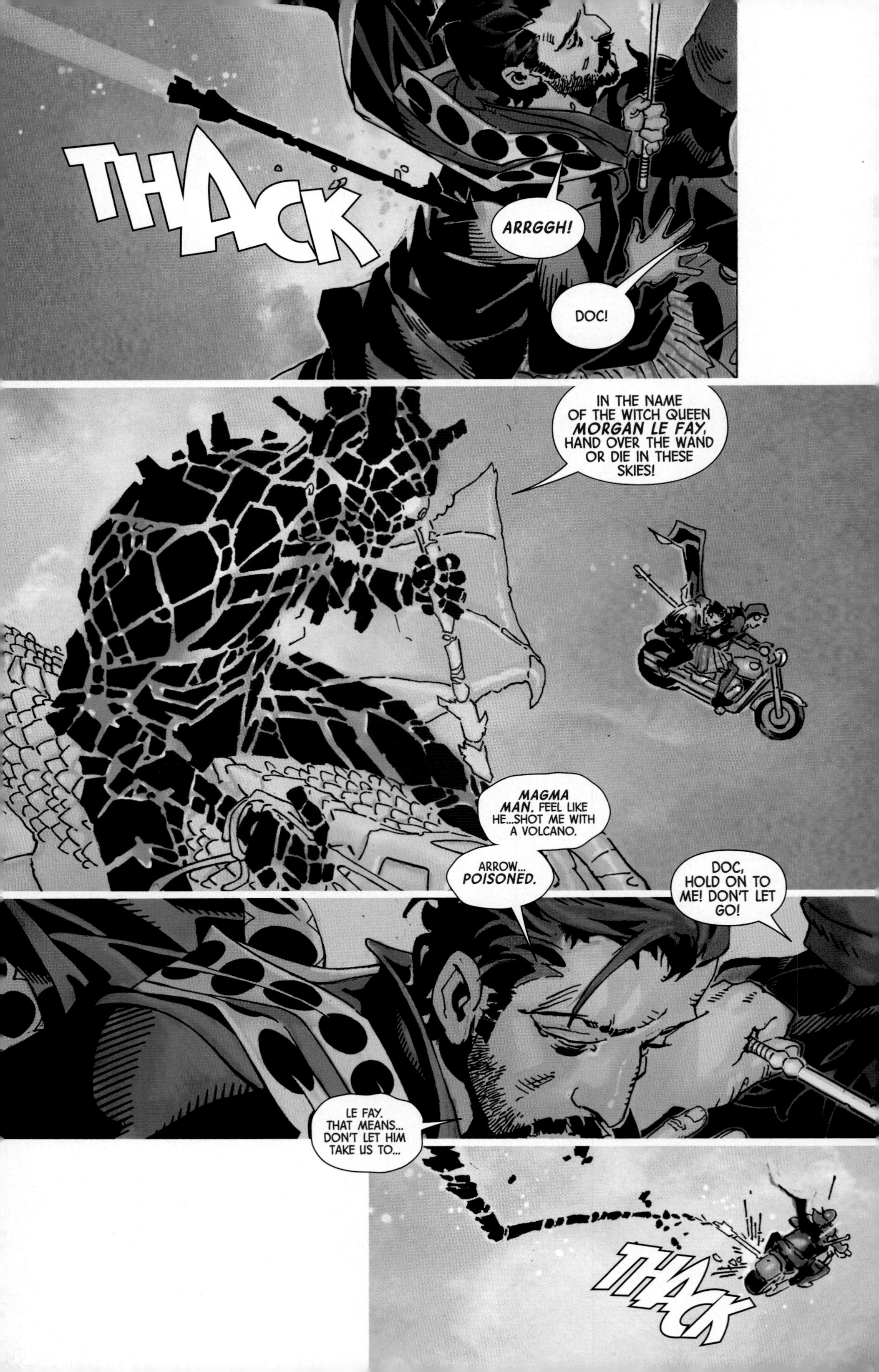
THACK
ARRGGH!
DOC!
IN THE NAME OF THE WITCH QUEEN MORGAN LE FAY, HAND OVER THE WAND OR DIE IN THESE SKIES!
MAGMA MAN. FEEL LIKE HE...SHOT ME WITH A VOLCANO.
ARROW... POISONED.
DOC, HOLD ON TO ME! DON'T LET GO!
LE FAY. THAT MEANS... DON'T LET HIM TAKE US TO...
THACK

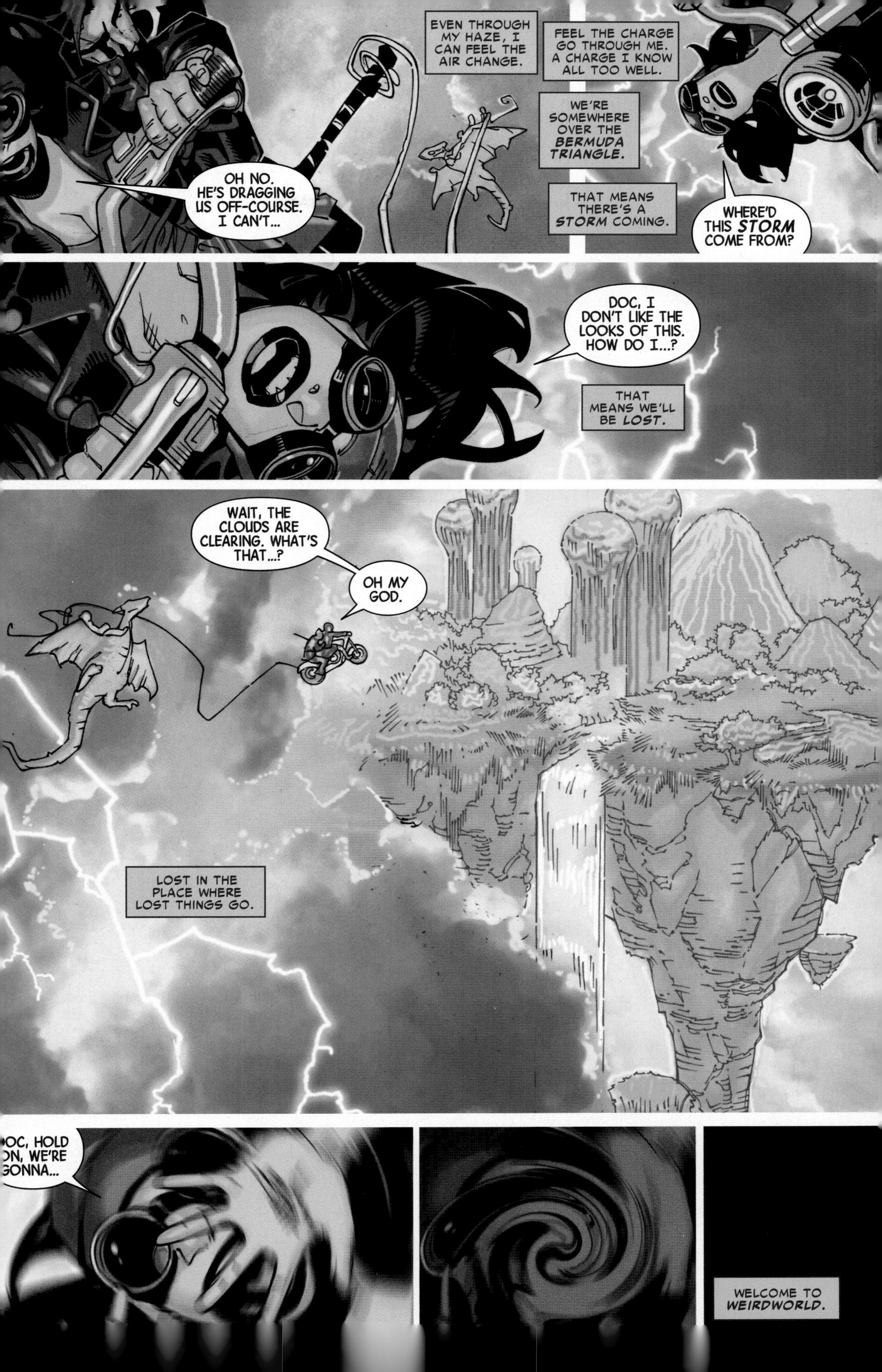
OH NO. HE'S DRAGGING US OFF-COURSE. I CAN'T...
EVEN THROUGH MY HAZE, I CAN FEEL THE AIR CHANGE.
FEEL THE CHARGE GO THROUGH ME. A CHARGE I KNOW ALL TOO WELL.
WE'RE SOMEWHERE OVER THE BERMUDA TRIANGLE.
THAT MEANS THERE'S A STORM COMING.
WHERE'D THIS STORM COME FROM?
DOC, I DON'T LIKE THE LOOKS OF THIS. HOW DO I...?
THAT MEANS WE'LL BE LOST.
WAIT, THE CLOUDS ARE CLEARING. WHAT'S THAT...?
OH MY GOD.
LOST IN THE PLACE WHERE LOST THINGS GO.
OC, HOLD N, WE'RE GONNA...
WELCOME TO WEIRDWORLD.

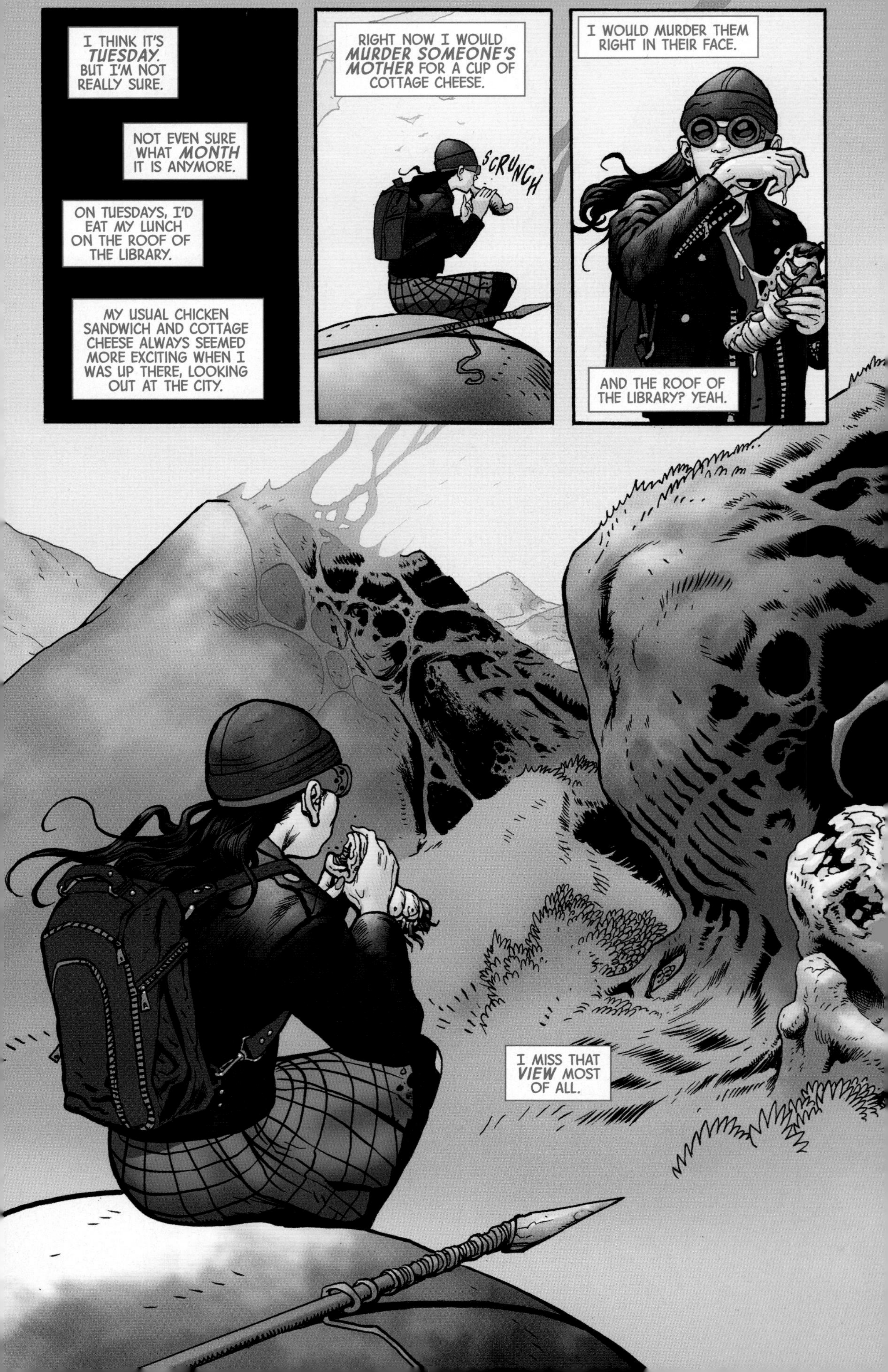
I THINK IT'S *TUESDAY.* BUT I'M NOT REALLY SURE.
NOT EVEN SURE WHAT *MONTH* IT IS ANYMORE.
ON TUESDAYS, I'D EAT MY LUNCH ON THE ROOF OF THE LIBRARY.
MY USUAL CHICKEN SANDWICH AND COTTAGE CHEESE ALWAYS SEEMED MORE EXCITING WHEN I WAS UP THERE, LOOKING OUT AT THE CITY.
RIGHT NOW I WOULD *MURDER SOMEONE'S MOTHER* FOR A CUP OF COTTAGE CHEESE.
SCRUNCH
I WOULD MURDER THEM RIGHT IN THEIR FACE.
AND THE ROOF OF THE LIBRARY? YEAH.
I MISS THAT *VIEW* MOST OF ALL.

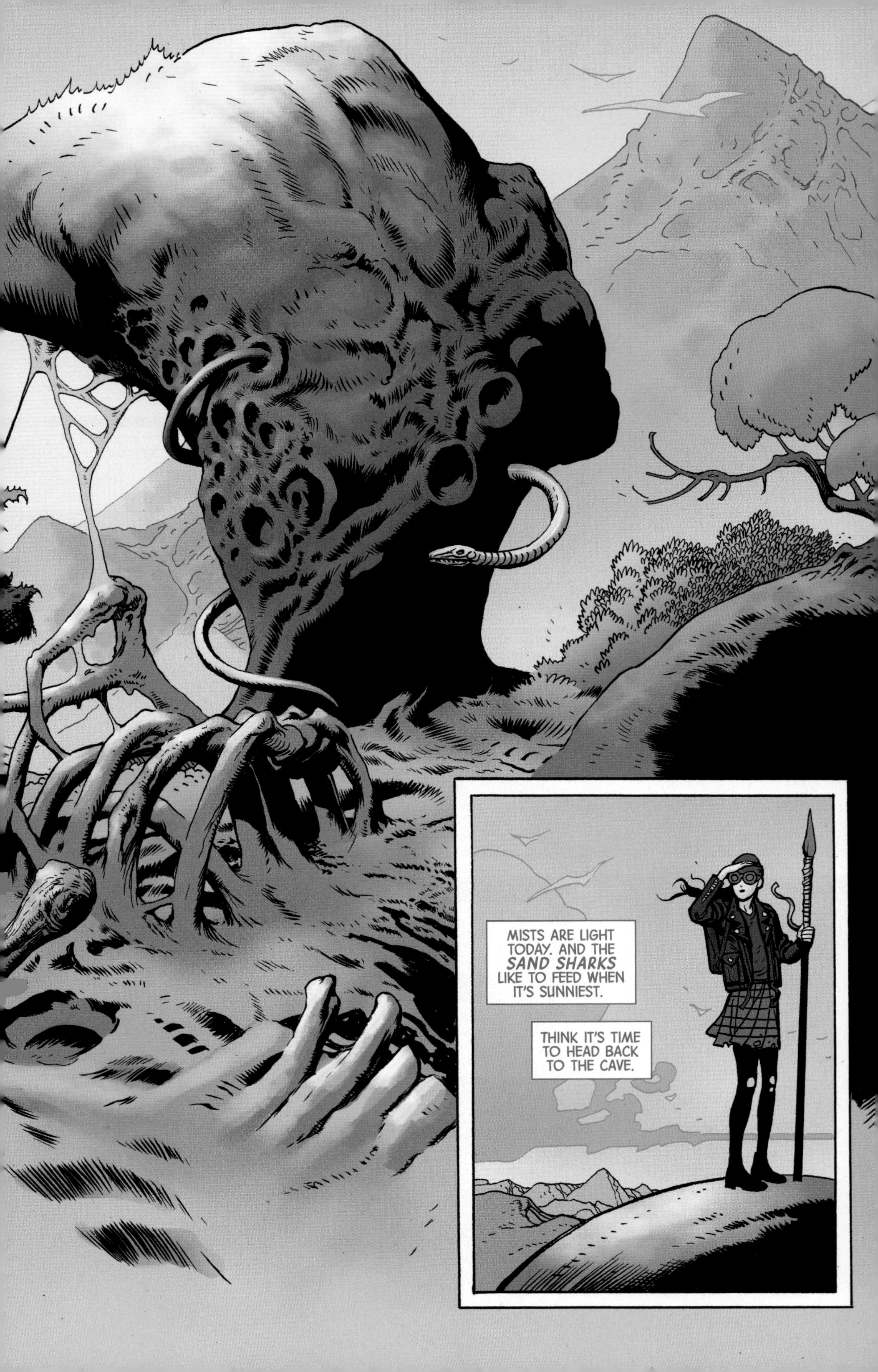
MISTS ARE LIGHT TODAY. AND THE SAND SHARKS LIKE TO FEED WHEN IT'S SUNNIEST.
THINK IT'S TIME TO HEAD BACK TO THE CAVE.

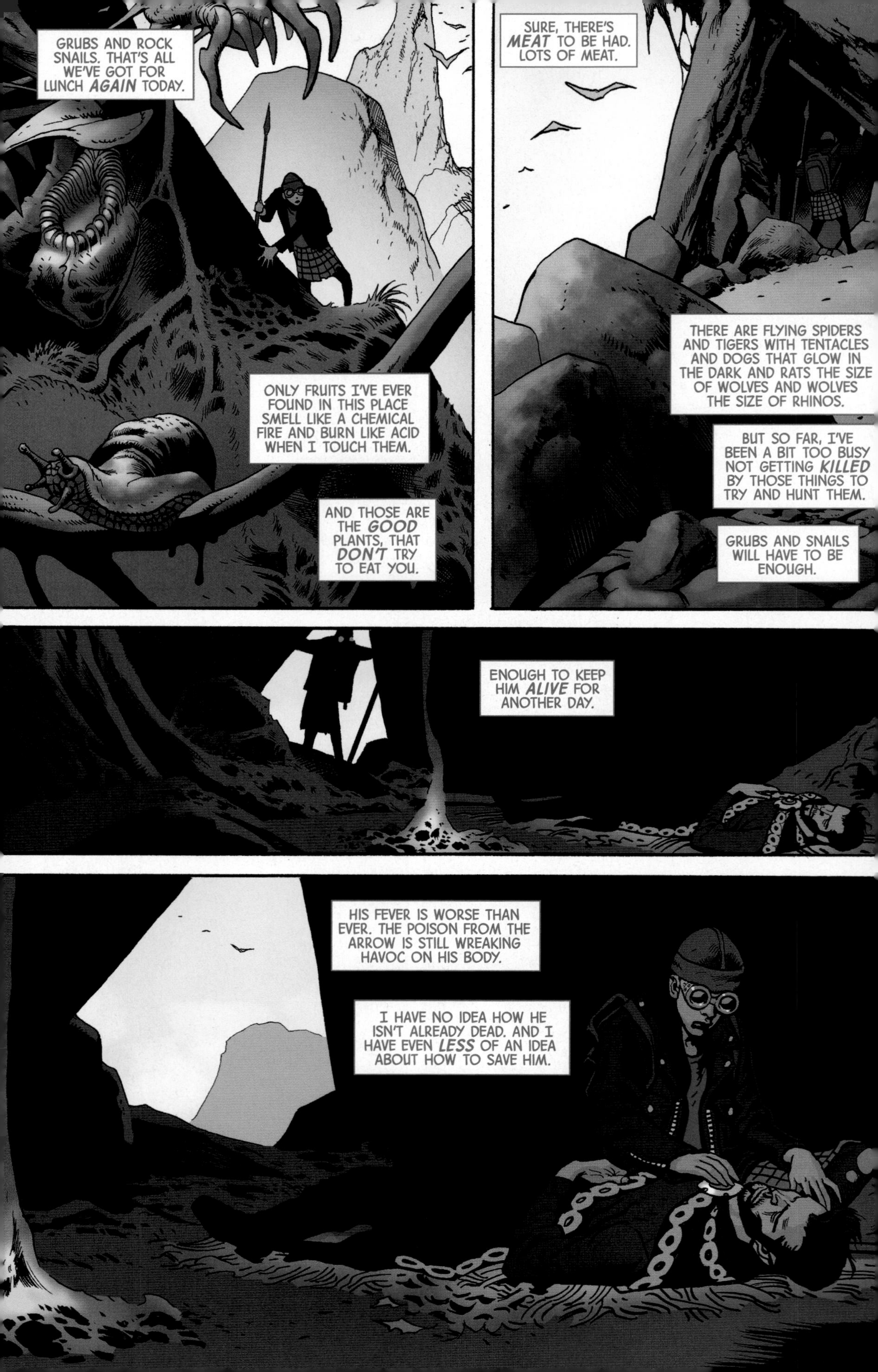
GRUBS AND ROCK SNAILS. THAT'S ALL WE'VE GOT FOR LUNCH AGAIN TODAY.
ONLY FRUITS I'VE EVER FOUND IN THIS PLACE SMELL LIKE A CHEMICAL FIRE AND BURN LIKE ACID WHEN I TOUCH THEM.
AND THOSE ARE THE GOOD PLANTS, THAT DON'T TRY TO EAT YOU.
SURE, THERE'S MEAT TO BE HAD. LOTS OF MEAT.
THERE ARE FLYING SPIDERS AND TIGERS WITH TENTACLES AND DOGS THAT GLOW IN THE DARK AND RATS THE SIZE OF WOLVES AND WOLVES THE SIZE OF RHINOS.
BUT SO FAR, I'VE BEEN A BIT TOO BUSY NOT GETTING KILLED BY THOSE THINGS TO TRY AND HUNT THEM.
GRUBS AND SNAILS WILL HAVE TO BE ENOUGH.
ENOUGH TO KEEP HIM ALIVE FOR ANOTHER DAY.
HIS FEVER IS WORSE THAN EVER. THE POISON FROM THE ARROW IS STILL WREAKING HAVOC ON HIS BODY.
I HAVE NO IDEA HOW HE ISN'T ALREADY DEAD. AND I HAVE EVEN LESS OF AN IDEA ABOUT HOW TO SAVE HIM.

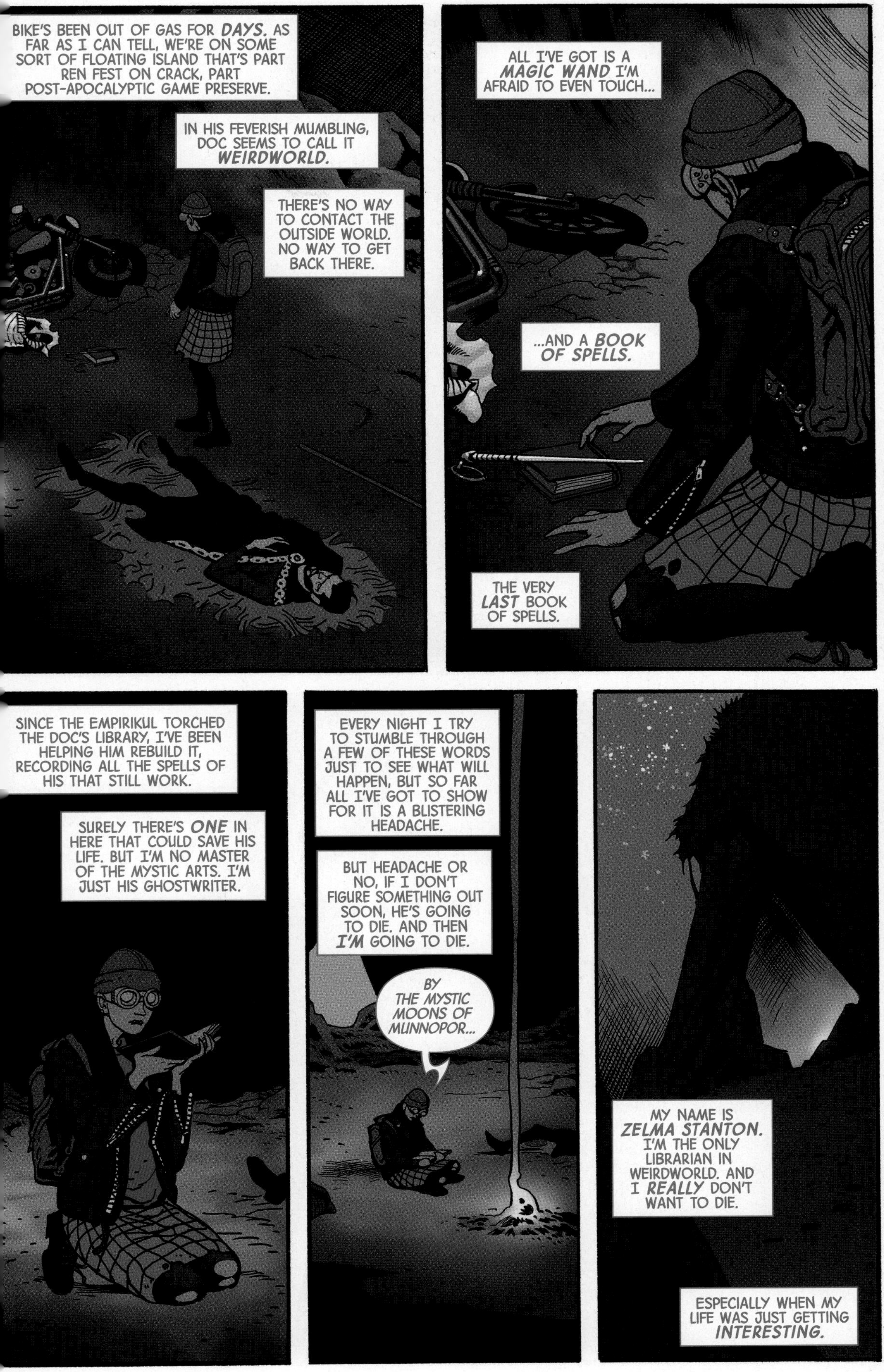
BIKE'S BEEN OUT OF GAS FOR DAYS. AS FAR AS I CAN TELL, WE'RE ON SOME SORT OF FLOATING ISLAND THAT'S PART REN FEST ON CRACK, PART POST-APOCALYPTIC GAME PRESERVE.
IN HIS FEVERISH MUMBLING, DOC SEEMS TO CALL IT WEIRDWORLD.
THERE'S NO WAY TO CONTACT THE OUTSIDE WORLD. NO WAY TO GET BACK THERE.
ALL I'VE GOT IS A MAGIC WAND I'M AFRAID TO EVEN TOUCH...
...AND A BOOK OF SPELLS.
THE VERY LAST BOOK OF SPELLS.
SINCE THE EMPIRIKUL TORCHED THE DOC'S LIBRARY, I'VE BEEN HELPING HIM REBUILD IT, RECORDING ALL THE SPELLS OF HIS THAT STILL WORK.
SURELY THERE'S ONE IN HERE THAT COULD SAVE HIS LIFE. BUT I'M NO MASTER OF THE MYSTIC ARTS. I'M JUST HIS GHOSTWRITER.
EVERY NIGHT I TRY TO STUMBLE THROUGH A FEW OF THESE WORDS JUST TO SEE WHAT WILL HAPPEN, BUT SO FAR ALL I'VE GOT TO SHOW FOR IT IS A BLISTERING HEADACHE.
BUT HEADACHE OR NO, IF I DON'T FIGURE SOMETHING OUT SOON, HE'S GOING TO DIE. AND THEN I'M GOING TO DIE.
BY THE MYSTIC MOONS OF MUNNOPOR...
MY NAME IS ZELMA STANTON. I'M THE ONLY LIBRARIAN IN WEIRDWORLD. AND I REALLY DON'T WANT TO DIE.
ESPECIALLY WHEN MY LIFE WAS JUST GETTING INTERESTING.

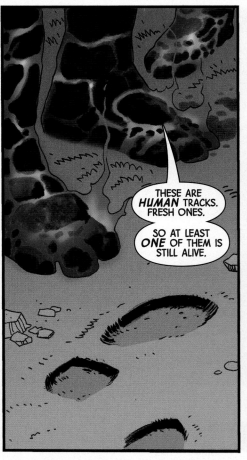

THESE ARE *HUMAN* TRACKS. FRESH ONES.

SO AT LEAST *ONE* OF THEM IS STILL ALIVE.

BUT WHICH? THE GIRL OR THE SORCERER?

I PUT AN ARROW IN THE WIZARD, ITS POINT DIPPED IN DRAGON BILE POISON. THERE'S NO WAY HE'S STILL BREATHING.

DOESN'T MATTER WHICH OF THEM IT IS. JUST AS LONG AS THEY'VE STILL GOT THE *WAND*.

BLOODBOARS HAVE GOT THE SCENT. WON'T BE LONG NOW.

SEND WORD TO MISTRESS LE FAY. TELL HER THE *MAGMA MEN* WILL SOON BE BRINGING HER THE WAND...

...AND THE HEAD OF THE *SORCERER SUPREME*.

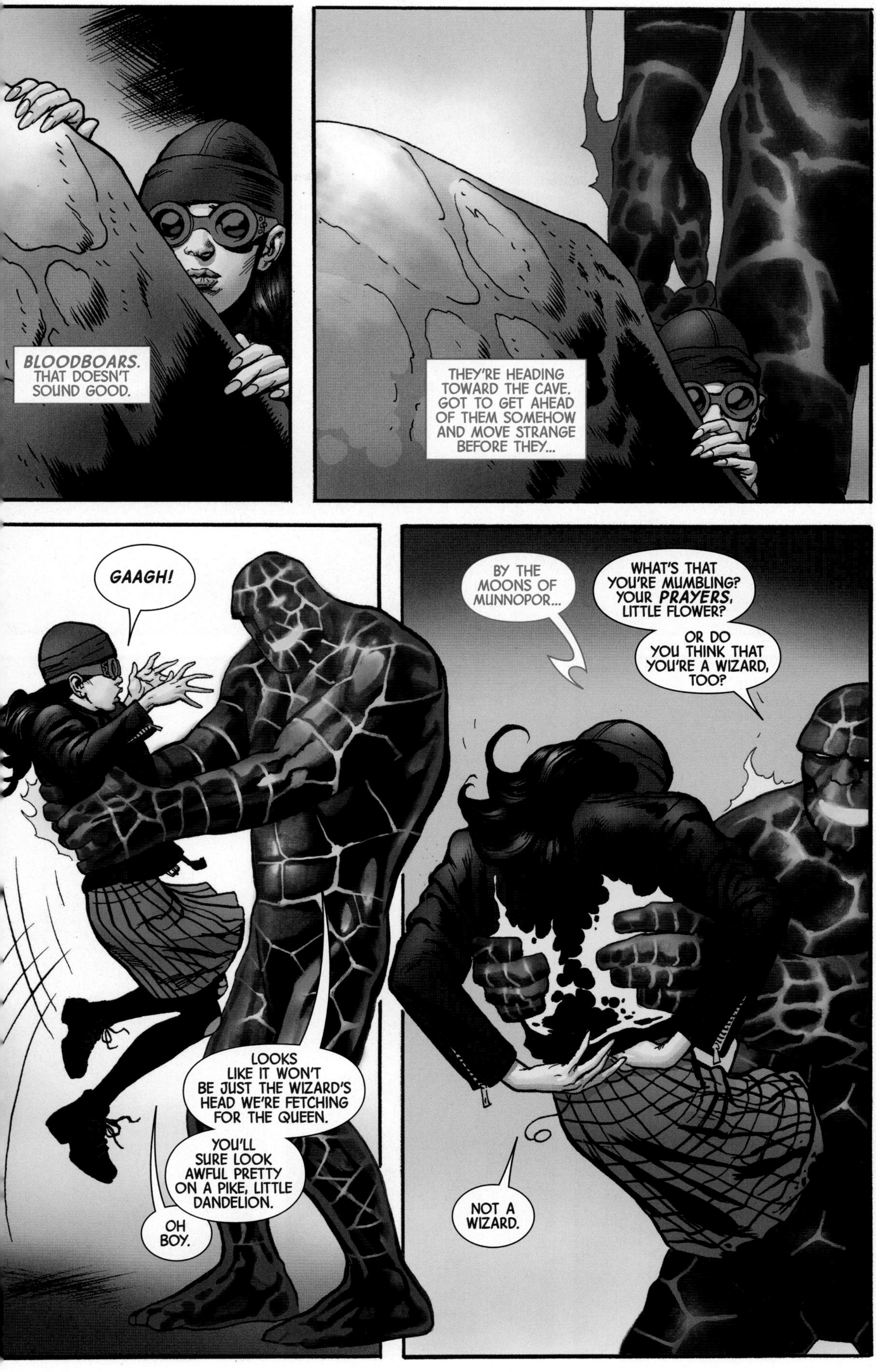
BLOODBOARS. THAT DOESN'T SOUND GOOD.
THEY'RE HEADING TOWARD THE CAVE. GOT TO GET AHEAD OF THEM SOMEHOW AND MOVE STRANGE BEFORE THEY...
GAAGH!
LOOKS LIKE IT WON'T BE JUST THE WIZARD'S HEAD WE'RE FETCHING FOR THE QUEEN.
YOU'LL SURE LOOK AWFUL PRETTY ON A PIKE, LITTLE DANDELION.
OH BOY.
BY THE MOONS OF MUNNOPOR...
WHAT'S THAT YOU'RE MUMBLING? YOUR PRAYERS, LITTLE FLOWER?
OR DO YOU THINK THAT YOU'RE A WIZARD, TOO?
NOT A WIZARD.

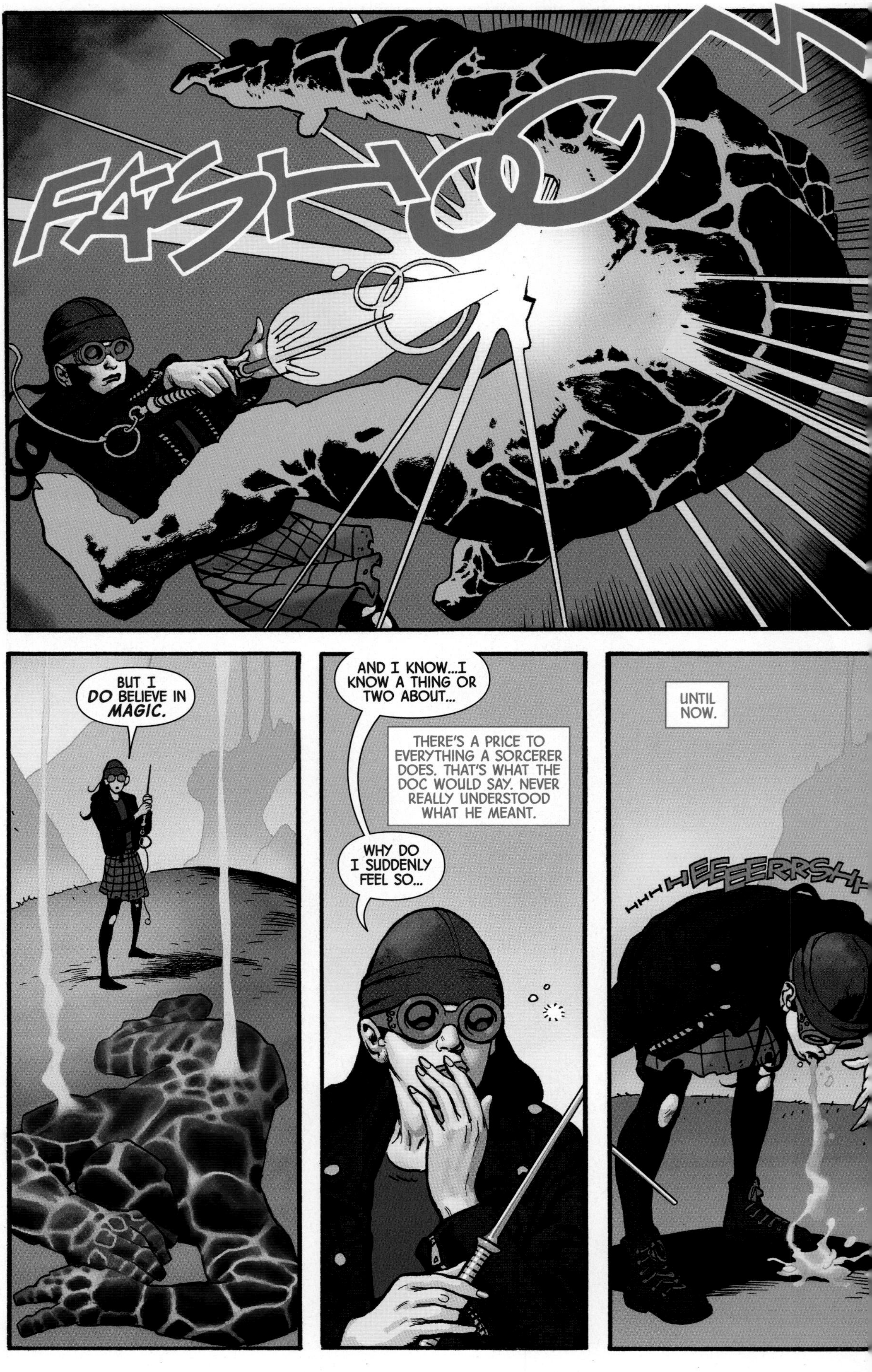
FASHOOOM
BUT I DO BELIEVE IN MAGIC.
AND I KNOW...I KNOW A THING OR TWO ABOUT...
THERE'S A PRICE TO EVERYTHING A SORCERER DOES. THAT'S WHAT THE DOC WOULD SAY. NEVER REALLY UNDERSTOOD WHAT HE MEANT.
WHY DO I SUDDENLY FEEL SO...
UNTIL NOW.
HHHHWEEEEERRSHH

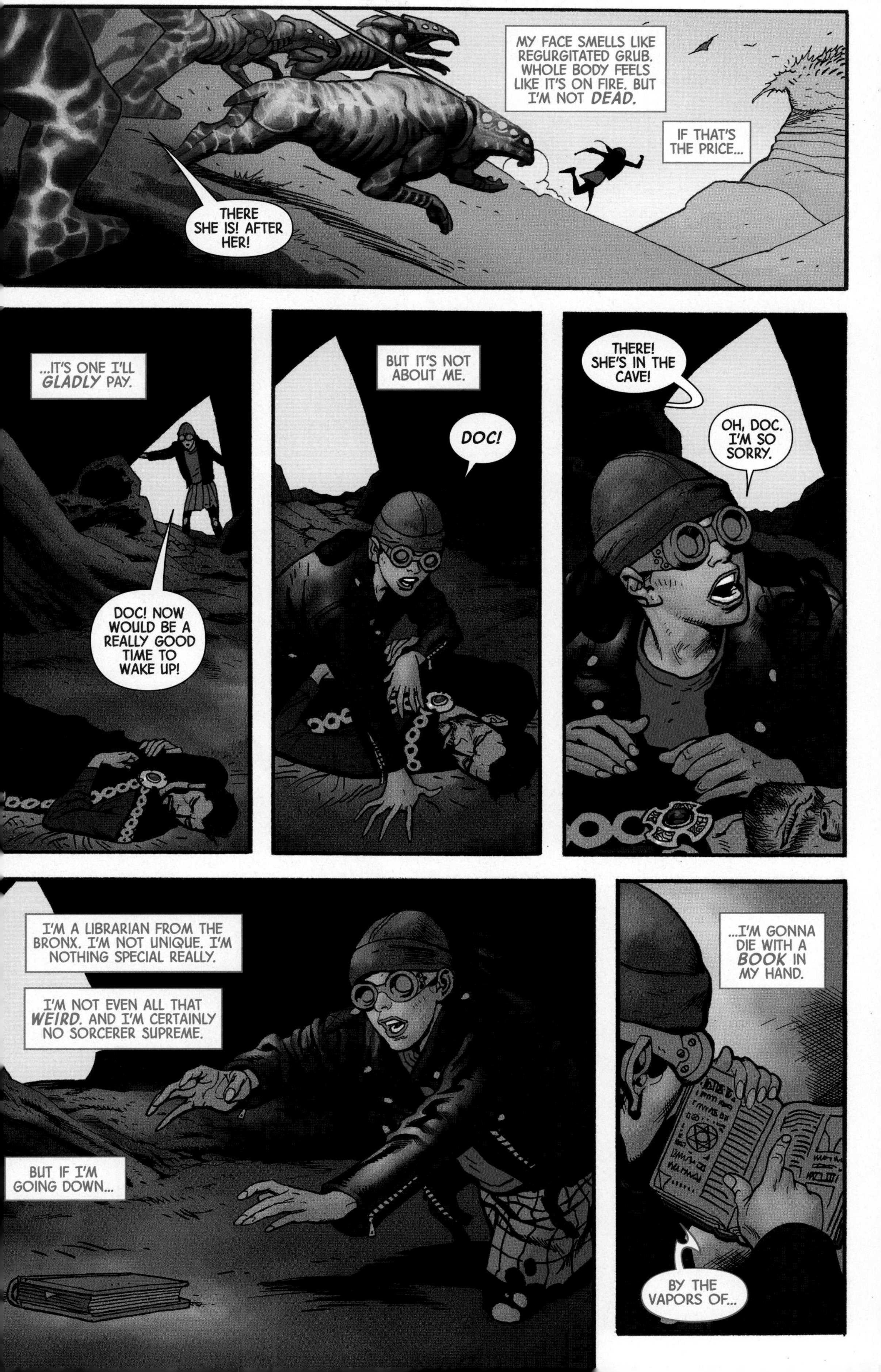

MY FACE SMELLS LIKE REGURGITATED GRUB. WHOLE BODY FEELS LIKE IT'S ON FIRE. BUT I'M NOT *DEAD.*
IF THAT'S THE PRICE...
THERE SHE IS! AFTER HER!
...IT'S ONE I'LL *GLADLY* PAY.
DOC! NOW WOULD BE A REALLY GOOD TIME TO WAKE UP!
BUT IT'S NOT ABOUT ME.
DOC!
THERE! SHE'S IN THE CAVE!
OH, DOC. I'M SO SORRY.
I'M A LIBRARIAN FROM THE BRONX. I'M NOT UNIQUE. I'M NOTHING SPECIAL REALLY.
I'M NOT EVEN ALL THAT *WEIRD.* AND I'M CERTAINLY NO SORCERER SUPREME.
BUT IF I'M GOING DOWN...
...I'M GONNA DIE WITH A *BOOK* IN MY HAND.
BY THE VAPORS OF...

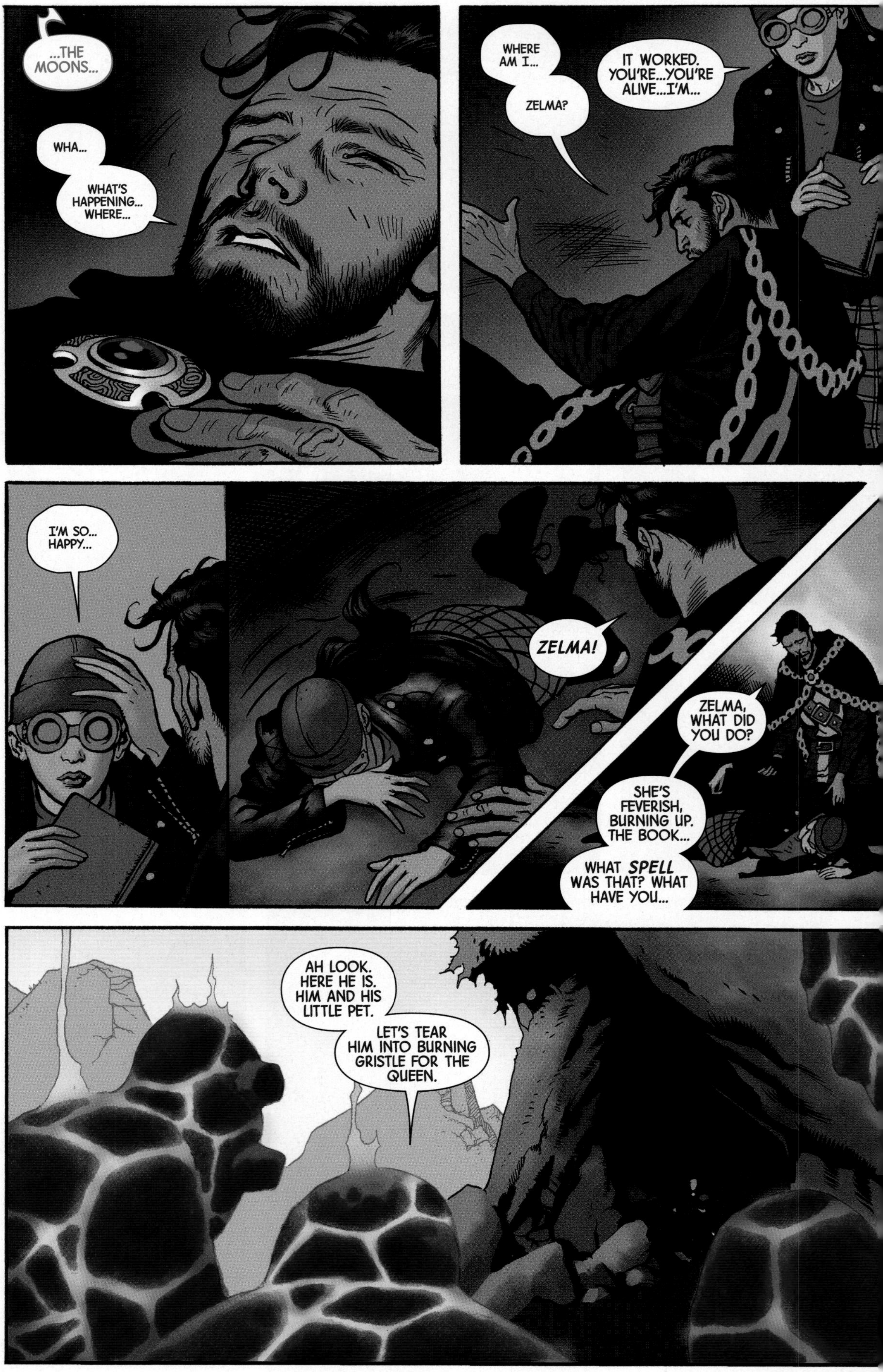
...THE MOONS...
WHA...
WHAT'S HAPPENING... WHERE...
WHERE AM I...
ZELMA?
IT WORKED. YOU'RE...YOU'RE ALIVE...I'M...
I'M SO... HAPPY...
ZELMA!
ZELMA, WHAT DID YOU DO?
SHE'S FEVERISH, BURNING UP. THE BOOK...
WHAT SPELL WAS THAT? WHAT HAVE YOU...
AH LOOK. HERE HE IS. HIM AND HIS LITTLE PET.
LET'S TEAR HIM INTO BURNING GRISTLE FOR THE QUEEN.

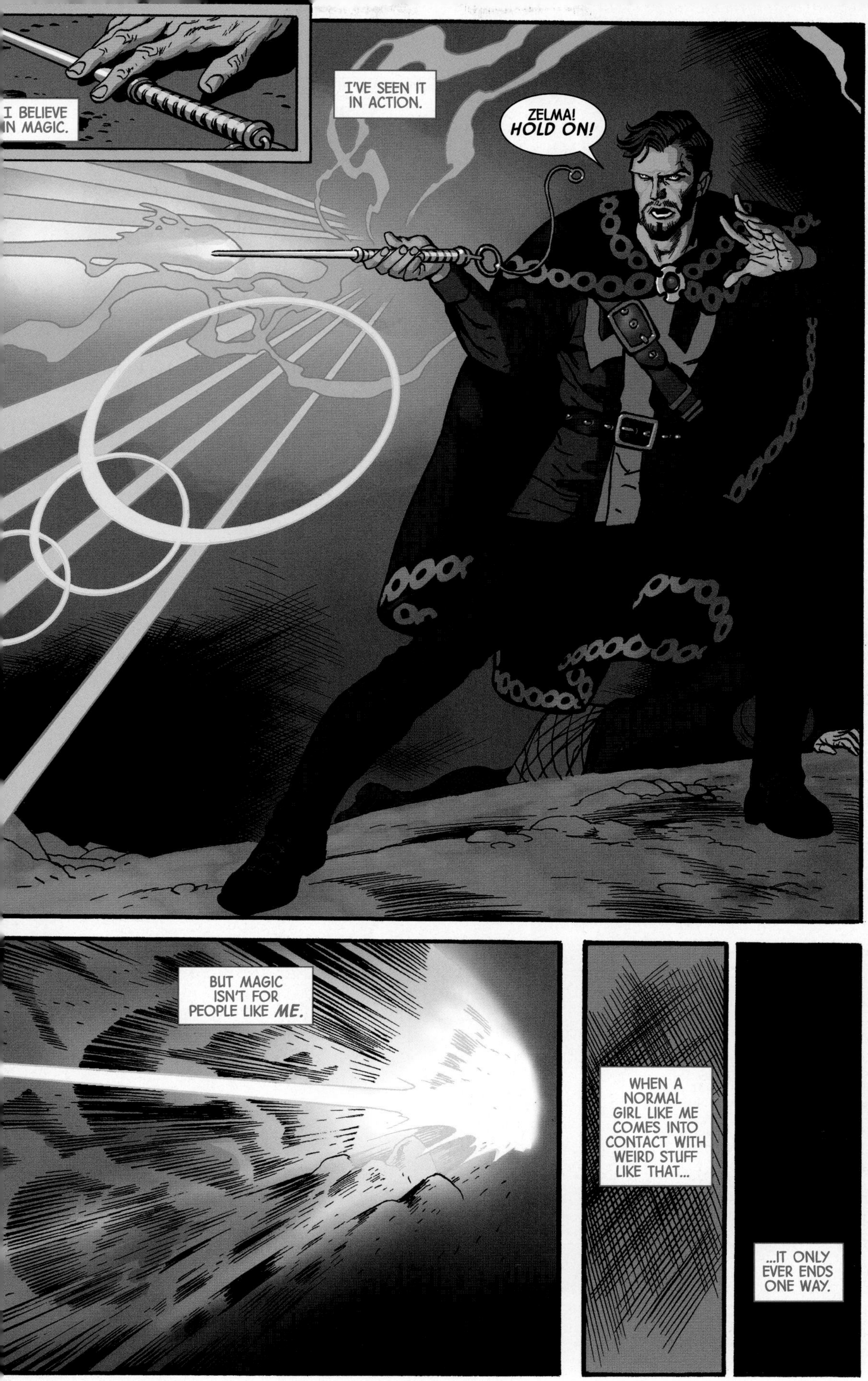

I BELIEVE IN MAGIC.
I'VE SEEN IT IN ACTION.
ZELMA! HOLD ON!
BUT MAGIC ISN'T FOR PEOPLE LIKE ME.
WHEN A NORMAL GIRL LIKE ME COMES INTO CONTACT WITH WEIRD STUFF LIKE THAT...
...IT ONLY EVER ENDS ONE WAY.

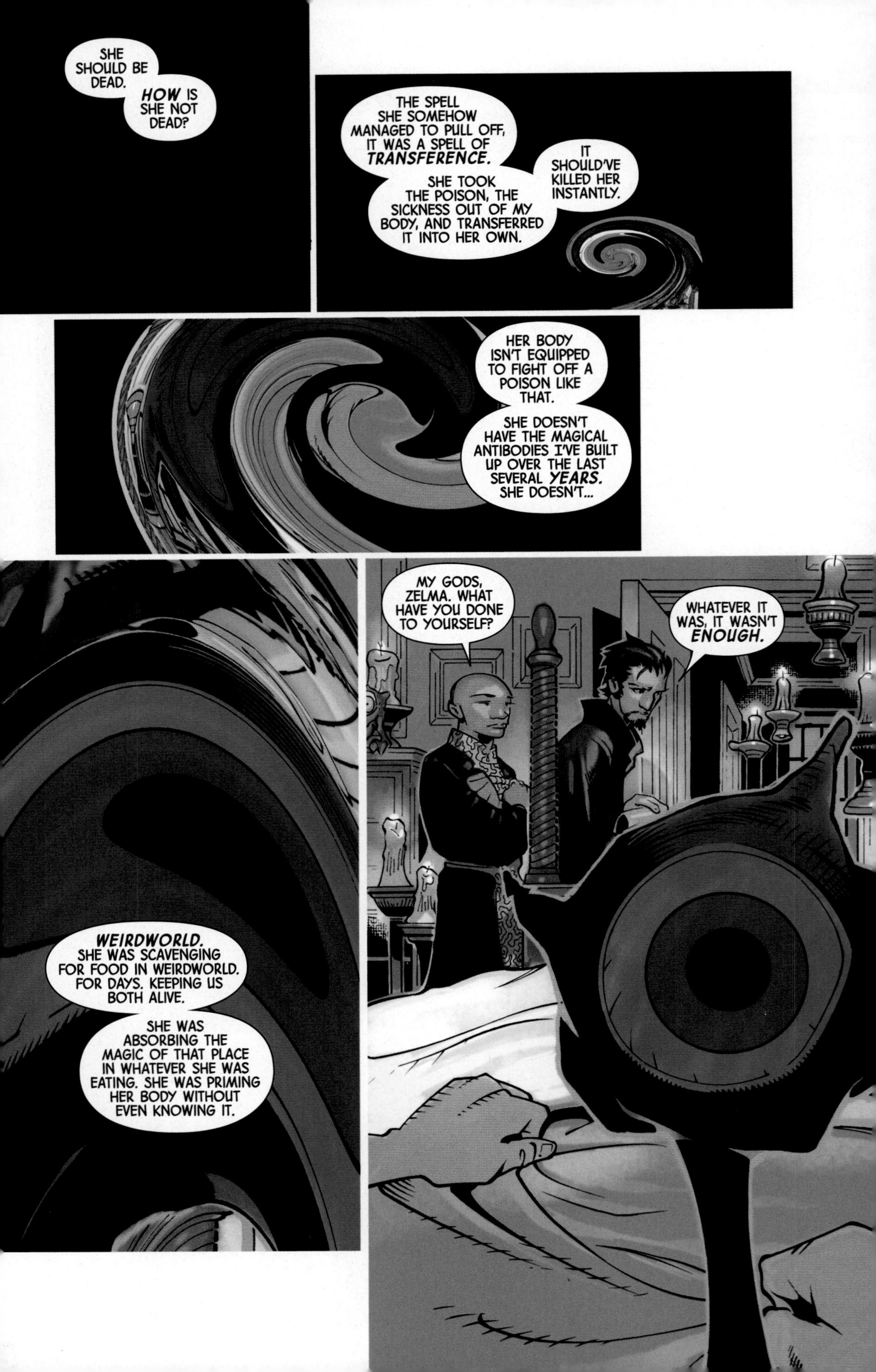
SHE SHOULD BE DEAD.
HOW IS SHE NOT DEAD?
THE SPELL SHE SOMEHOW MANAGED TO PULL OFF, IT WAS A SPELL OF TRANSFERENCE.
SHE TOOK THE POISON, THE SICKNESS OUT OF MY BODY, AND TRANSFERRED IT INTO HER OWN.
IT SHOULD'VE KILLED HER INSTANTLY.
HER BODY ISN'T EQUIPPED TO FIGHT OFF A POISON LIKE THAT.
SHE DOESN'T HAVE THE MAGICAL ANTIBODIES I'VE BUILT UP OVER THE LAST SEVERAL YEARS. SHE DOESN'T...
WEIRDWORLD. SHE WAS SCAVENGING FOR FOOD IN WEIRDWORLD. FOR DAYS. KEEPING US BOTH ALIVE.
SHE WAS ABSORBING THE MAGIC OF THAT PLACE IN WHATEVER SHE WAS EATING. SHE WAS PRIMING HER BODY WITHOUT EVEN KNOWING IT.
MY GODS, ZELMA. WHAT HAVE YOU DONE TO YOURSELF?
WHATEVER IT WAS, IT WASN'T ENOUGH.

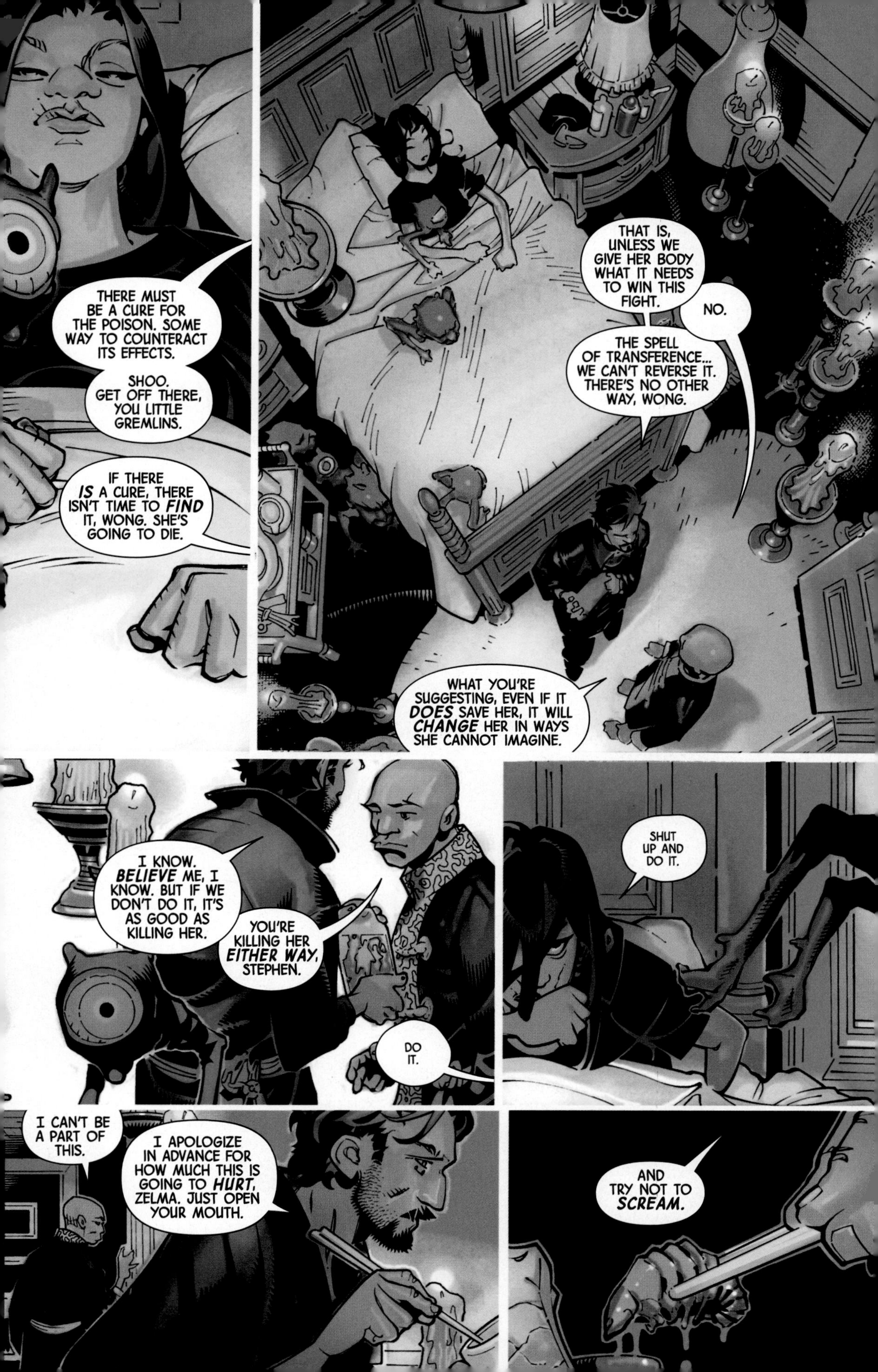
THERE MUST BE A CURE FOR THE POISON. SOME WAY TO COUNTERACT ITS EFFECTS.
SHOO. GET OFF THERE, YOU LITTLE GREMLINS.
IF THERE *IS* A CURE, THERE ISN'T TIME TO *FIND* IT, WONG. SHE'S GOING TO DIE.
THAT IS, UNLESS WE GIVE HER BODY WHAT IT NEEDS TO WIN THIS FIGHT.
NO.
THE SPELL OF TRANSFERENCE... WE CAN'T REVERSE IT. THERE'S NO OTHER WAY, WONG.
WHAT YOU'RE SUGGESTING, EVEN IF IT *DOES* SAVE HER, IT WILL *CHANGE* HER IN WAYS SHE CANNOT IMAGINE.
I KNOW. *BELIEVE* ME, I KNOW. BUT IF WE DON'T DO IT, IT'S AS GOOD AS KILLING HER.
YOU'RE KILLING HER *EITHER WAY*, STEPHEN.
DO IT.
SHUT UP AND DO IT.
I CAN'T BE A PART OF THIS.
I APOLOGIZE IN ADVANCE FOR HOW MUCH THIS IS GOING TO *HURT*, ZELMA. JUST OPEN YOUR MOUTH.
AND TRY NOT TO *SCREAM.*

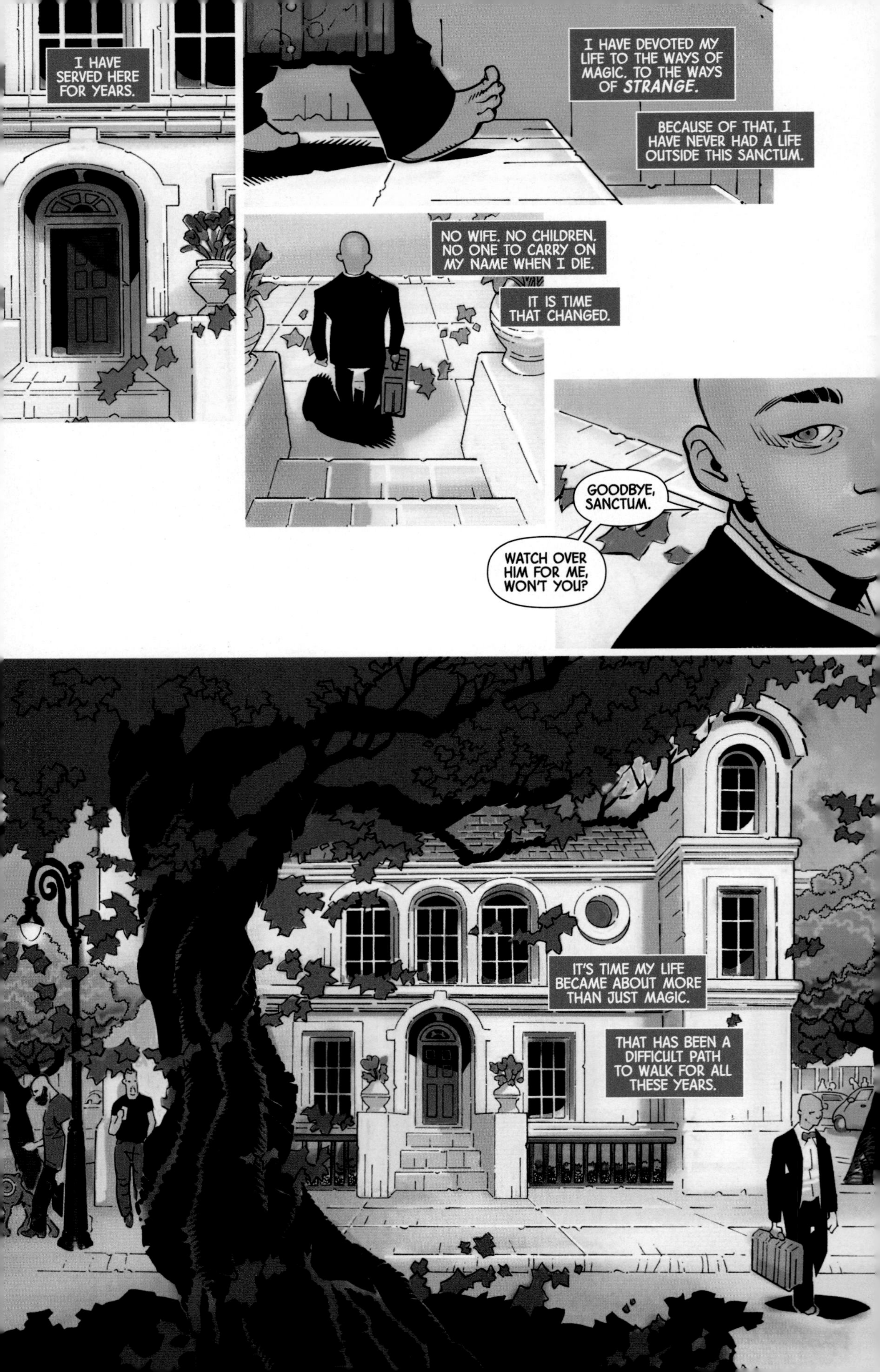
I HAVE SERVED HERE FOR YEARS.
I HAVE DEVOTED MY LIFE TO THE WAYS OF MAGIC. TO THE WAYS OF STRANGE.
BECAUSE OF THAT, I HAVE NEVER HAD A LIFE OUTSIDE THIS SANCTUM.
NO WIFE. NO CHILDREN. NO ONE TO CARRY ON MY NAME WHEN I DIE.
IT IS TIME THAT CHANGED.
GOODBYE, SANCTUM.
WATCH OVER HIM FOR ME, WON'T YOU?
IT'S TIME MY LIFE BECAME ABOUT MORE THAN JUST MAGIC.
THAT HAS BEEN A DIFFICULT PATH TO WALK FOR ALL THESE YEARS.

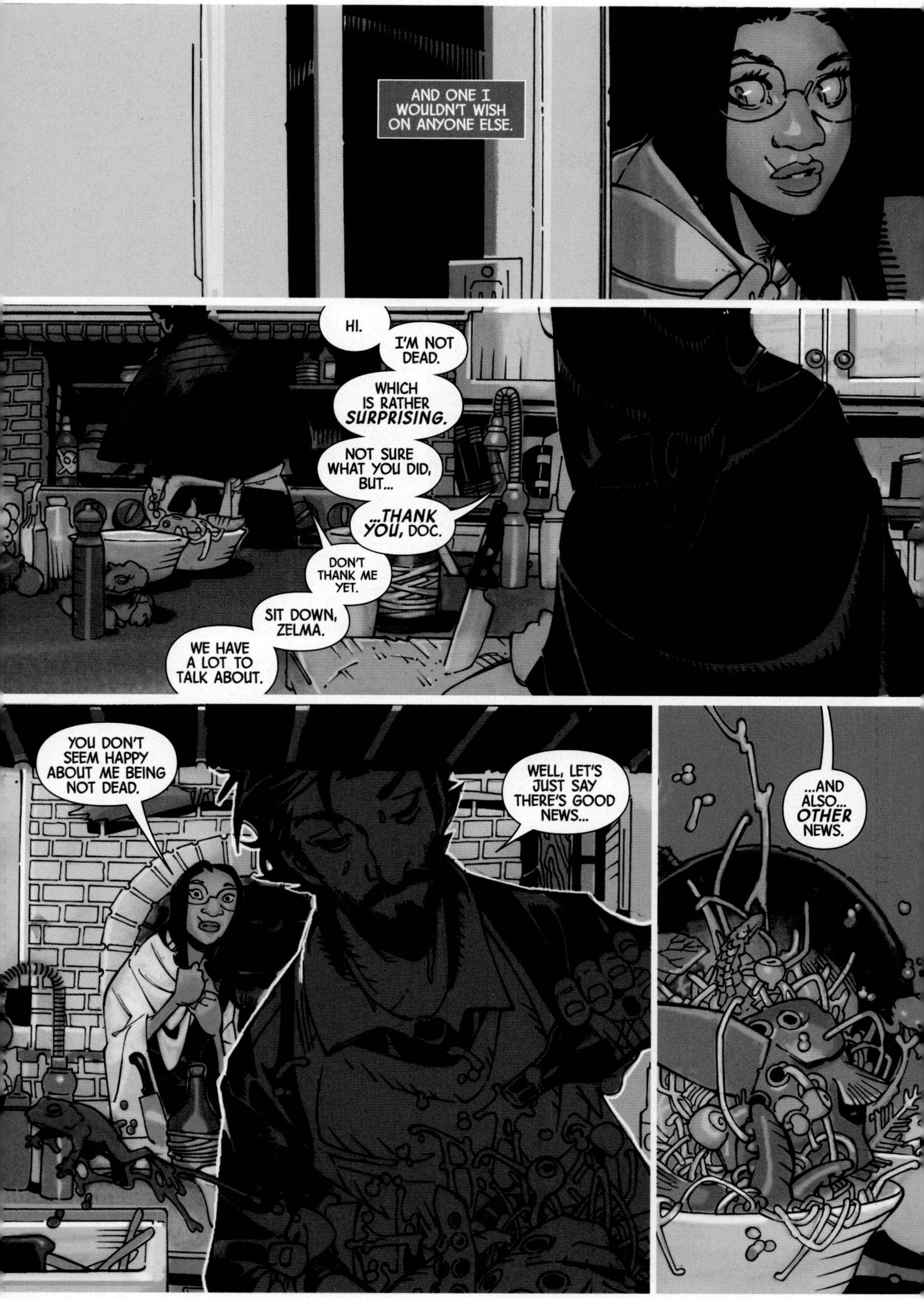
AND ONE I WOULDN'T WISH ON ANYONE ELSE.
HI.
I'M NOT DEAD.
WHICH IS RATHER SURPRISING.
NOT SURE WHAT YOU DID, BUT...
...THANK YOU, DOC.
DON'T THANK ME YET.
SIT DOWN, ZELMA.
WE HAVE A LOT TO TALK ABOUT.
YOU DON'T SEEM HAPPY ABOUT ME BEING NOT DEAD.
WELL, LET'S JUST SAY THERE'S GOOD NEWS...
...AND ALSO... OTHER NEWS.

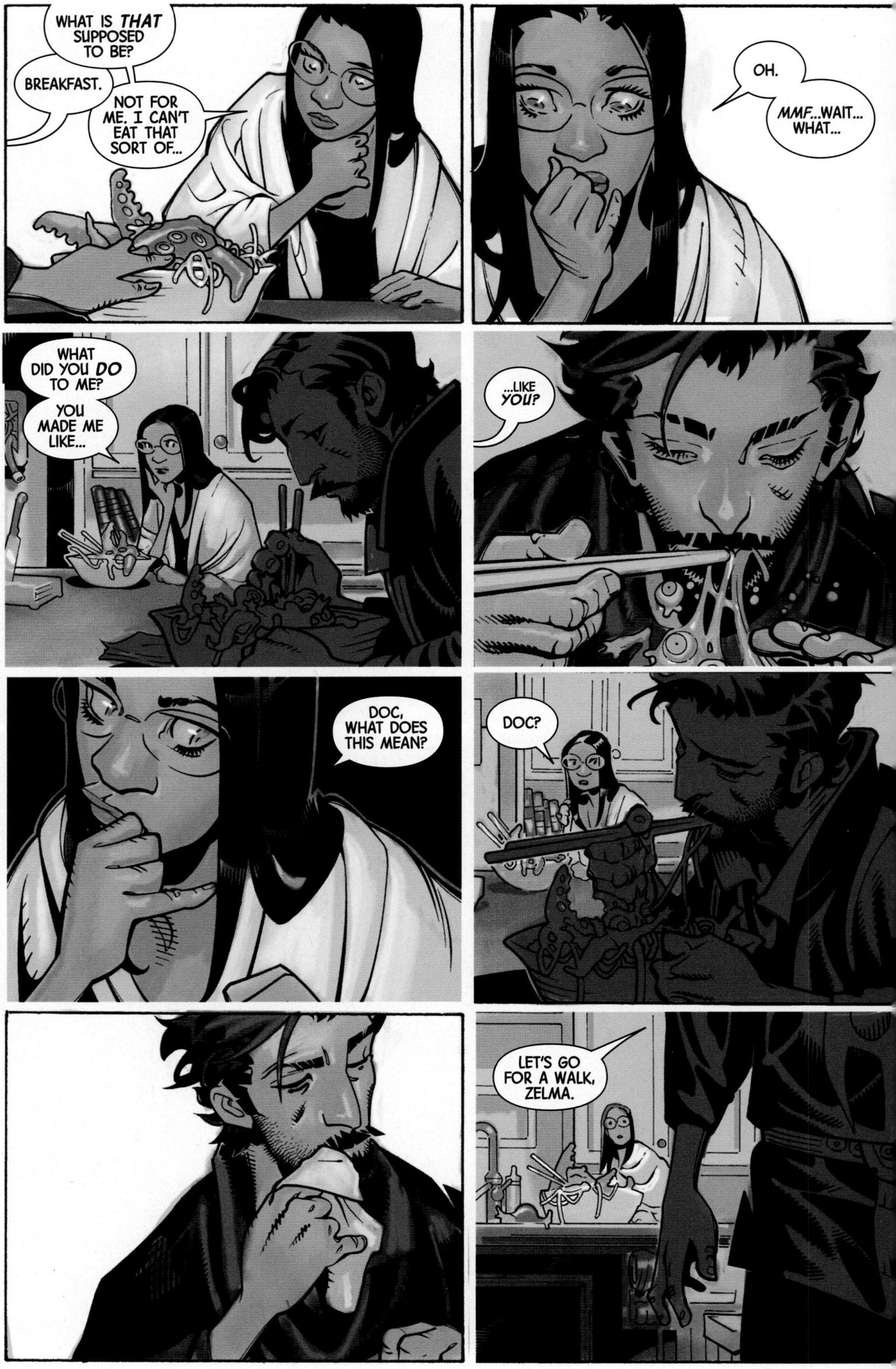
WHAT IS THAT SUPPOSED TO BE?
BREAKFAST.
NOT FOR ME. I CAN'T EAT THAT SORT OF...
OH.
MMF...WAIT... WHAT...
WHAT DID YOU DO TO ME?
YOU MADE ME LIKE...
...LIKE YOU?
DOC, WHAT DOES THIS MEAN?
DOC?
LET'S GO FOR A WALK, ZELMA.

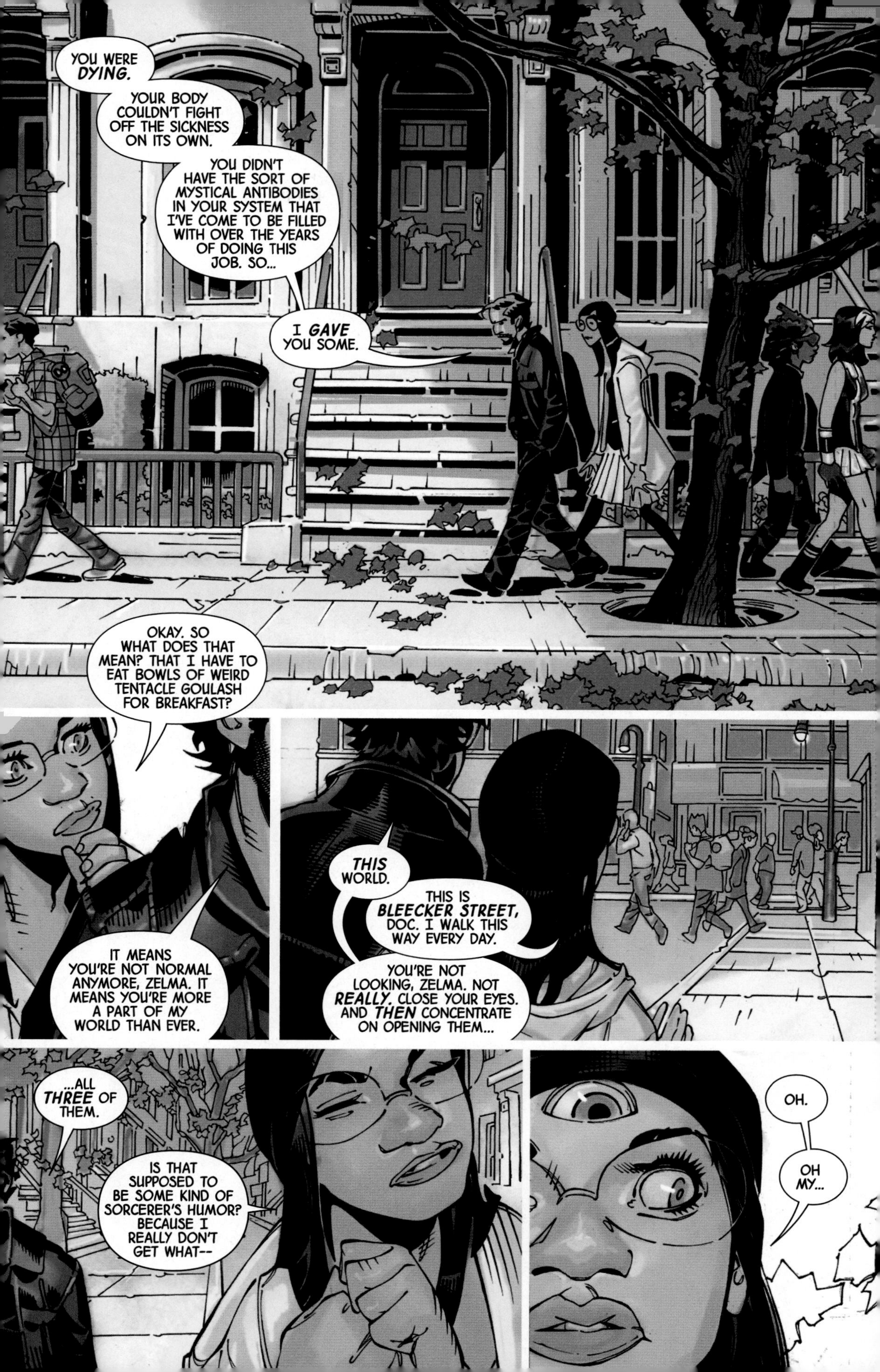
YOU WERE DYING.
YOUR BODY COULDN'T FIGHT OFF THE SICKNESS ON ITS OWN.
YOU DIDN'T HAVE THE SORT OF MYSTICAL ANTIBODIES IN YOUR SYSTEM THAT I'VE COME TO BE FILLED WITH OVER THE YEARS OF DOING THIS JOB. SO...
I GAVE YOU SOME.
OKAY. SO WHAT DOES THAT MEAN? THAT I HAVE TO EAT BOWLS OF WEIRD TENTACLE GOULASH FOR BREAKFAST?
IT MEANS YOU'RE NOT NORMAL ANYMORE, ZELMA. IT MEANS YOU'RE MORE A PART OF MY WORLD THAN EVER.
THIS WORLD.
THIS IS BLEECKER STREET, DOC. I WALK THIS WAY EVERY DAY.
YOU'RE NOT LOOKING, ZELMA. NOT REALLY. CLOSE YOUR EYES. AND THEN CONCENTRATE ON OPENING THEM...
...ALL THREE OF THEM.
IS THAT SUPPOSED TO BE SOME KIND OF SORCERER'S HUMOR? BECAUSE I REALLY DON'T GET WHAT--
OH.
OH MY...

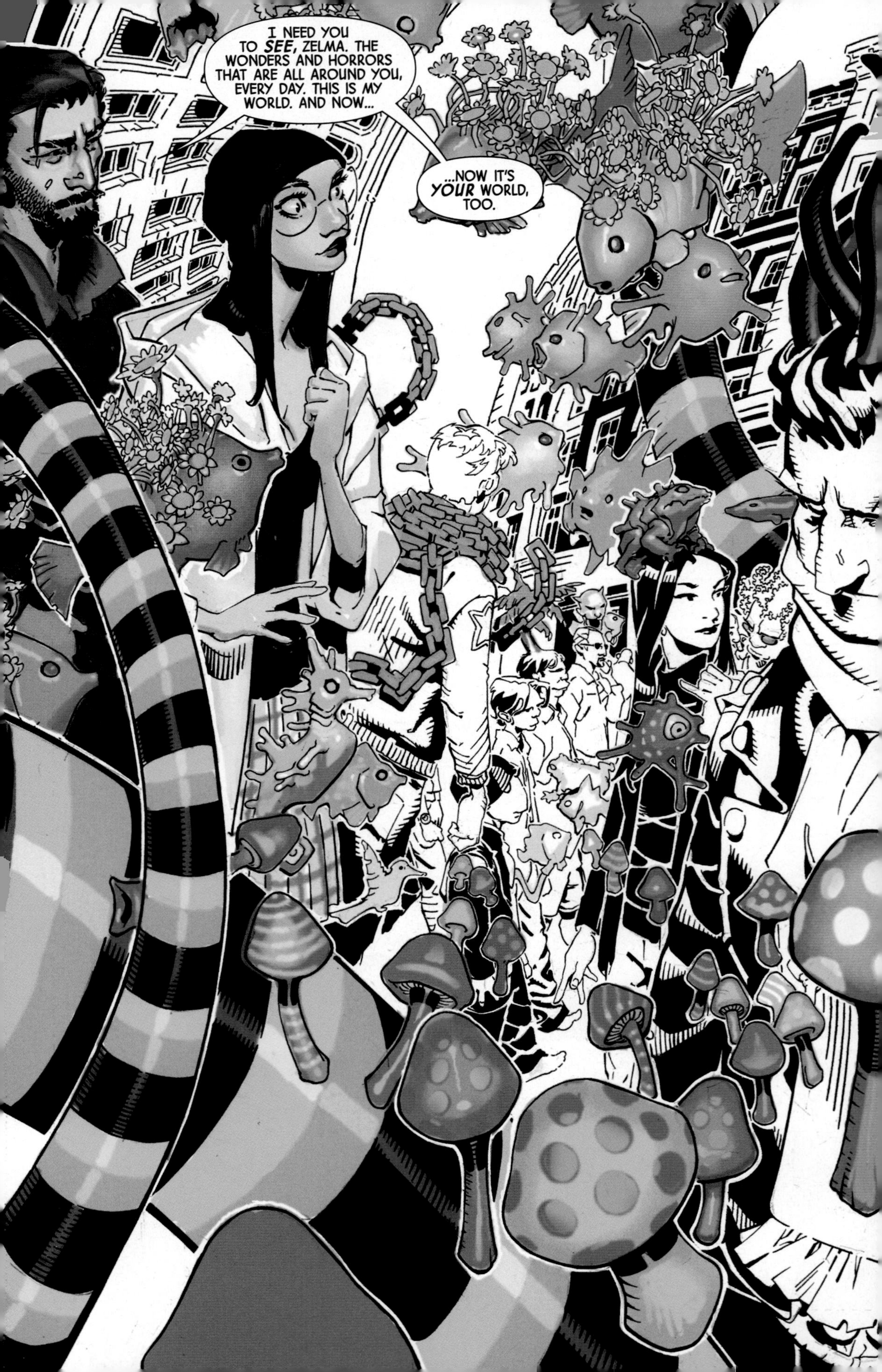
I NEED YOU TO SEE, ZELMA. THE WONDERS AND HORRORS THAT ARE ALL AROUND YOU, EVERY DAY. THIS IS MY WORLD. AND NOW...
...NOW IT'S YOUR WORLD, TOO.

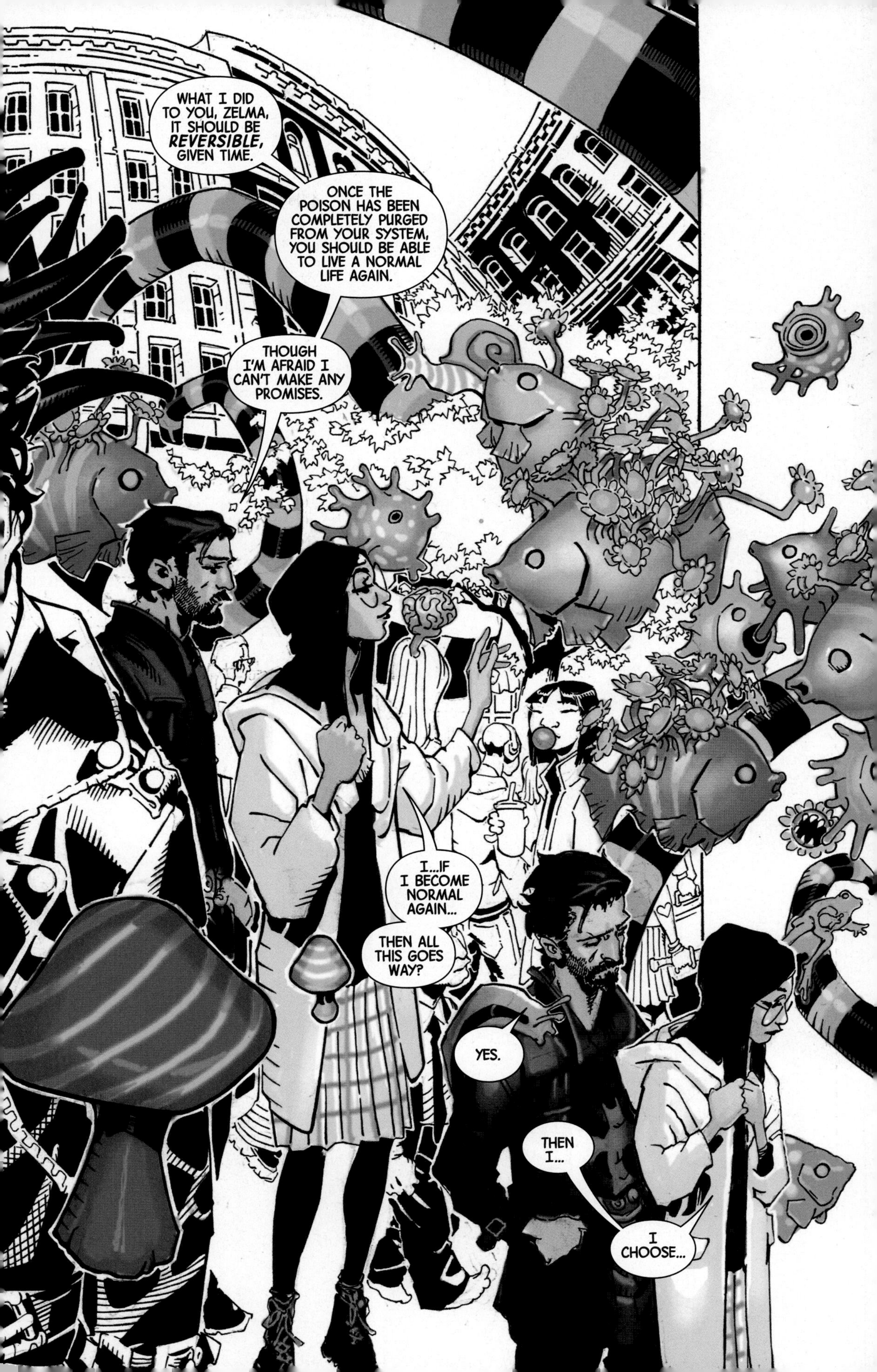
WHAT I DID TO YOU, ZELMA, IT SHOULD BE REVERSIBLE, GIVEN TIME.
ONCE THE POISON HAS BEEN COMPLETELY PURGED FROM YOUR SYSTEM, YOU SHOULD BE ABLE TO LIVE A NORMAL LIFE AGAIN.
THOUGH I'M AFRAID I CAN'T MAKE ANY PROMISES.
I...IF I BECOME NORMAL AGAIN...
THEN ALL THIS GOES WAY?
YES.
THEN I...
I CHOOSE...

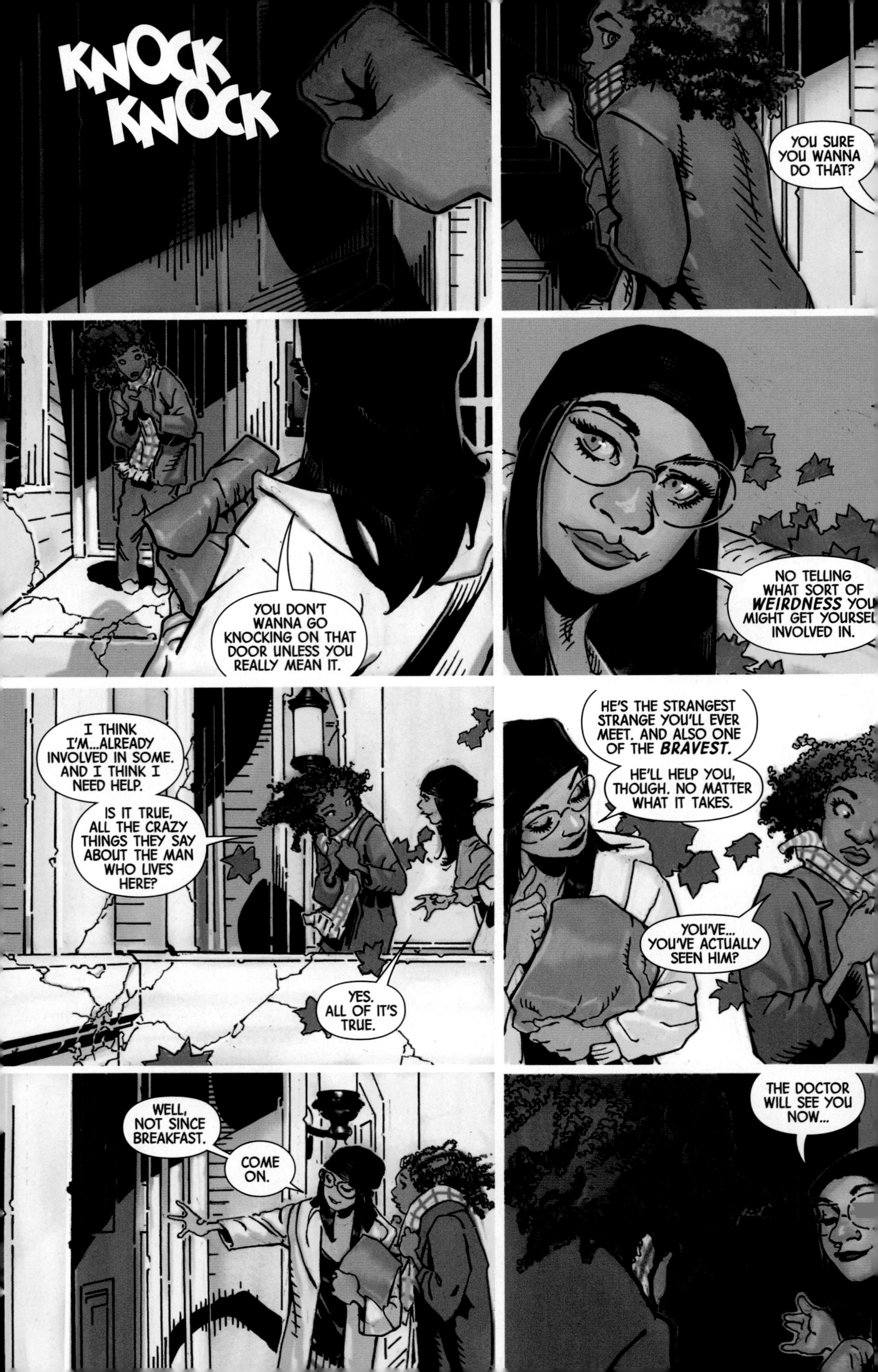
KNOCK KNOCK
YOU SURE YOU WANNA DO THAT?
YOU DON'T WANNA GO KNOCKING ON THAT DOOR UNLESS YOU REALLY MEAN IT.
NO TELLING WHAT SORT OF WEIRDNESS YOU MIGHT GET YOURSEL INVOLVED IN.
I THINK I'M...ALREADY INVOLVED IN SOME. AND I THINK I NEED HELP.
IS IT TRUE, ALL THE CRAZY THINGS THEY SAY ABOUT THE MAN WHO LIVES HERE?
YES. ALL OF IT'S TRUE.
HE'S THE STRANGEST STRANGE YOU'LL EVER MEET. AND ALSO ONE OF THE BRAVEST.
HE'LL HELP YOU, THOUGH. NO MATTER WHAT IT TAKES.
YOU'VE... YOU'VE ACTUALLY SEEN HIM?
WELL, NOT SINCE BREAKFAST.
COME ON.
THE DOCTOR WILL SEE YOU NOW...

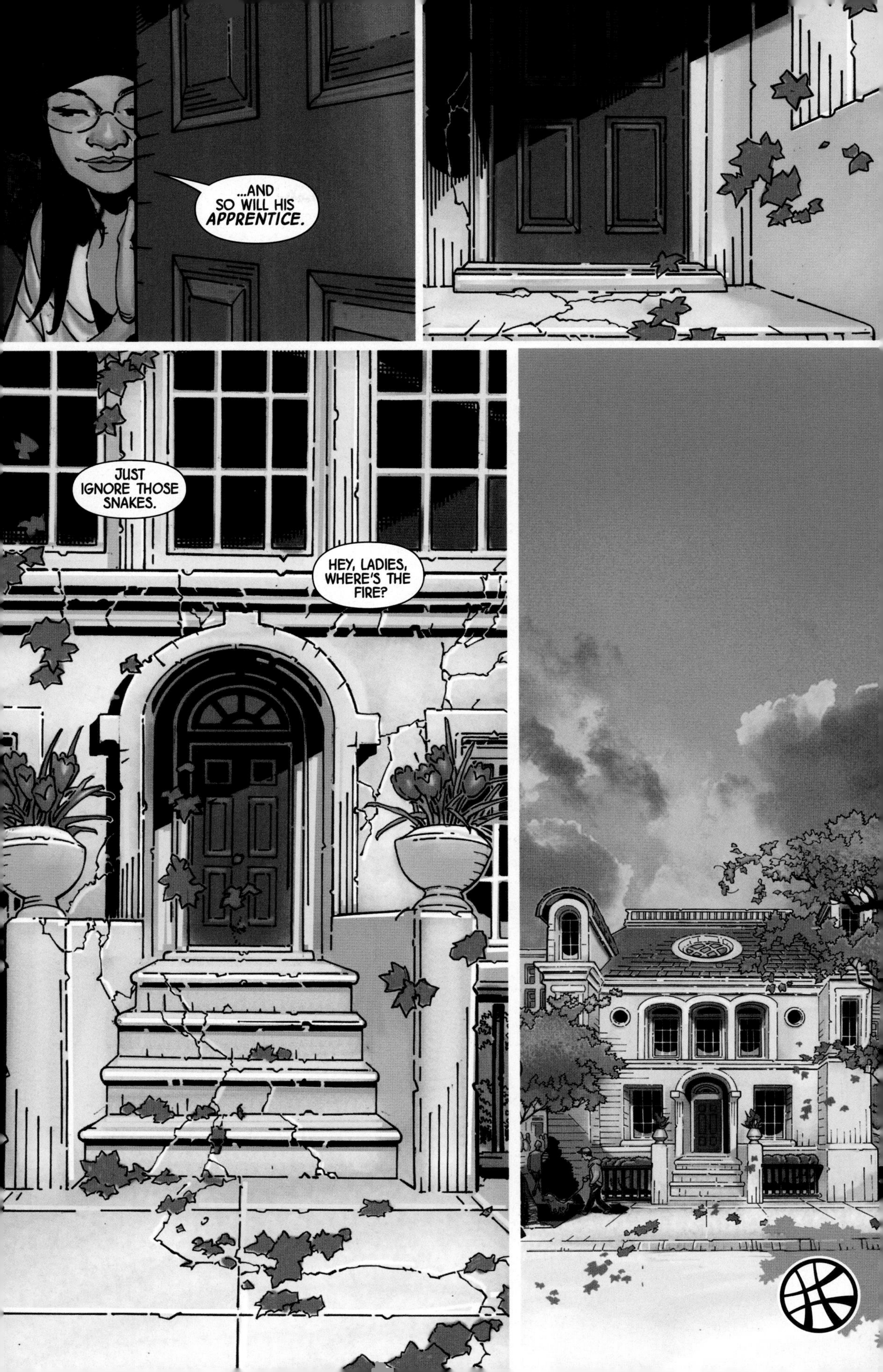
...AND SO WILL HIS *APPRENTICE.*
JUST IGNORE THOSE SNAKES.
HEY, LADIES, WHERE'S THE FIRE?

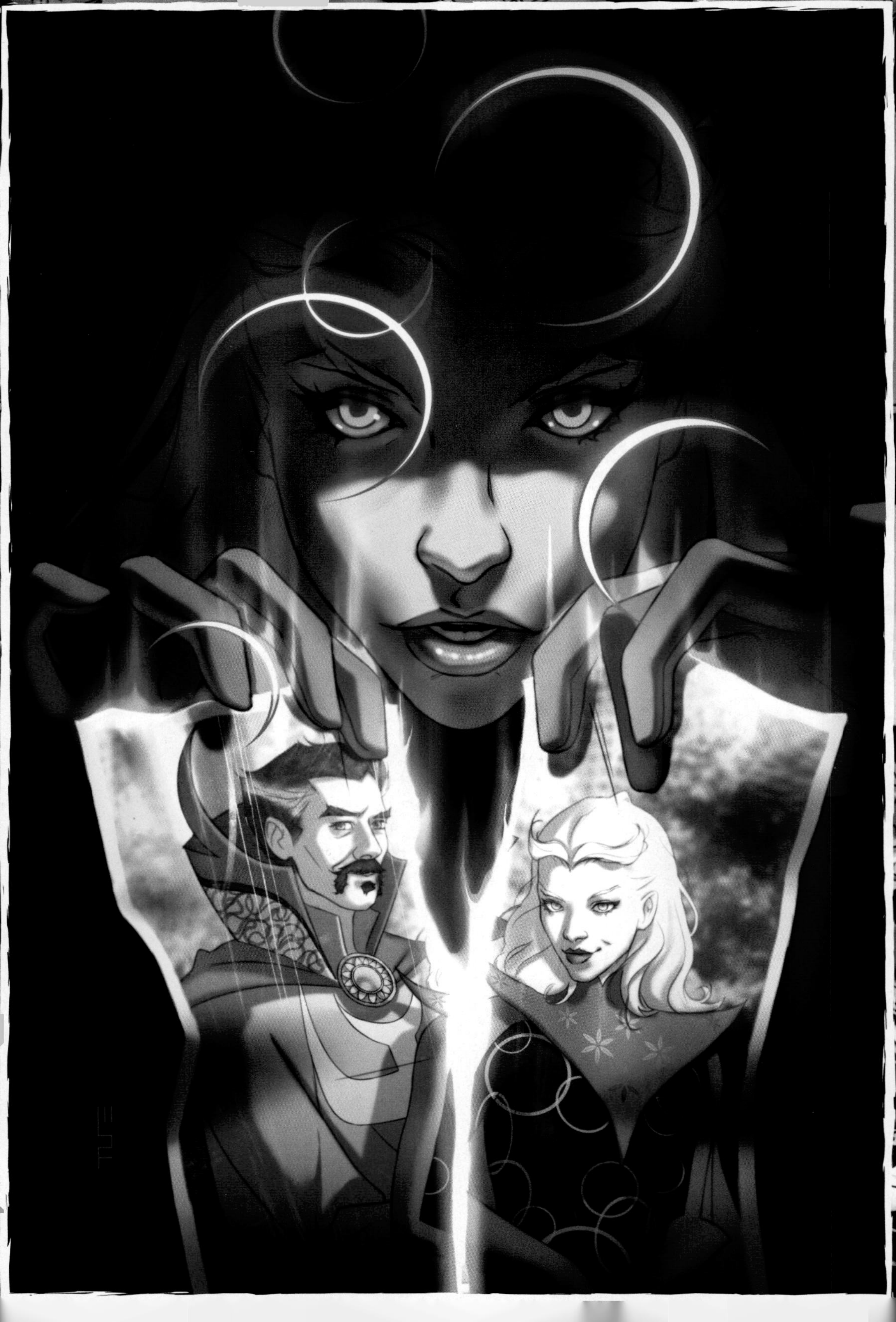

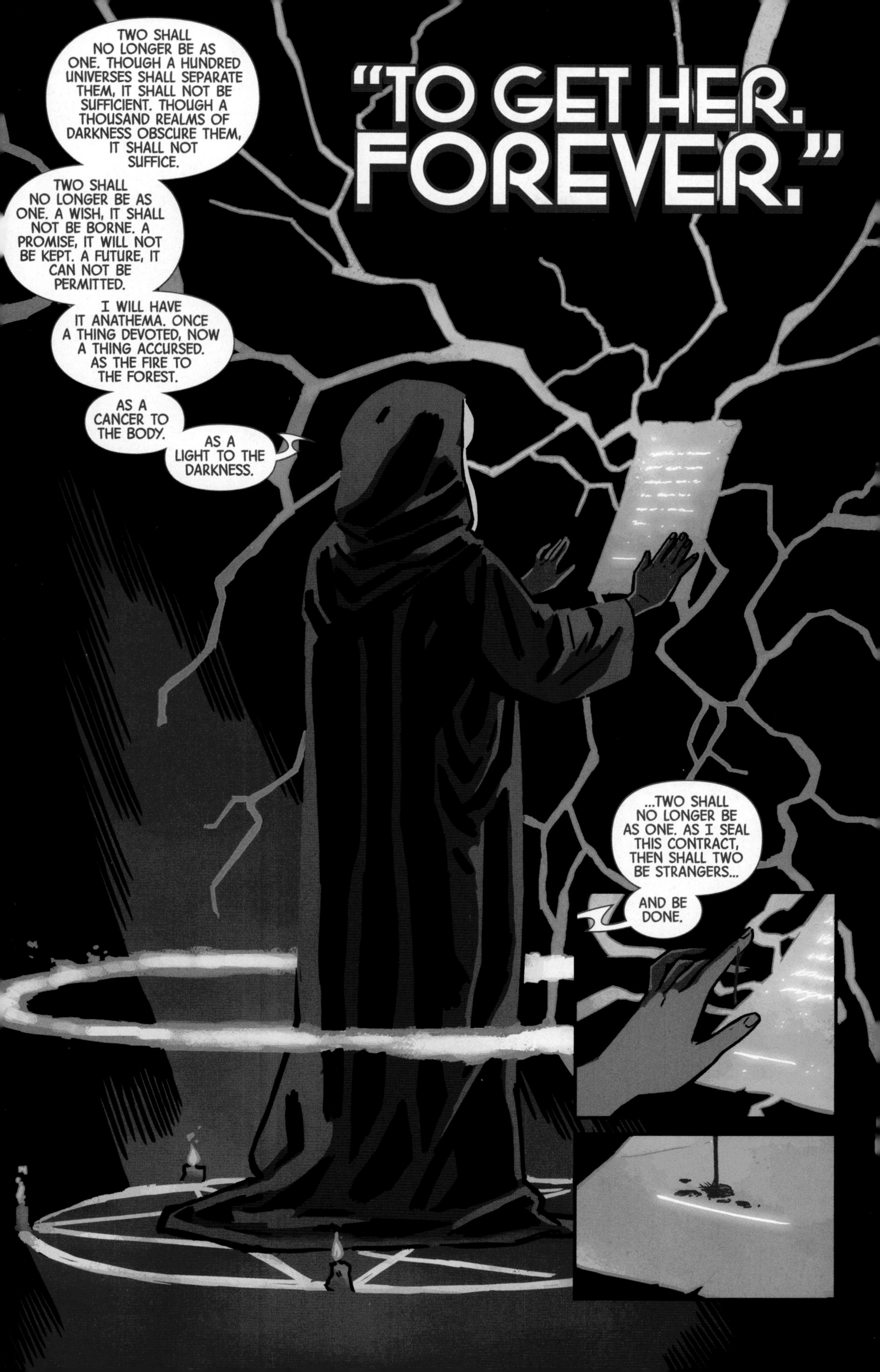

TWO SHALL NO LONGER BE AS ONE. THOUGH A HUNDRED UNIVERSES SHALL SEPARATE THEM, IT SHALL NOT BE SUFFICIENT. THOUGH A THOUSAND REALMS OF DARKNESS OBSCURE THEM, IT SHALL NOT SUFFICE.
"TO GET HER. FOREVER."
TWO SHALL NO LONGER BE AS ONE. A WISH, IT SHALL NOT BE BORNE. A PROMISE, IT WILL NOT BE KEPT. A FUTURE, IT CAN NOT BE PERMITTED.
I WILL HAVE IT ANATHEMA. ONCE A THING DEVOTED, NOW A THING ACCURSED. AS THE FIRE TO THE FOREST.
AS A CANCER TO THE BODY.
AS A LIGHT TO THE DARKNESS.
...TWO SHALL NO LONGER BE AS ONE. AS I SEAL THIS CONTRACT, THEN SHALL TWO BE STRANGERS...
AND BE DONE.

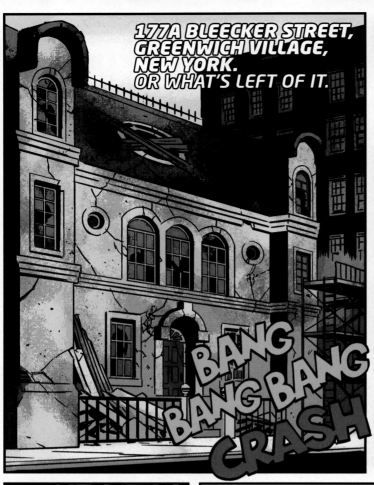

177A BLEECKER STREET, GREENWICH VILLAGE, NEW YORK. OR WHAT'S LEFT OF IT.

BANG BANG BANG CRASH

→SNARRLL←

STOP! STOP IT!!!

WHAT ARE YOU *DOING?!* YOU WERE HIRED TO EFFECT REPAIRS NOT CREATE *MORE* RUBBLE!

TWO STEPS FORWARD, ONE STEP BACK IS ALWAYS THE WAY. ROOT OUT THE *ROT.* IMPROVE THE *STOCK.* STAY OUTTA MY WAY.

YOU WERE CONTRACTED FOR FLOORS AND TILE. AND SPEAKING OF TILE, THE DOWNSTAIRS BATH IS UNACCEPTABLE.

IF YOU HAVE OUTSTANDING ISSUES, THEN PUT 'EM ON THE PUNCH LIST.

THE *PUNCH LIST* IS AS LONG AS MY ARM.

FUNNY, THAT. MINE'S ONLY GOT THE ONE THING ON IT AT THE MOMENT. STRANGE, INNIT?

NOT STRANGE AT ALL, YOU CORDLESS-TOOLED GORILLA. BUT IF YOU THINK I'M GOING TO TOLERATE IDLE--

STRANGE. BEHIND YOU.

TWITCH

STEPHEN?

JUST PULLING YOUR LEG. CAN I GET BACK TO WORK, YOUR WORSHIP?

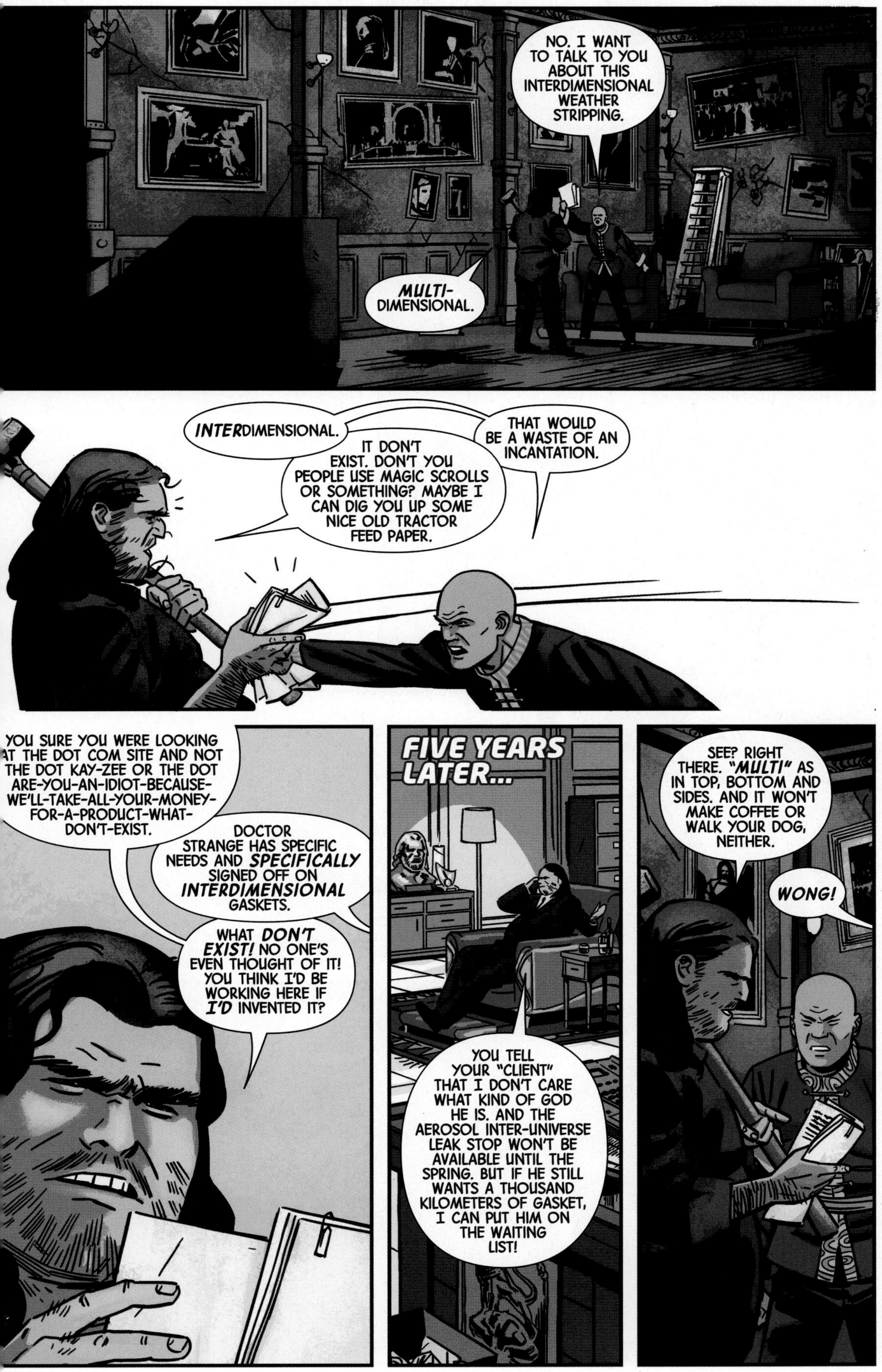
NO. I WANT TO TALK TO YOU ABOUT THIS INTERDIMENSIONAL WEATHER STRIPPING.
MULTI-DIMENSIONAL.
INTERDIMENSIONAL.
IT DON'T EXIST. DON'T YOU PEOPLE USE MAGIC SCROLLS OR SOMETHING? MAYBE I CAN DIG YOU UP SOME NICE OLD TRACTOR FEED PAPER.
THAT WOULD BE A WASTE OF AN INCANTATION.
YOU SURE YOU WERE LOOKING AT THE DOT COM SITE AND NOT THE DOT KAY-ZEE OR THE DOT ARE-YOU-AN-IDIOT-BECAUSE-WE'LL-TAKE-ALL-YOUR-MONEY-FOR-A-PRODUCT-WHAT-DON'T-EXIST.
DOCTOR STRANGE HAS SPECIFIC NEEDS AND SPECIFICALLY SIGNED OFF ON INTERDIMENSIONAL GASKETS.
WHAT DON'T EXIST! NO ONE'S EVEN THOUGHT OF IT! YOU THINK I'D BE WORKING HERE IF I'D INVENTED IT?
FIVE YEARS LATER...
YOU TELL YOUR "CLIENT" THAT I DON'T CARE WHAT KIND OF GOD HE IS. AND THE AEROSOL INTER-UNIVERSE LEAK STOP WON'T BE AVAILABLE UNTIL THE SPRING. BUT IF HE STILL WANTS A THOUSAND KILOMETERS OF GASKET, I CAN PUT HIM ON THE WAITING LIST!
SEE? RIGHT THERE. "MULTI" AS IN TOP, BOTTOM AND SIDES. AND IT WON'T MAKE COFFEE OR WALK YOUR DOG, NEITHER.
WONG!

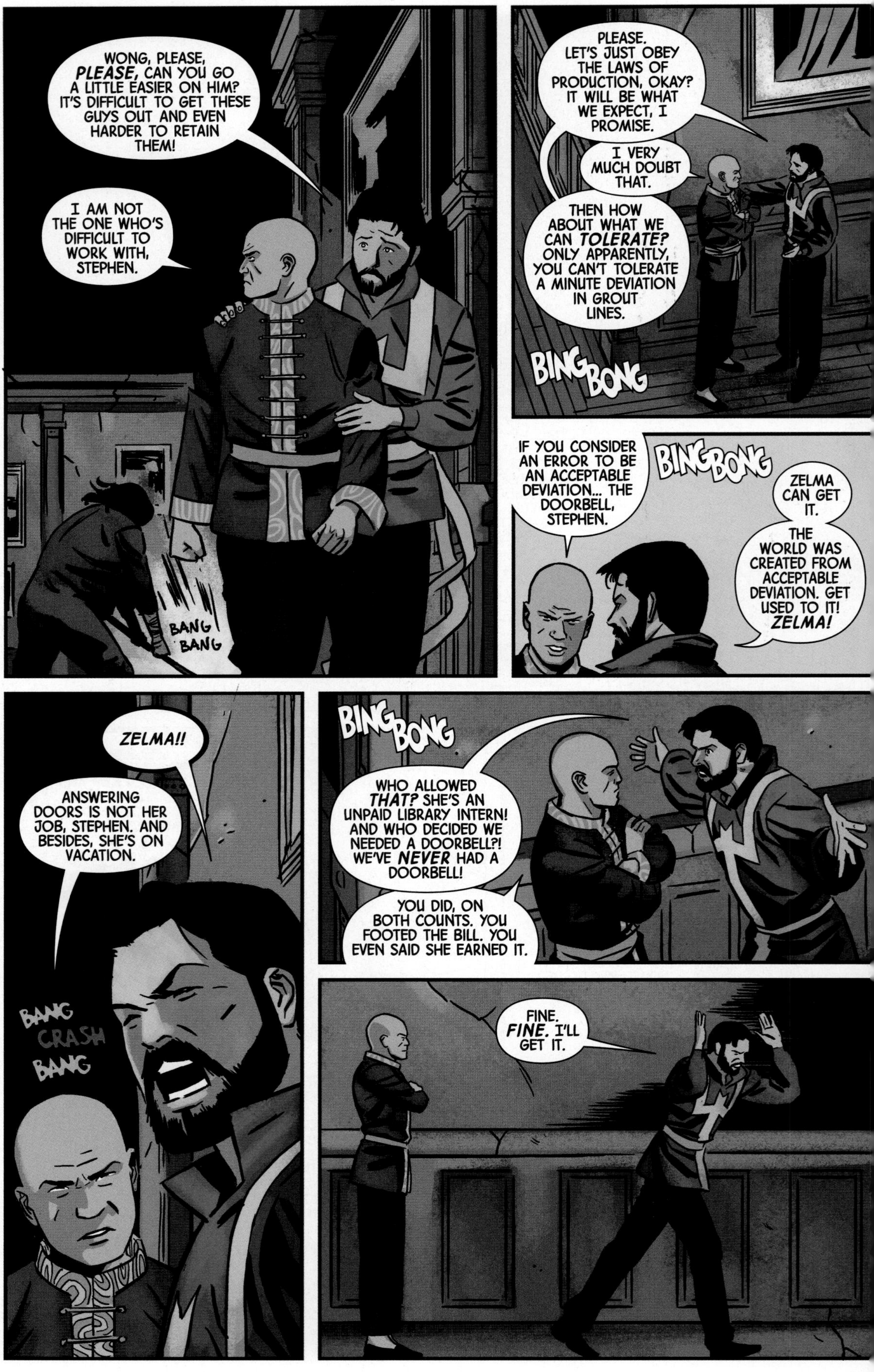
WONG, PLEASE, *PLEASE,* CAN YOU GO A LITTLE EASIER ON HIM? IT'S DIFFICULT TO GET THESE GUYS OUT AND EVEN HARDER TO RETAIN THEM!
I AM NOT THE ONE WHO'S DIFFICULT TO WORK WITH, STEPHEN.
BANG BANG
PLEASE. LET'S JUST OBEY THE LAWS OF PRODUCTION, OKAY? IT WILL BE WHAT WE EXPECT, I PROMISE.
I VERY MUCH DOUBT THAT.
THEN HOW ABOUT WHAT WE CAN *TOLERATE?* ONLY APPARENTLY, YOU CAN'T TOLERATE A MINUTE DEVIATION IN GROUT LINES.
BING BONG
IF YOU CONSIDER AN ERROR TO BE AN ACCEPTABLE DEVIATION... THE DOORBELL, STEPHEN.
BING BONG
ZELMA CAN GET IT.
THE WORLD WAS CREATED FROM ACCEPTABLE DEVIATION. GET USED TO IT! *ZELMA!*
ZELMA!!
ANSWERING DOORS IS NOT HER JOB, STEPHEN. AND BESIDES, SHE'S ON VACATION.
BANG CRASH BANG
BING BONG
WHO ALLOWED *THAT?* SHE'S AN UNPAID LIBRARY INTERN! AND WHO DECIDED WE NEEDED A DOORBELL?! WE'VE *NEVER* HAD A DOORBELL!
YOU DID, ON BOTH COUNTS. YOU FOOTED THE BILL. YOU EVEN SAID SHE EARNED IT.
FINE. *FINE.* I'LL GET IT.

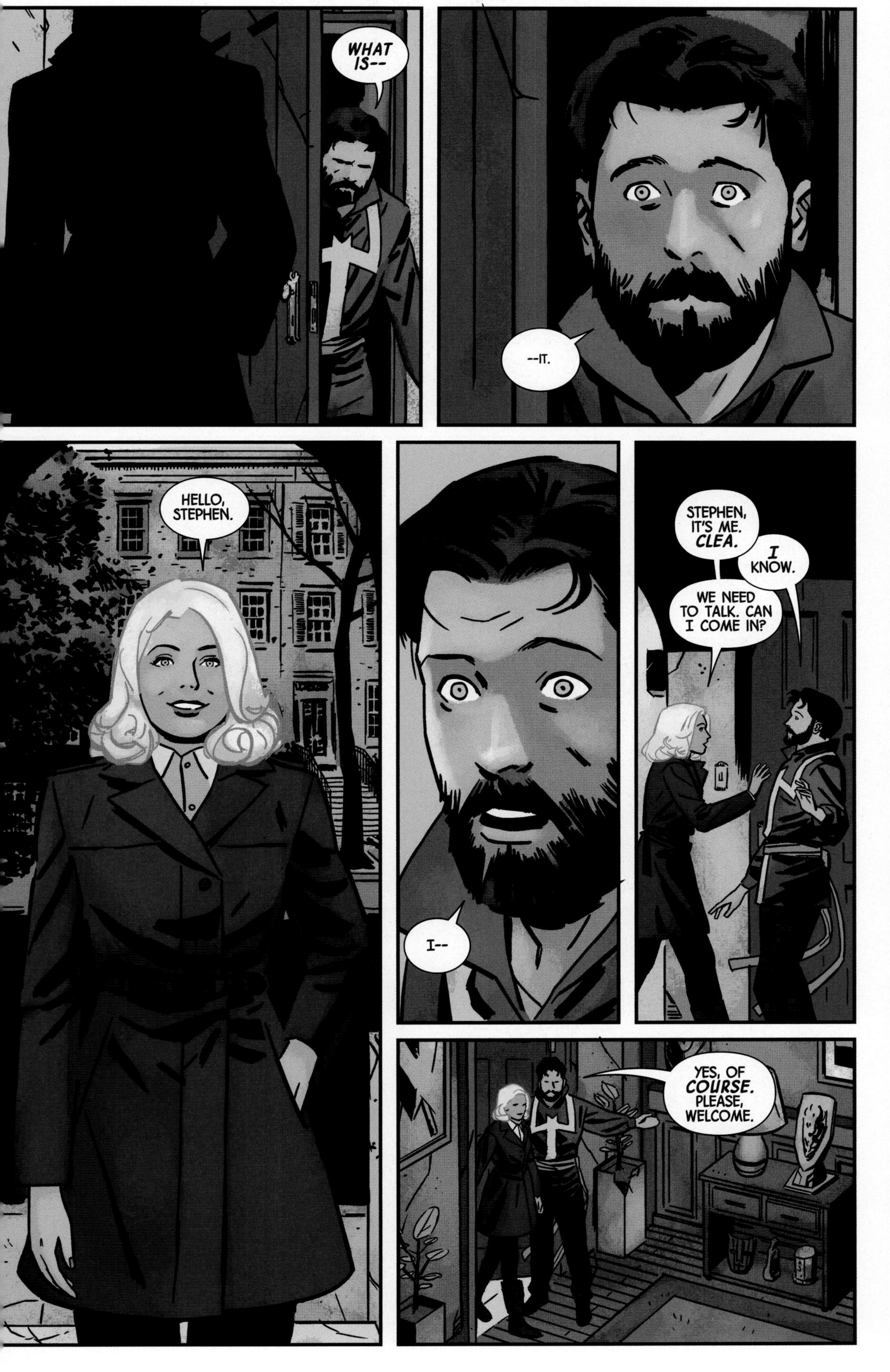
WHAT IS--
--IT.
HELLO, STEPHEN.
I--
STEPHEN, IT'S ME. CLEA.
I KNOW.
WE NEED TO TALK. CAN I COME IN?
YES, OF COURSE. PLEASE, WELCOME.

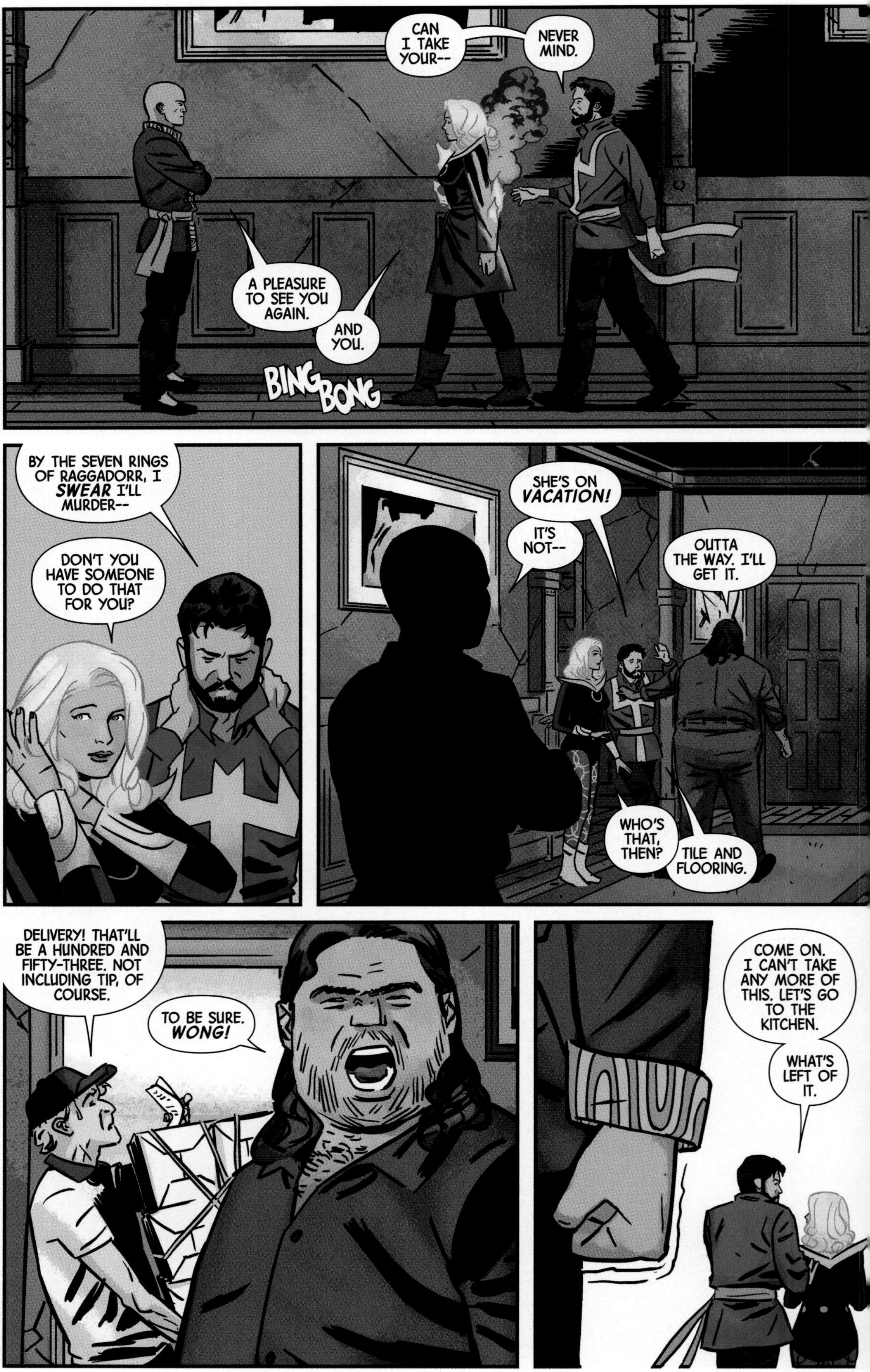
CAN I TAKE YOUR--
NEVER MIND.
A PLEASURE TO SEE YOU AGAIN.
AND YOU.
BING BONG
BY THE SEVEN RINGS OF RAGGADORR, I *SWEAR* I'LL MURDER--
DON'T YOU HAVE SOMEONE TO DO THAT FOR YOU?
SHE'S ON *VACATION!*
IT'S NOT--
OUTTA THE WAY. I'LL GET IT.
WHO'S THAT, THEN?
TILE AND FLOORING.
DELIVERY! THAT'LL BE A HUNDRED AND FIFTY-THREE. NOT INCLUDING TIP, OF COURSE.
TO BE SURE. *WONG!*
COME ON. I CAN'T TAKE ANY MORE OF THIS. LET'S GO TO THE KITCHEN.
WHAT'S LEFT OF IT.

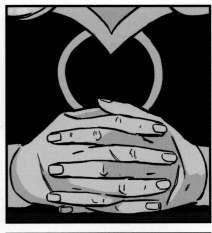

TEA?

YES!

HOW DOES ANYONE FIND A DAMN THING IN THIS MESS? I CAN'T BELIEVE--

STEPHEN.

STEPHEN.

CLEA, ARE YOU HERE TO HELP ME?

NOT PRECISELY. MAYBE. I'M NOT SURE.

BECAUSE I COULD REALLY USE YOU RIGHT NOW.

THAT'S WHAT I'M AFRAID OF.

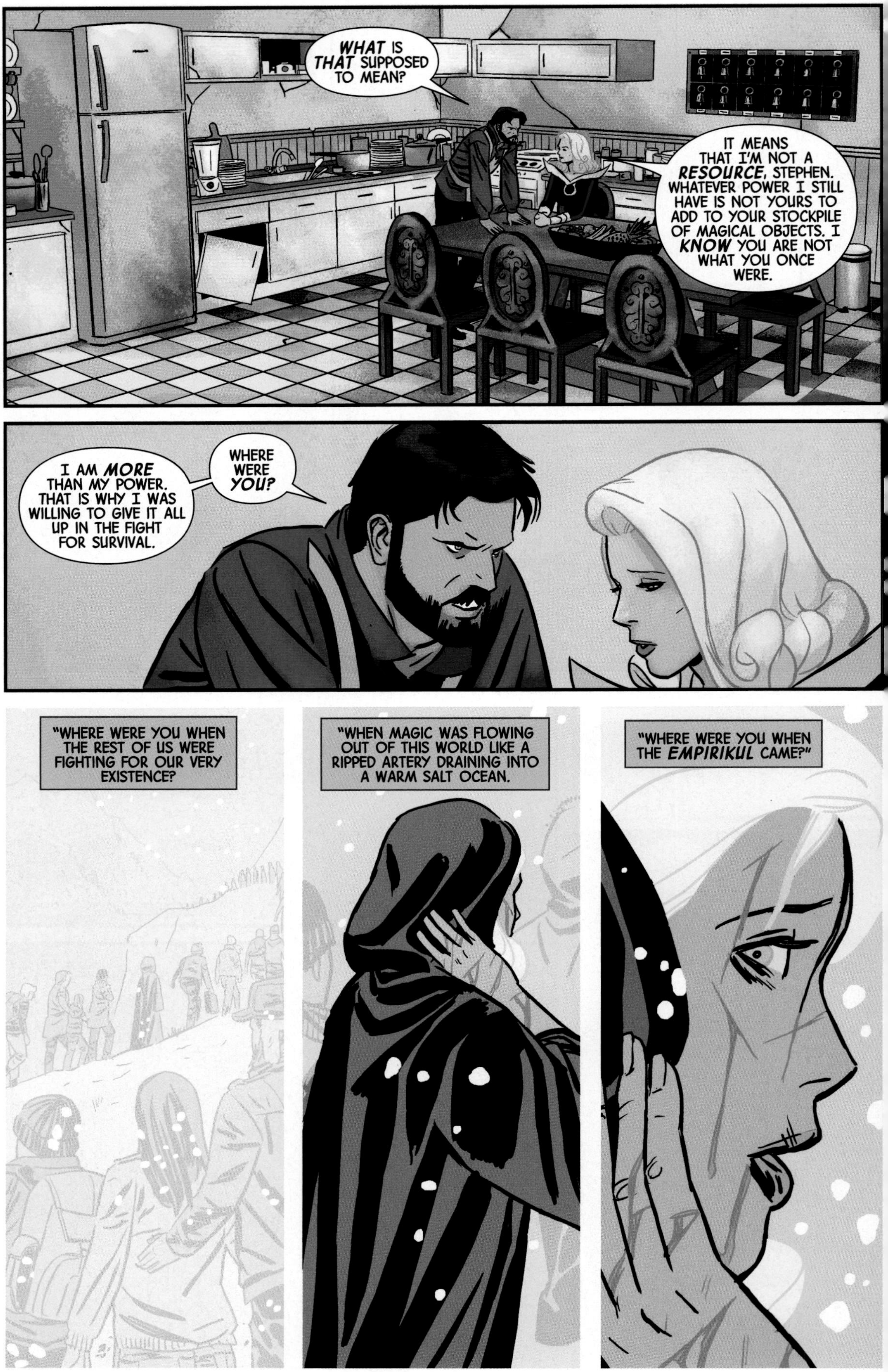
WHAT IS THAT SUPPOSED TO MEAN?
IT MEANS THAT I'M NOT A RESOURCE, STEPHEN. WHATEVER POWER I STILL HAVE IS NOT YOURS TO ADD TO YOUR STOCKPILE OF MAGICAL OBJECTS. I KNOW YOU ARE NOT WHAT YOU ONCE WERE.
I AM MORE THAN MY POWER. THAT IS WHY I WAS WILLING TO GIVE IT ALL UP IN THE FIGHT FOR SURVIVAL.
WHERE WERE YOU?
"WHERE WERE YOU WHEN THE REST OF US WERE FIGHTING FOR OUR VERY EXISTENCE?
"WHEN MAGIC WAS FLOWING OUT OF THIS WORLD LIKE A RIPPED ARTERY DRAINING INTO A WARM SALT OCEAN.
"WHERE WERE YOU WHEN THE EMPIRIKUL CAME?"

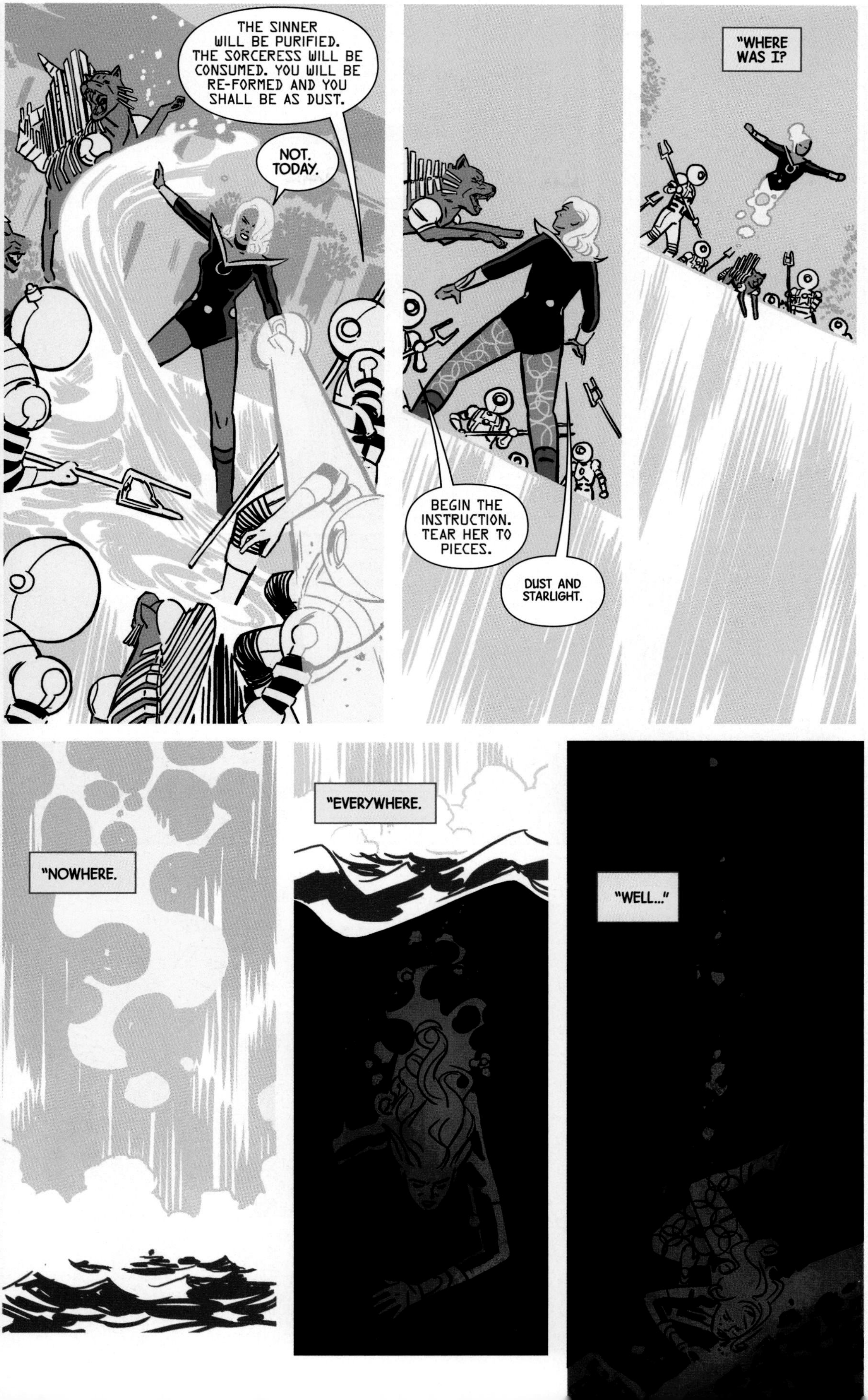
THE SINNER WILL BE PURIFIED. THE SORCERESS WILL BE CONSUMED. YOU WILL BE RE-FORMED AND YOU SHALL BE AS DUST.
NOT. TODAY.
BEGIN THE INSTRUCTION. TEAR HER TO PIECES.
DUST AND STARLIGHT.
"WHERE WAS I?
"NOWHERE.
"EVERYWHERE.
"WELL..."

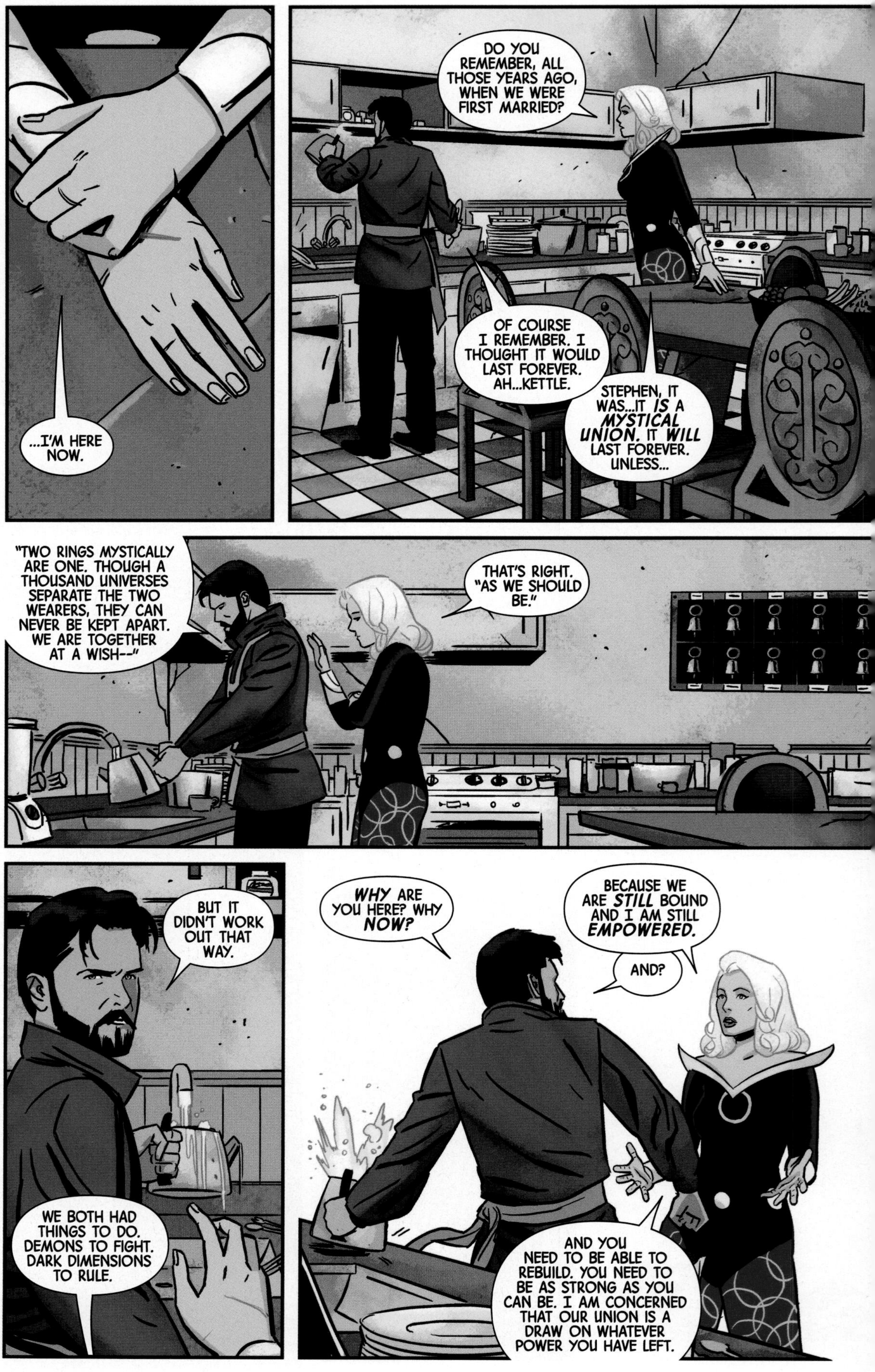
...I'M HERE NOW.
DO YOU REMEMBER, ALL THOSE YEARS AGO, WHEN WE WERE FIRST MARRIED?
OF COURSE I REMEMBER. I THOUGHT IT WOULD LAST FOREVER. AH...KETTLE.
STEPHEN, IT WAS...IT IS A MYSTICAL UNION. IT WILL LAST FOREVER. UNLESS...
"TWO RINGS MYSTICALLY ARE ONE. THOUGH A THOUSAND UNIVERSES SEPARATE THE TWO WEARERS, THEY CAN NEVER BE KEPT APART. WE ARE TOGETHER AT A WISH--"
THAT'S RIGHT. "AS WE SHOULD BE."
BUT IT DIDN'T WORK OUT THAT WAY.
WE BOTH HAD THINGS TO DO. DEMONS TO FIGHT. DARK DIMENSIONS TO RULE.
WHY ARE YOU HERE? WHY NOW?
BECAUSE WE ARE STILL BOUND AND I AM STILL EMPOWERED.
AND?
AND YOU NEED TO BE ABLE TO REBUILD. YOU NEED TO BE AS STRONG AS YOU CAN BE. I AM CONCERNED THAT OUR UNION IS A DRAW ON WHATEVER POWER YOU HAVE LEFT.

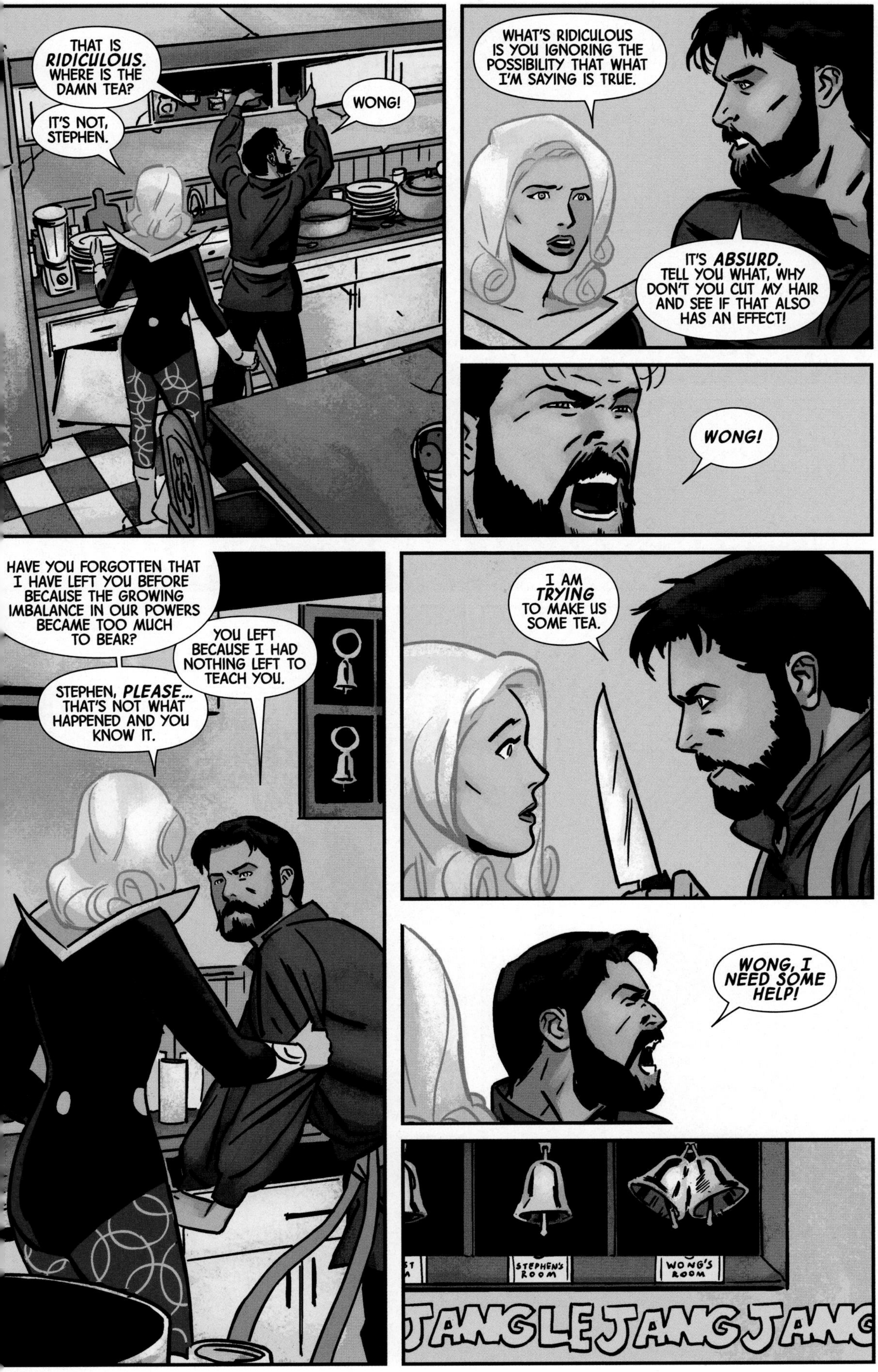
THAT IS RIDICULOUS. WHERE IS THE DAMN TEA?
IT'S NOT, STEPHEN.
WONG!
WHAT'S RIDICULOUS IS YOU IGNORING THE POSSIBILITY THAT WHAT I'M SAYING IS TRUE.
IT'S ABSURD. TELL YOU WHAT, WHY DON'T YOU CUT MY HAIR AND SEE IF THAT ALSO HAS AN EFFECT!
WONG!
HAVE YOU FORGOTTEN THAT I HAVE LEFT YOU BEFORE BECAUSE THE GROWING IMBALANCE IN OUR POWERS BECAME TOO MUCH TO BEAR?
YOU LEFT BECAUSE I HAD NOTHING LEFT TO TEACH YOU.
STEPHEN, PLEASE... THAT'S NOT WHAT HAPPENED AND YOU KNOW IT.
I AM TRYING TO MAKE US SOME TEA.
WONG, I NEED SOME HELP!
STEPHEN'S ROOM
WONG'S ROOM
JANGLE JANG JANG

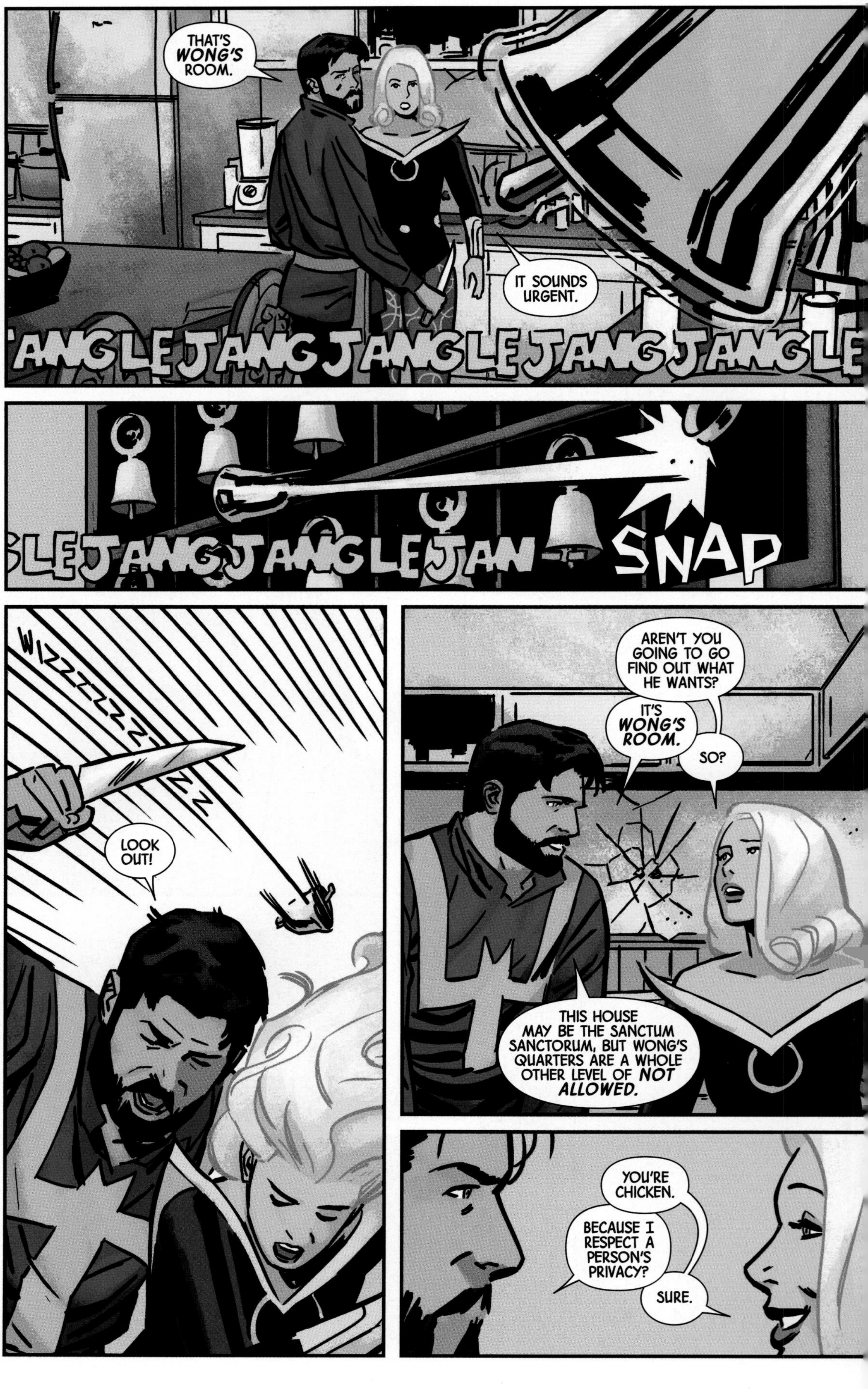

THAT'S WONG'S ROOM.
IT SOUNDS URGENT.
JANGLE JANG JANGLE JANG JANGLE
LE JANG JANGLE JAN
SNAP
WIZZZZZZZZZ
LOOK OUT!
AREN'T YOU GOING TO GO FIND OUT WHAT HE WANTS?
IT'S WONG'S ROOM.
SO?
THIS HOUSE MAY BE THE SANCTUM SANCTORUM, BUT WONG'S QUARTERS ARE A WHOLE OTHER LEVEL OF NOT ALLOWED.
YOU'RE CHICKEN.
BECAUSE I RESPECT A PERSON'S PRIVACY?
SURE.

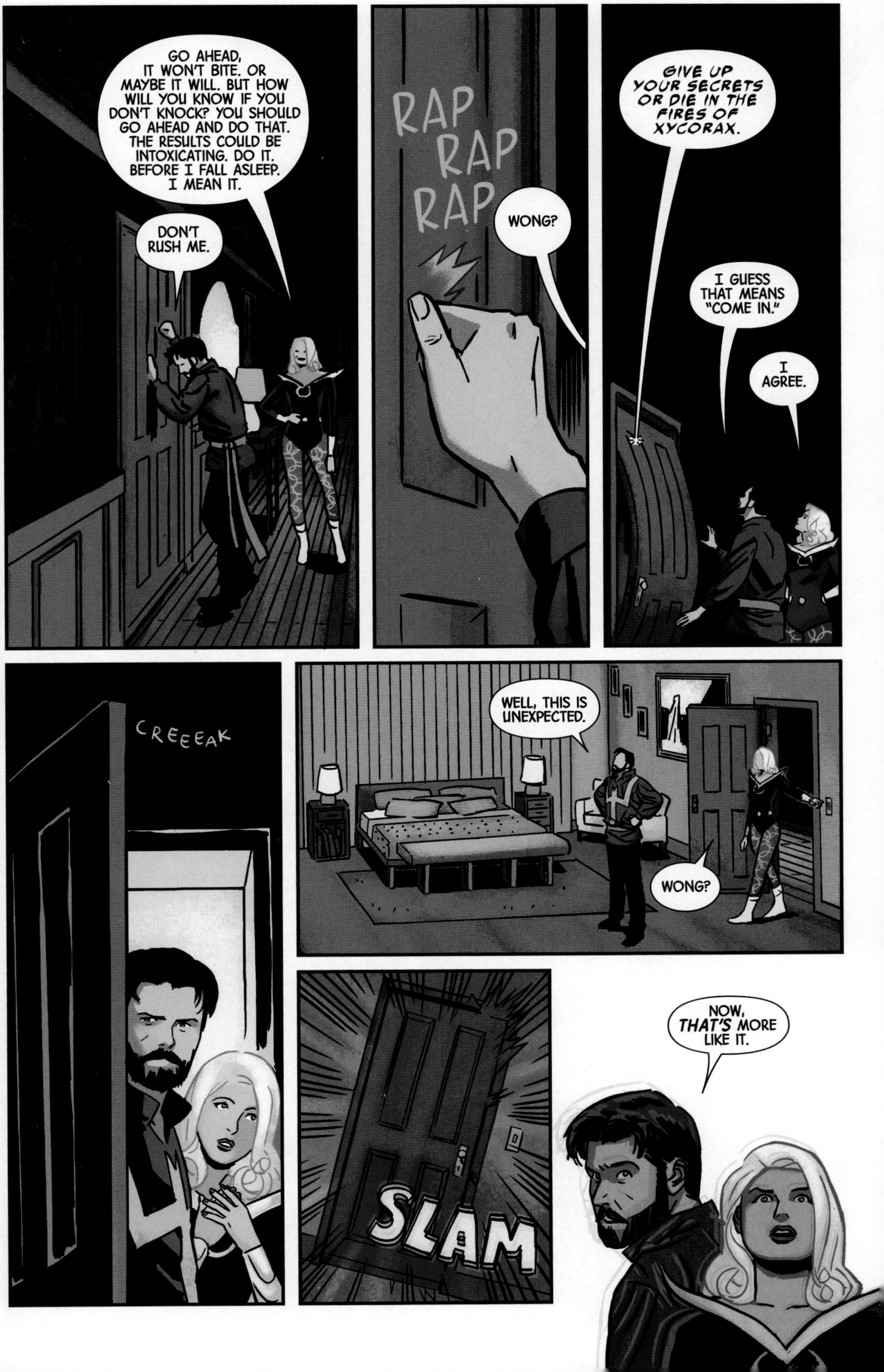
GO AHEAD, IT WON'T BITE. OR MAYBE IT WILL. BUT HOW WILL YOU KNOW IF YOU DON'T KNOCK? YOU SHOULD GO AHEAD AND DO THAT. THE RESULTS COULD BE INTOXICATING. DO IT. BEFORE I FALL ASLEEP. I MEAN IT.
DON'T RUSH ME.
RAP RAP RAP
WONG?
GIVE UP YOUR SECRETS OR DIE IN THE FIRES OF XYCORAX.
I GUESS THAT MEANS "COME IN."
I AGREE.
CREEEAK
WELL, THIS IS UNEXPECTED.
WONG?
SLAM
NOW, THAT'S MORE LIKE IT.

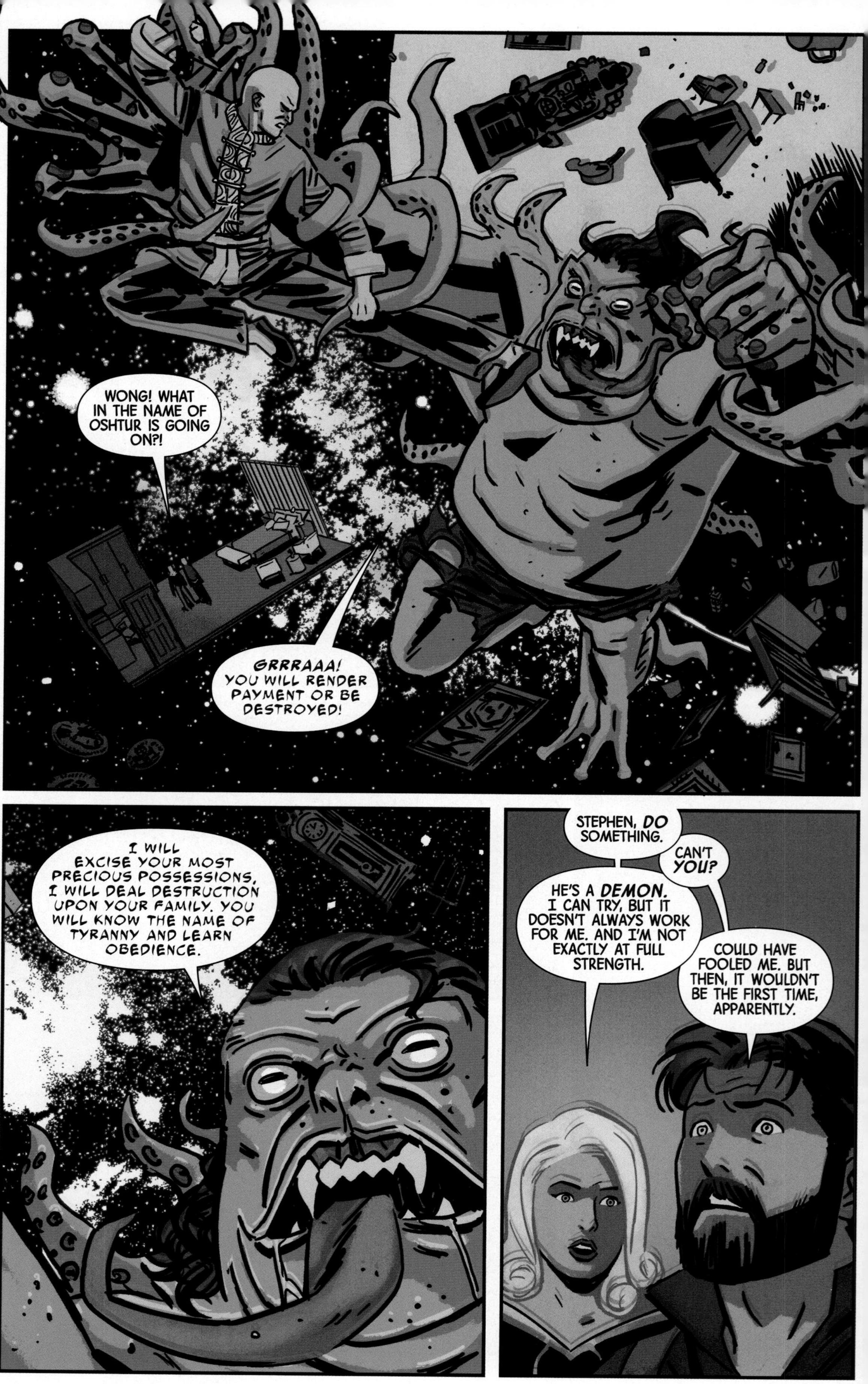
WONG! WHAT IN THE NAME OF OSHTUR IS GOING ON?!
GRRRAAA! YOU WILL RENDER PAYMENT OR BE DESTROYED!
I WILL EXCISE YOUR MOST PRECIOUS POSSESSIONS. I WILL DEAL DESTRUCTION UPON YOUR FAMILY. YOU WILL KNOW THE NAME OF TYRANNY AND LEARN OBEDIENCE.
STEPHEN, DO SOMETHING.
CAN'T YOU?
HE'S A DEMON. I CAN TRY, BUT IT DOESN'T ALWAYS WORK FOR ME. AND I'M NOT EXACTLY AT FULL STRENGTH.
COULD HAVE FOOLED ME. BUT THEN, IT WOULDN'T BE THE FIRST TIME, APPARENTLY.

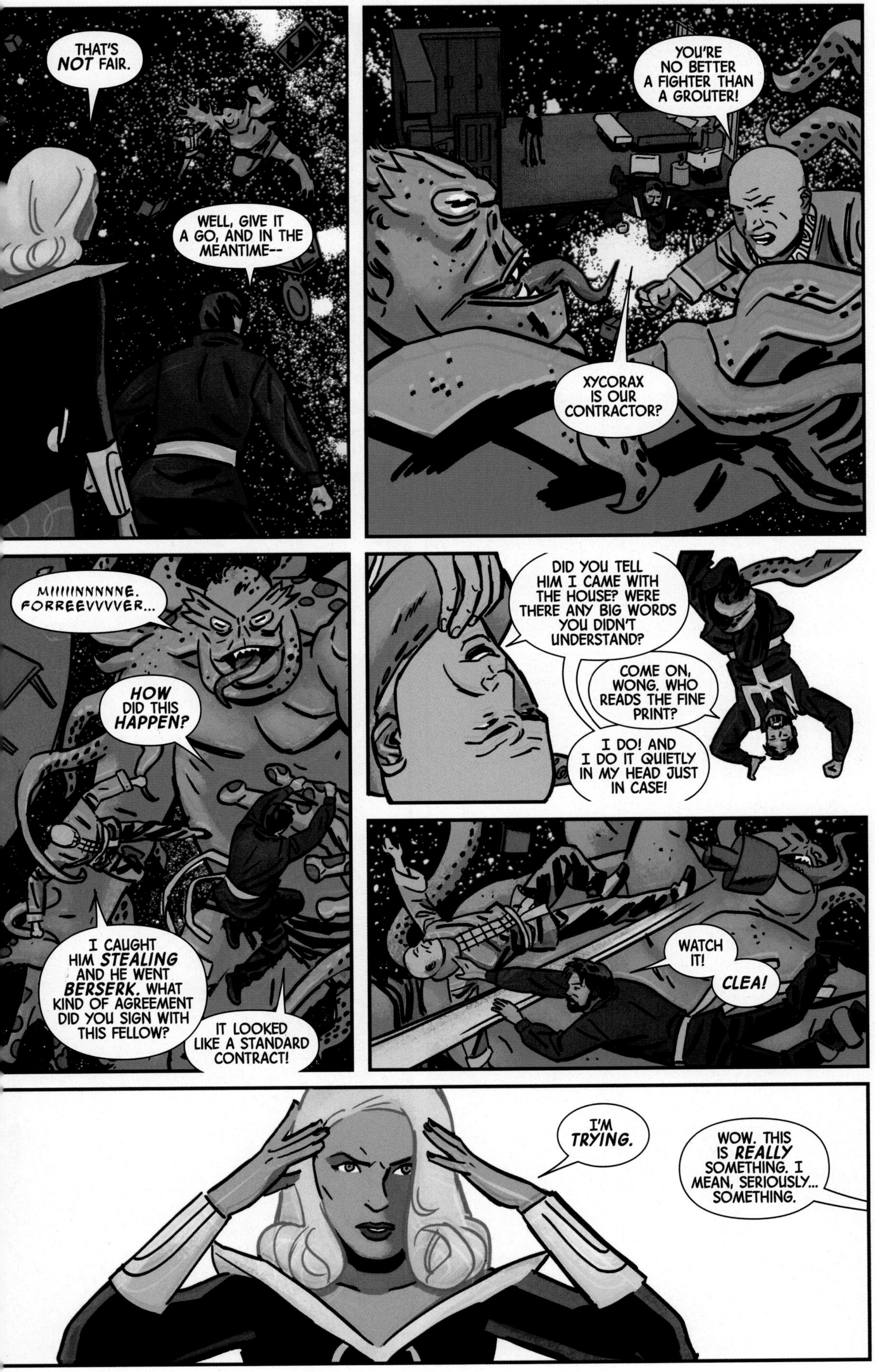
THAT'S NOT FAIR.
WELL, GIVE IT A GO, AND IN THE MEANTIME--
YOU'RE NO BETTER A FIGHTER THAN A GROUTER!
XYCORAX IS OUR CONTRACTOR?
MIIIIINNNNNE. FORREEVVVVVER...
HOW DID THIS HAPPEN?
I CAUGHT HIM STEALING AND HE WENT BERSERK. WHAT KIND OF AGREEMENT DID YOU SIGN WITH THIS FELLOW?
IT LOOKED LIKE A STANDARD CONTRACT!
DID YOU TELL HIM I CAME WITH THE HOUSE? WERE THERE ANY BIG WORDS YOU DIDN'T UNDERSTAND?
COME ON, WONG. WHO READS THE FINE PRINT?
I DO! AND I DO IT QUIETLY IN MY HEAD JUST IN CASE!
WATCH IT!
CLEA!
I'M TRYING.
WOW. THIS IS REALLY SOMETHING. I MEAN, SERIOUSLY... SOMETHING.

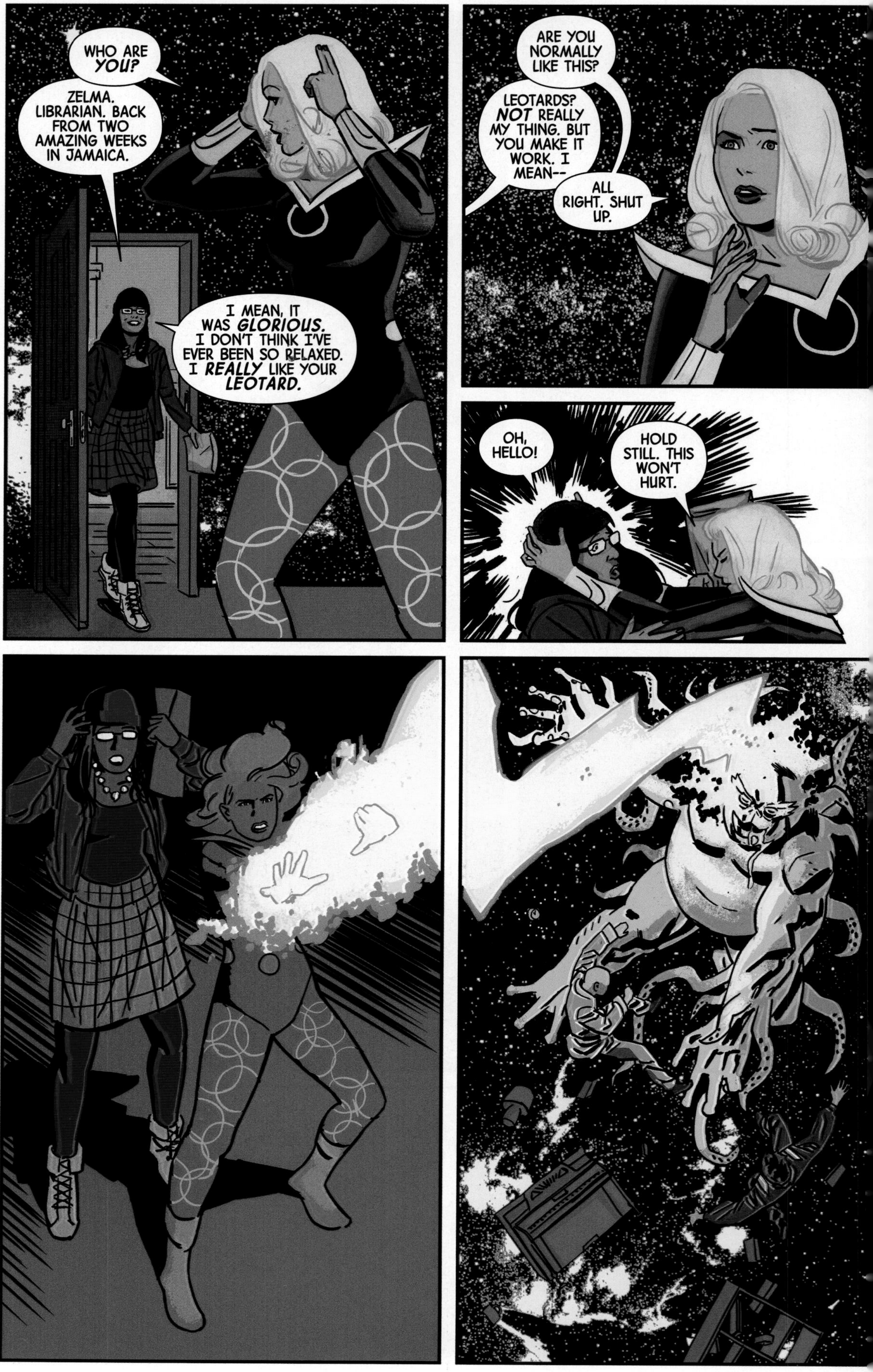
WHO ARE YOU?
ZELMA. LIBRARIAN. BACK FROM TWO AMAZING WEEKS IN JAMAICA.
I MEAN, IT WAS GLORIOUS. I DON'T THINK I'VE EVER BEEN SO RELAXED. I REALLY LIKE YOUR LEOTARD.
ARE YOU NORMALLY LIKE THIS?
LEOTARDS? NOT REALLY MY THING. BUT YOU MAKE IT WORK. I MEAN--
ALL RIGHT. SHUT UP.
OH, HELLO!
HOLD STILL. THIS WON'T HURT.

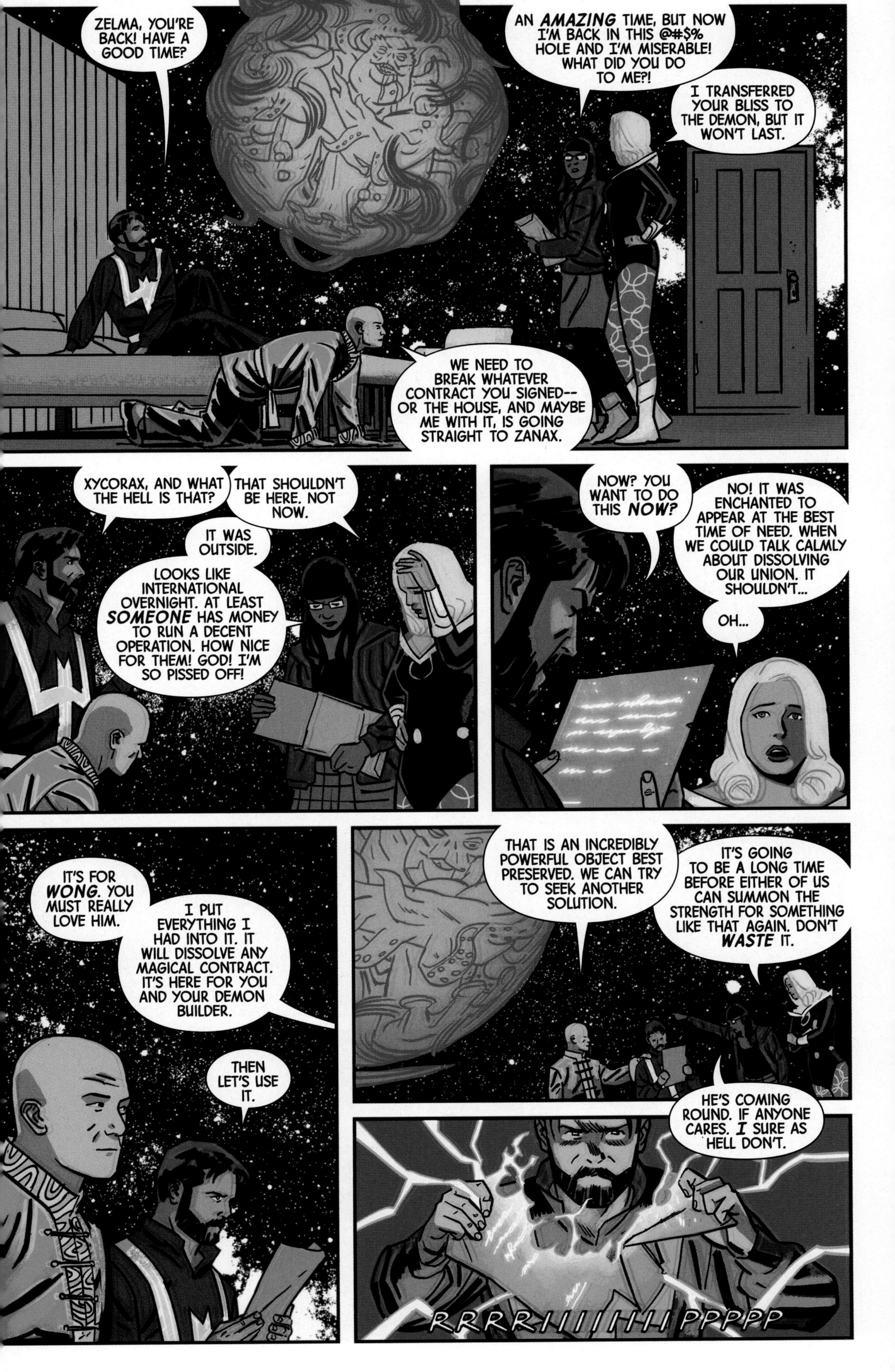
ZELMA, YOU'RE BACK! HAVE A GOOD TIME?
AN AMAZING TIME, BUT NOW I'M BACK IN THIS @#$% HOLE AND I'M MISERABLE! WHAT DID YOU DO TO ME?!
I TRANSFERRED YOUR BLISS TO THE DEMON, BUT IT WON'T LAST.
WE NEED TO BREAK WHATEVER CONTRACT YOU SIGNED-- OR THE HOUSE, AND MAYBE ME WITH IT, IS GOING STRAIGHT TO ZANAX.
XYCORAX, AND WHAT THE HELL IS THAT?
THAT SHOULDN'T BE HERE. NOT NOW.
IT WAS OUTSIDE.
LOOKS LIKE INTERNATIONAL OVERNIGHT. AT LEAST SOMEONE HAS MONEY TO RUN A DECENT OPERATION. HOW NICE FOR THEM! GOD! I'M SO PISSED OFF!
NOW? YOU WANT TO DO THIS NOW?
NO! IT WAS ENCHANTED TO APPEAR AT THE BEST TIME OF NEED. WHEN WE COULD TALK CALMLY ABOUT DISSOLVING OUR UNION. IT SHOULDN'T...
OH...
IT'S FOR WONG. YOU MUST REALLY LOVE HIM.
I PUT EVERYTHING I HAD INTO IT. IT WILL DISSOLVE ANY MAGICAL CONTRACT. IT'S HERE FOR YOU AND YOUR DEMON BUILDER.
THEN LET'S USE IT.
THAT IS AN INCREDIBLY POWERFUL OBJECT BEST PRESERVED. WE CAN TRY TO SEEK ANOTHER SOLUTION.
IT'S GOING TO BE A LONG TIME BEFORE EITHER OF US CAN SUMMON THE STRENGTH FOR SOMETHING LIKE THAT AGAIN. DON'T WASTE IT.
HE'S COMING ROUND. IF ANYONE CARES. I SURE AS HELL DON'T.
RRRRRIIIIIIIIII PPPPPP

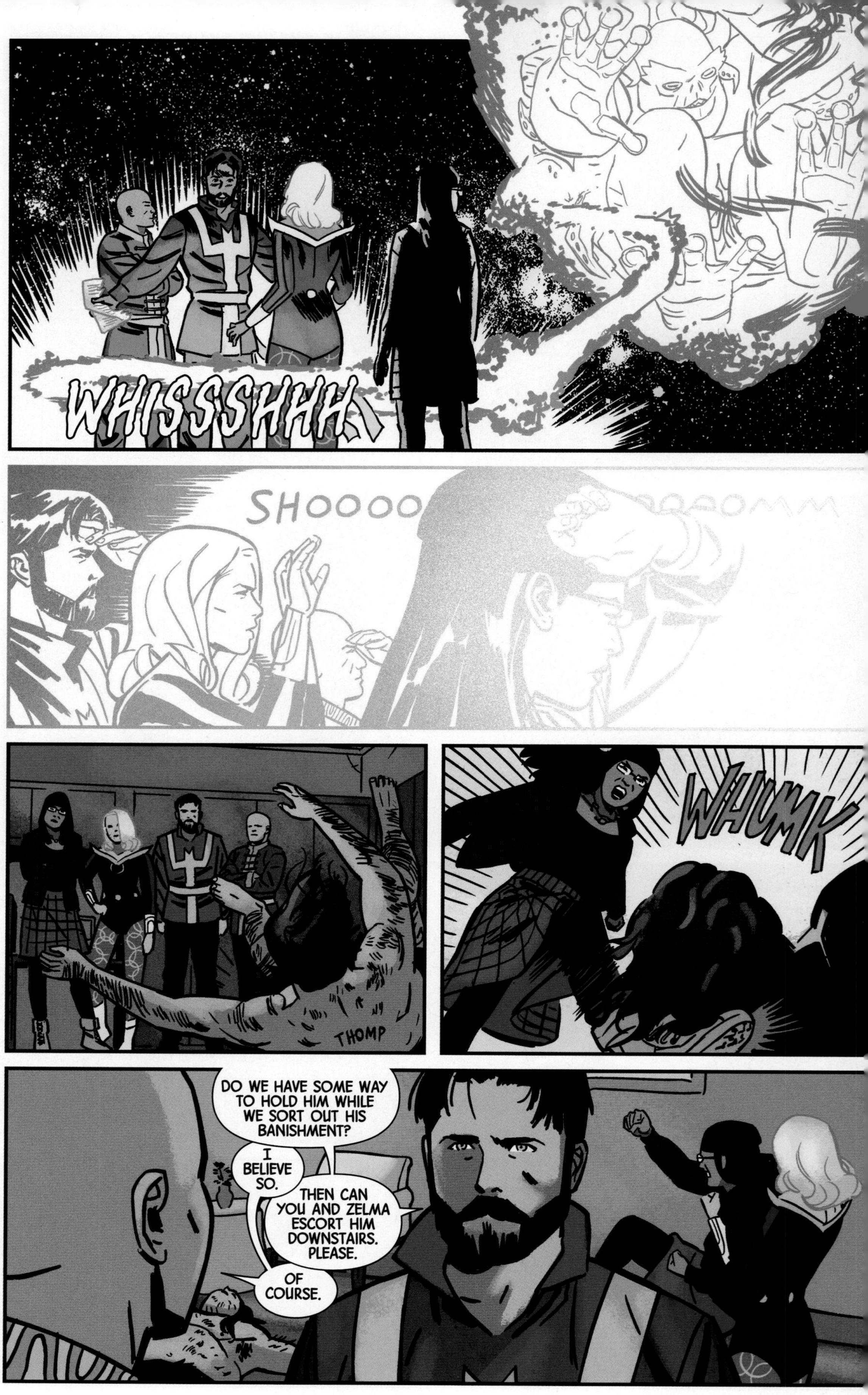
WHISSSHHH
SHOOOO
OOOOOOMM
THOMP
WHUMK
DO WE HAVE SOME WAY TO HOLD HIM WHILE WE SORT OUT HIS BANISHMENT?
I BELIEVE SO.
THEN CAN YOU AND ZELMA ESCORT HIM DOWNSTAIRS. PLEASE.
OF COURSE.

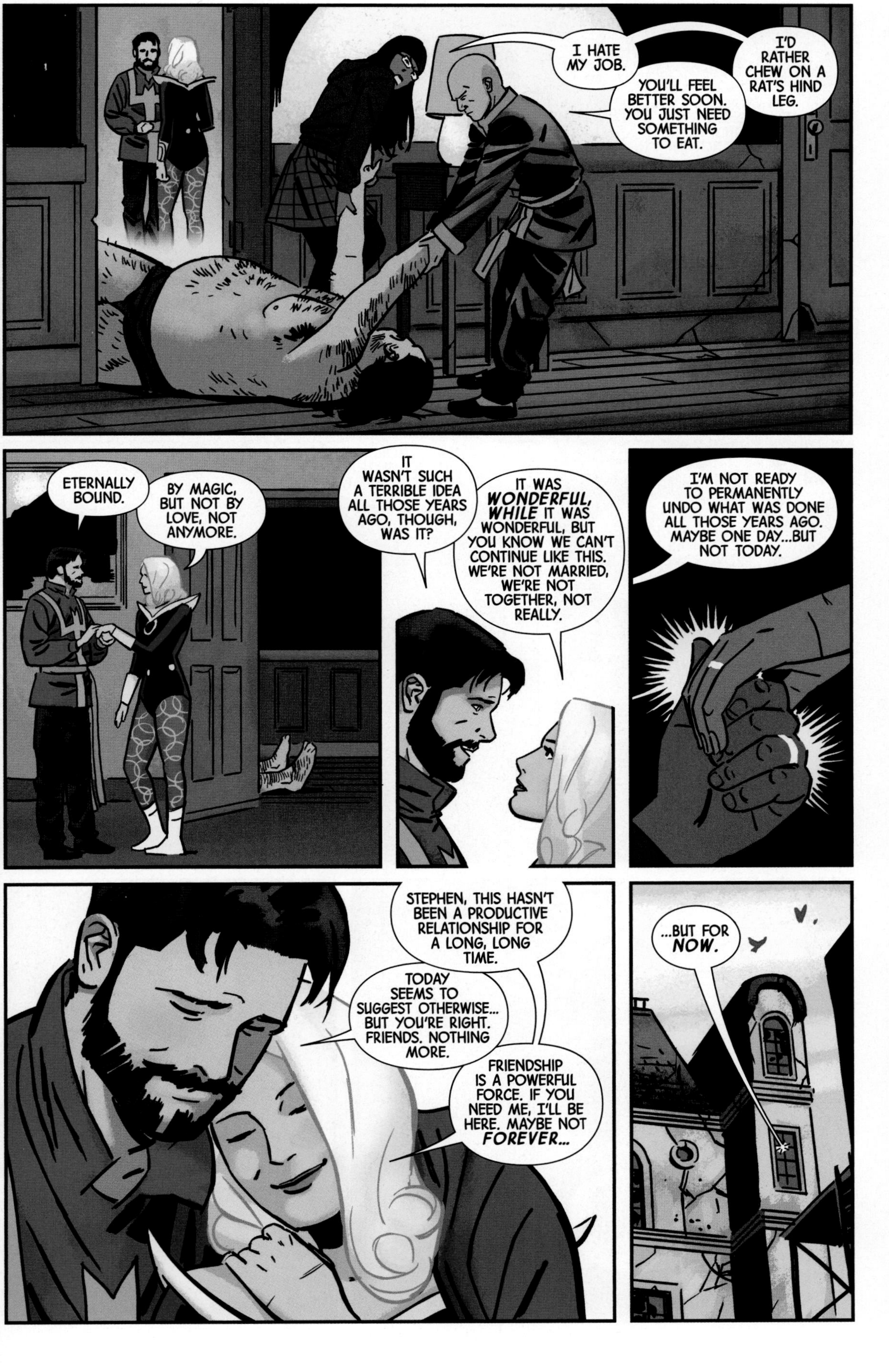
I HATE MY JOB.
YOU'LL FEEL BETTER SOON. YOU JUST NEED SOMETHING TO EAT.
I'D RATHER CHEW ON A RAT'S HIND LEG.
ETERNALLY BOUND.
BY MAGIC, BUT NOT BY LOVE, NOT ANYMORE.
IT WASN'T SUCH A TERRIBLE IDEA ALL THOSE YEARS AGO, THOUGH, WAS IT?
IT WAS *WONDERFUL, WHILE* IT WAS WONDERFUL, BUT YOU KNOW WE CAN'T CONTINUE LIKE THIS. WE'RE NOT MARRIED, WE'RE NOT TOGETHER, NOT REALLY.
I'M NOT READY TO PERMANENTLY UNDO WHAT WAS DONE ALL THOSE YEARS AGO. MAYBE ONE DAY...BUT NOT TODAY.
STEPHEN, THIS HASN'T BEEN A PRODUCTIVE RELATIONSHIP FOR A LONG, LONG TIME.
TODAY SEEMS TO SUGGEST OTHERWISE... BUT YOU'RE RIGHT. FRIENDS. NOTHING MORE.
FRIENDSHIP IS A POWERFUL FORCE. IF YOU NEED ME, I'LL BE HERE. MAYBE NOT *FOREVER*...
...BUT FOR *NOW*.

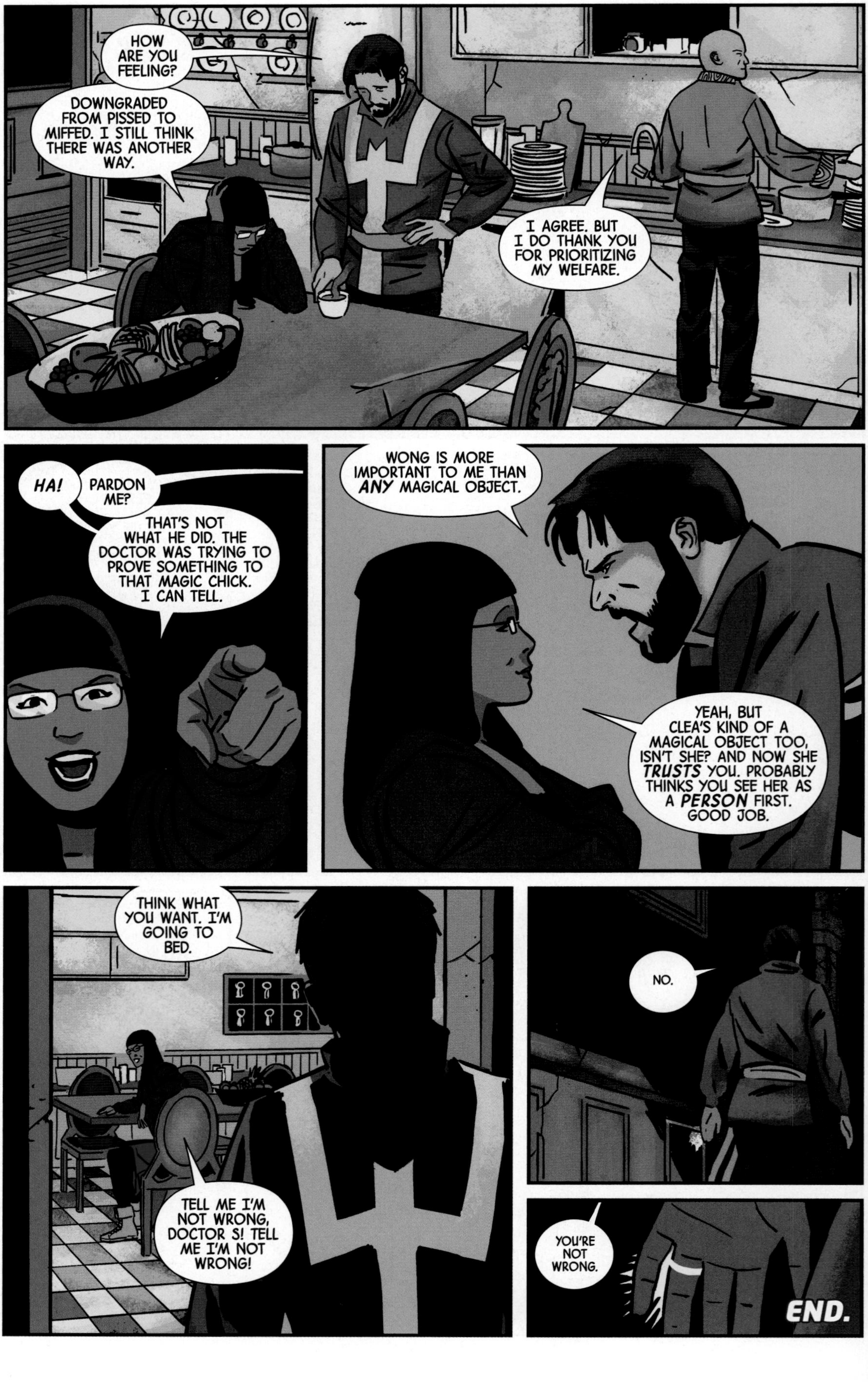
HOW ARE YOU FEELING?
DOWNGRADED FROM PISSED TO MIFFED. I STILL THINK THERE WAS ANOTHER WAY.
I AGREE. BUT I DO THANK YOU FOR PRIORITIZING MY WELFARE.
HA!
PARDON ME?
THAT'S NOT WHAT HE DID. THE DOCTOR WAS TRYING TO PROVE SOMETHING TO THAT MAGIC CHICK. I CAN TELL.
WONG IS MORE IMPORTANT TO ME THAN ANY MAGICAL OBJECT.
YEAH, BUT CLEA'S KIND OF A MAGICAL OBJECT TOO, ISN'T SHE? AND NOW SHE TRUSTS YOU. PROBABLY THINKS YOU SEE HER AS A PERSON FIRST. GOOD JOB.
THINK WHAT YOU WANT. I'M GOING TO BED.
TELL ME I'M NOT WRONG, DOCTOR S! TELL ME I'M NOT WRONG!
NO.
YOU'RE NOT WRONG.
END.

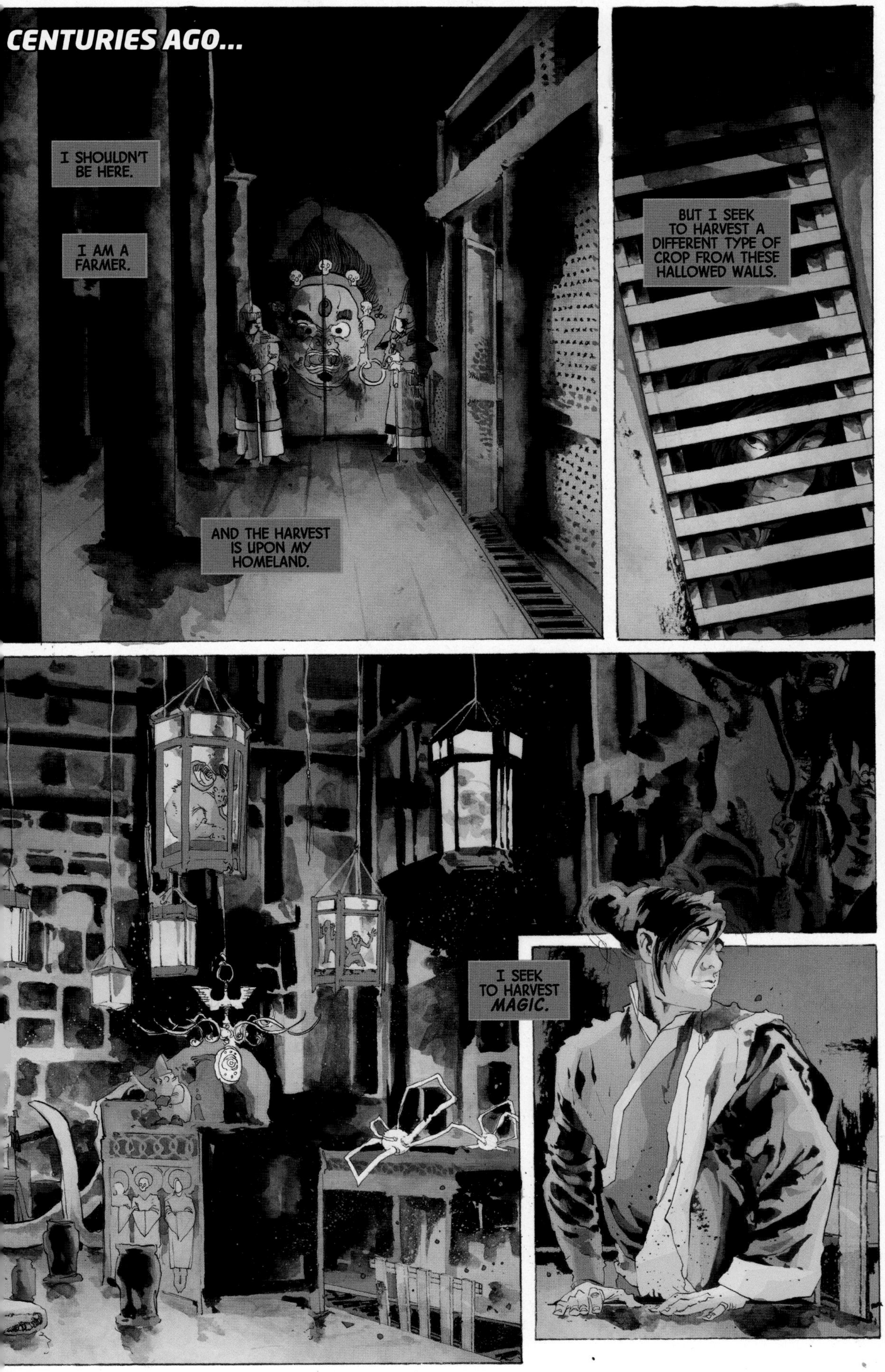
CENTURIES AGO...
I SHOULDN'T BE HERE.
I AM A FARMER.
AND THE HARVEST IS UPON MY HOMELAND.
BUT I SEEK TO HARVEST A DIFFERENT TYPE OF CROP FROM THESE HALLOWED WALLS.
I SEEK TO HARVEST *MAGIC*.

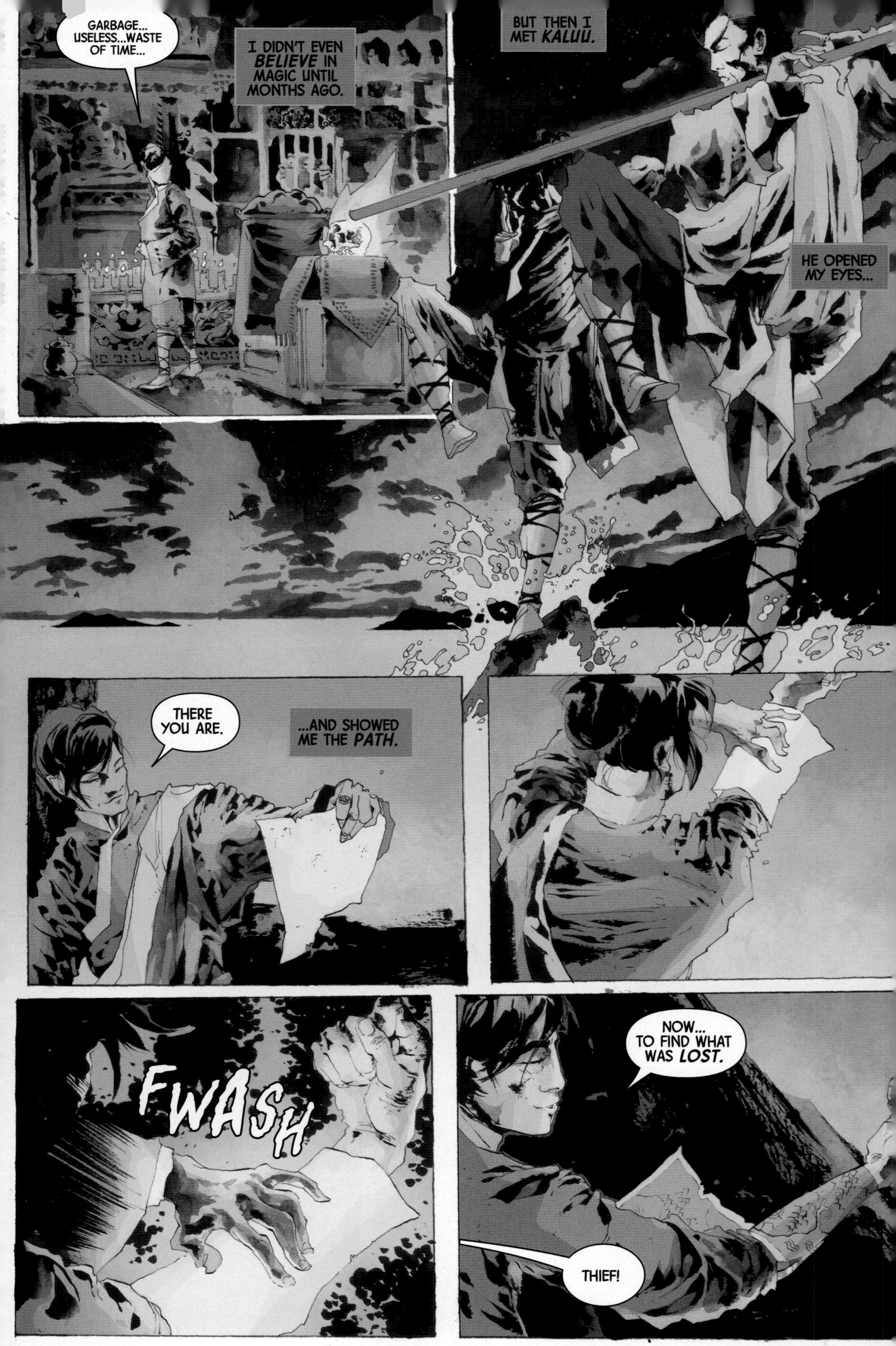
GARBAGE... USELESS...WASTE OF TIME...
I DIDN'T EVEN BELIEVE IN MAGIC UNTIL MONTHS AGO.
BUT THEN I MET KALUU.
HE OPENED MY EYES...
THERE YOU ARE.
...AND SHOWED ME THE PATH.
FWASH
NOW... TO FIND WHAT WAS LOST.
THIEF!

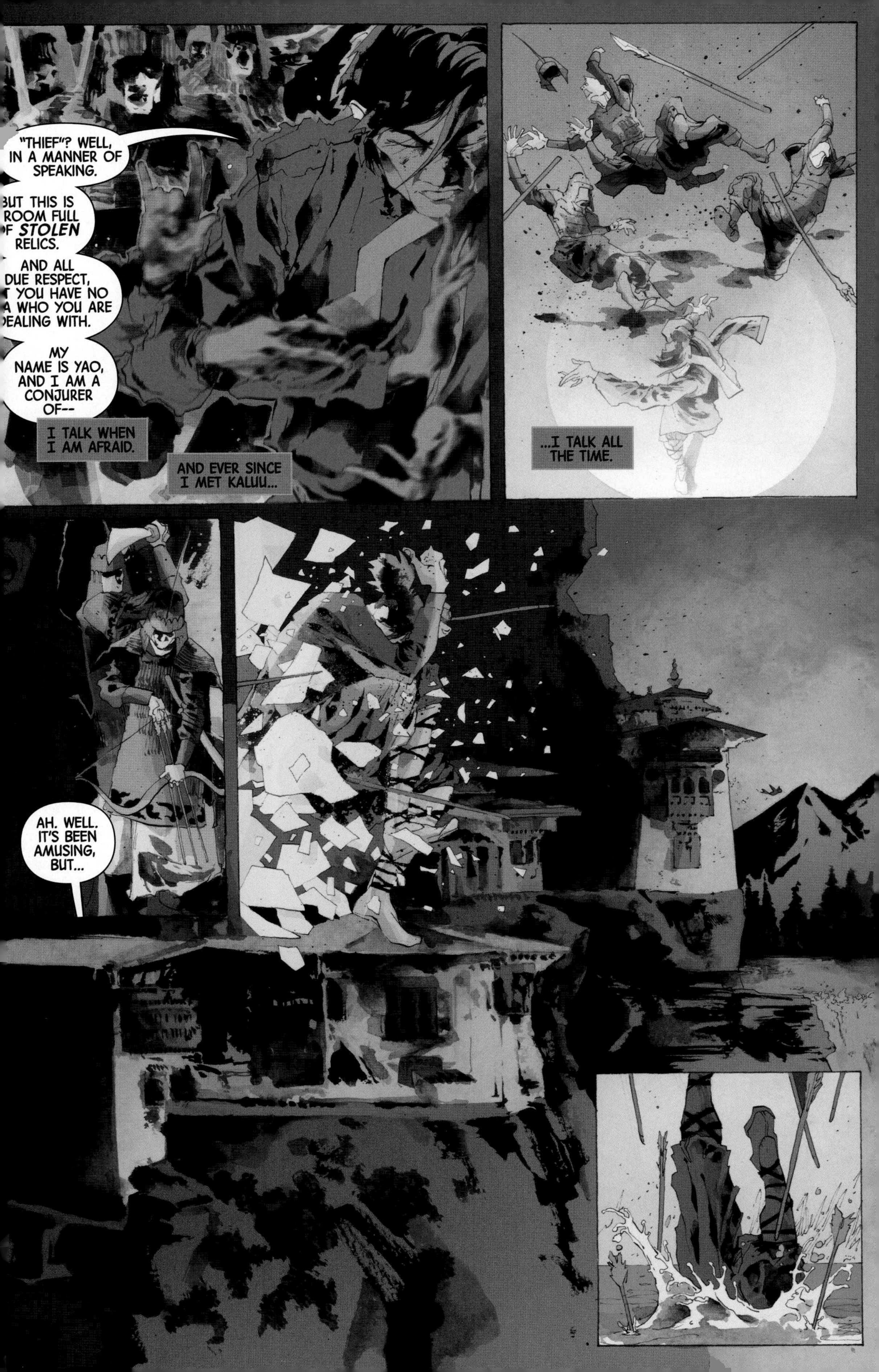
"THIEF"? WELL, IN A MANNER OF SPEAKING.
BUT THIS IS ROOM FULL OF STOLEN RELICS.
AND ALL DUE RESPECT, YOU HAVE NO A WHO YOU ARE DEALING WITH.
MY NAME IS YAO, AND I AM A CONJURER OF--
I TALK WHEN I AM AFRAID.
AND EVER SINCE I MET KALUU...
...I TALK ALL THE TIME.
AH. WELL. IT'S BEEN AMUSING, BUT...

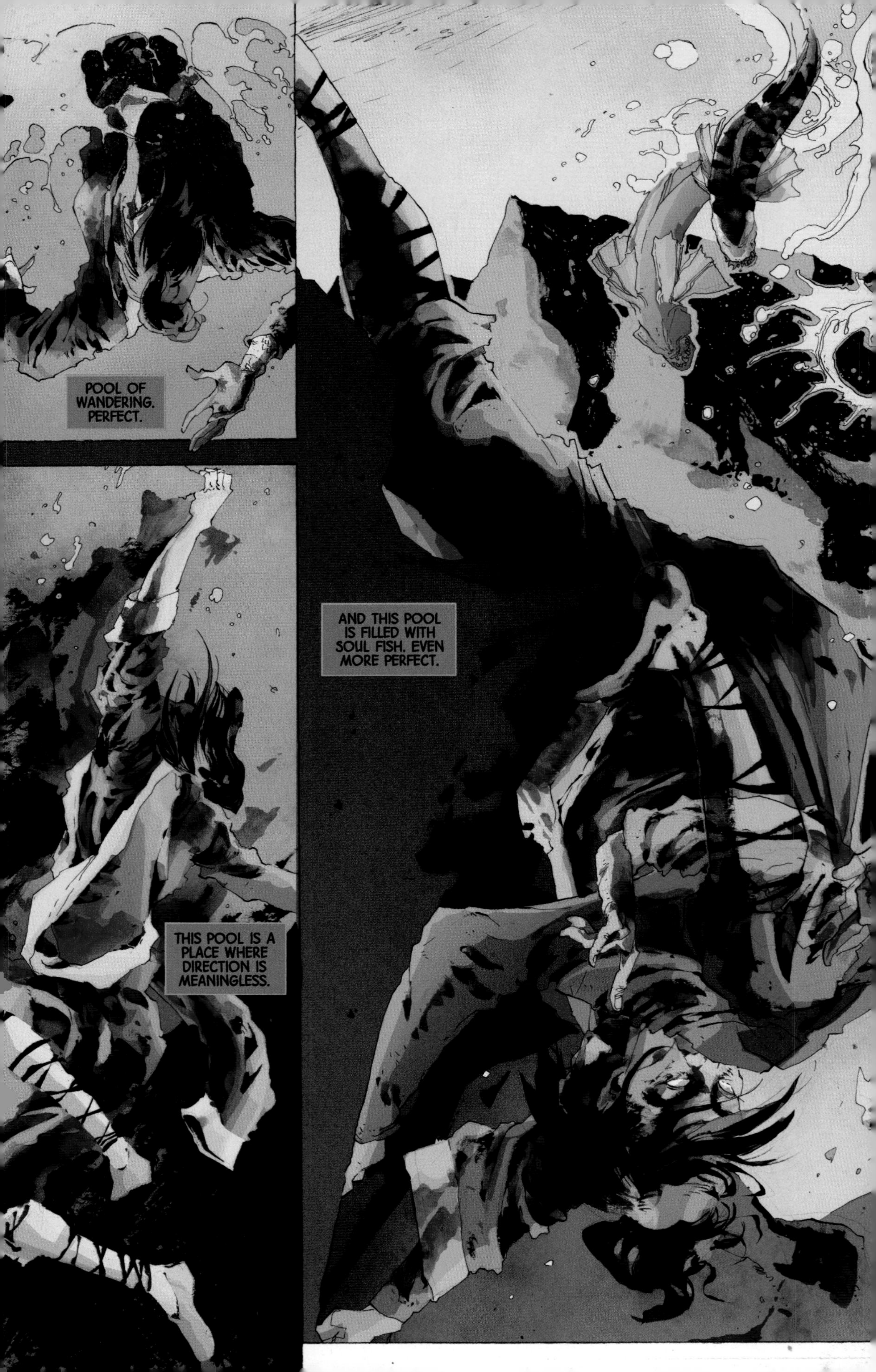
POOL OF WANDERING. PERFECT.
THIS POOL IS A PLACE WHERE DIRECTION IS MEANINGLESS.
AND THIS POOL IS FILLED WITH SOUL FISH. EVEN MORE PERFECT.

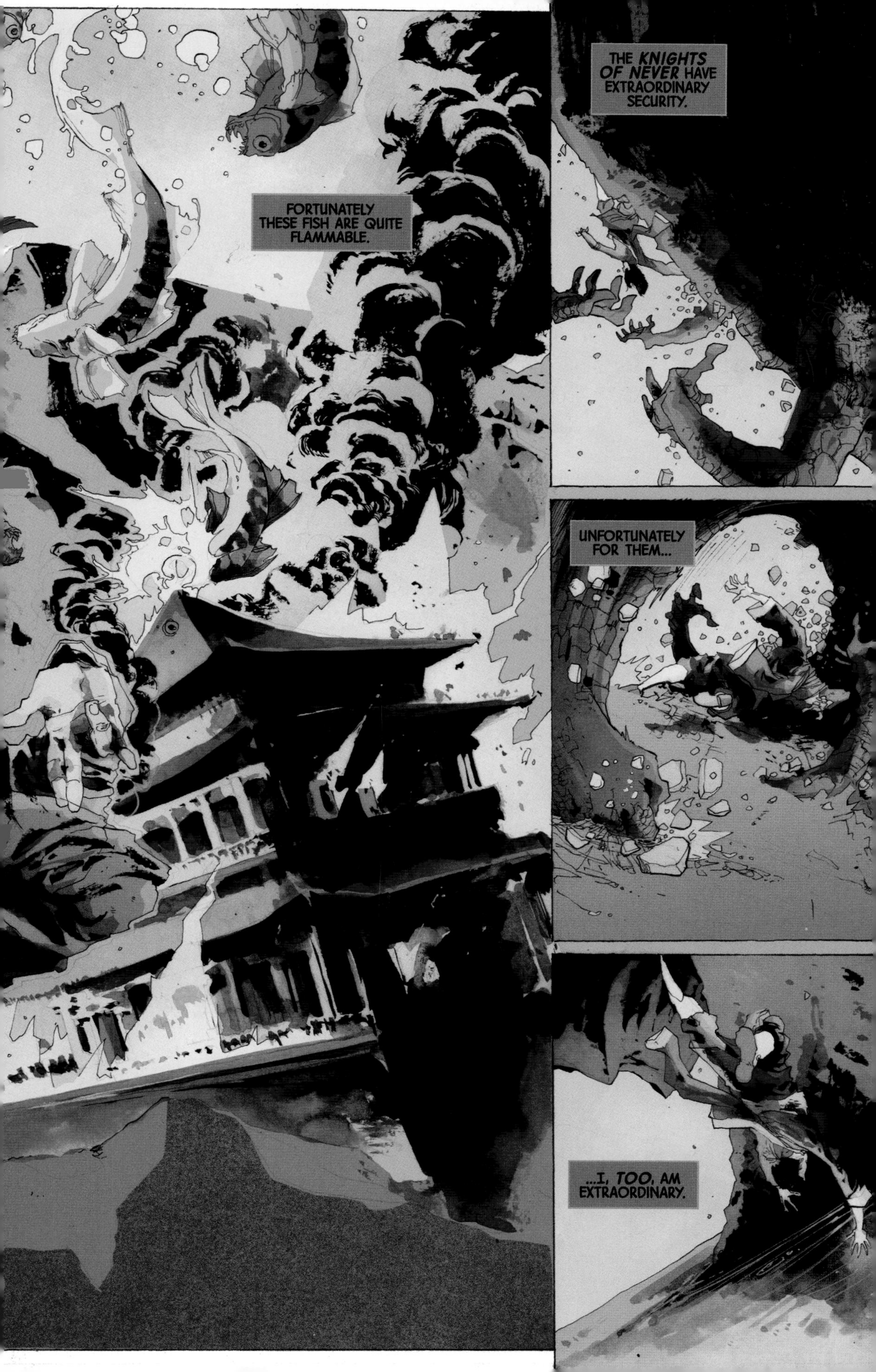
FORTUNATELY THESE FISH ARE QUITE FLAMMABLE.
THE *KNIGHTS OF NEVER* HAVE EXTRAORDINARY SECURITY.
UNFORTUNATELY FOR THEM...
...I, *TOO*, AM EXTRAORDINARY.

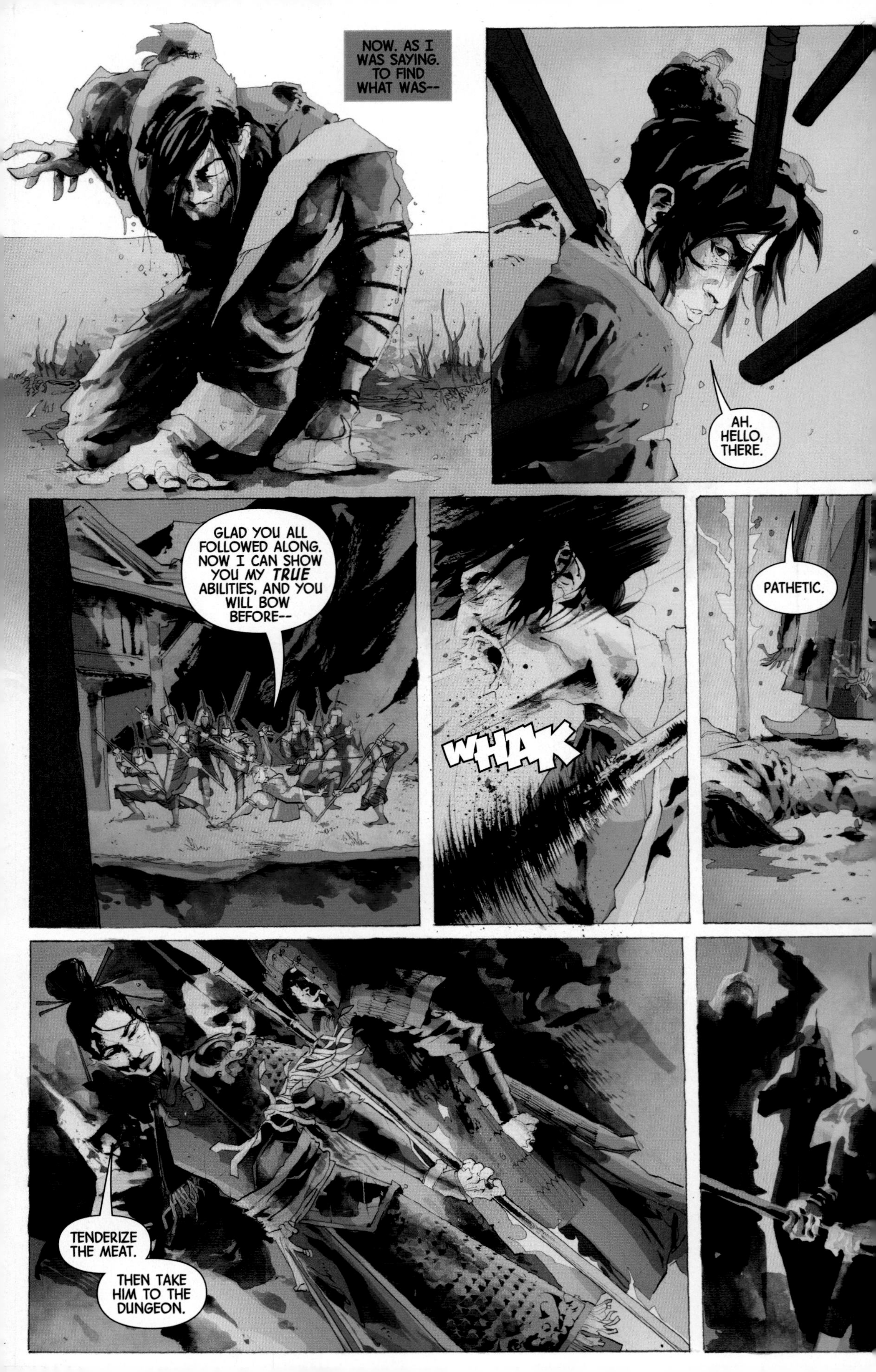
NOW. AS I WAS SAYING. TO FIND WHAT WAS--
AH. HELLO, THERE.
GLAD YOU ALL FOLLOWED ALONG. NOW I CAN SHOW YOU MY *TRUE* ABILITIES, AND YOU WILL BOW BEFORE--
WHAK
PATHETIC.
TENDERIZE THE MEAT.
THEN TAKE HIM TO THE DUNGEON.

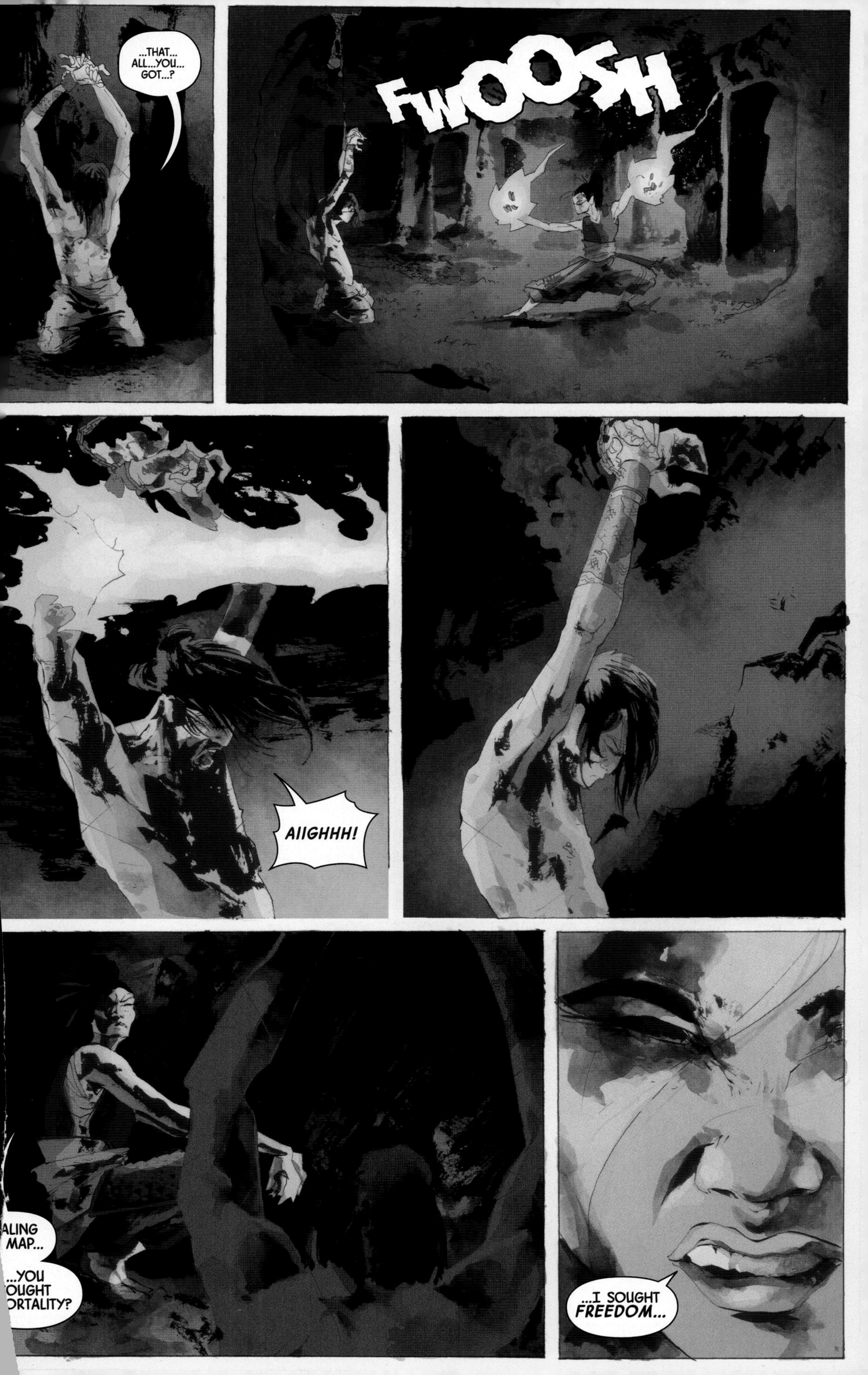
...THAT... ALL...YOU... GOT...?
FWOOSH
AIIGHHH!
ALING MAP...
...YOU OUGHT ORTALITY?
...I SOUGHT FREEDOM...

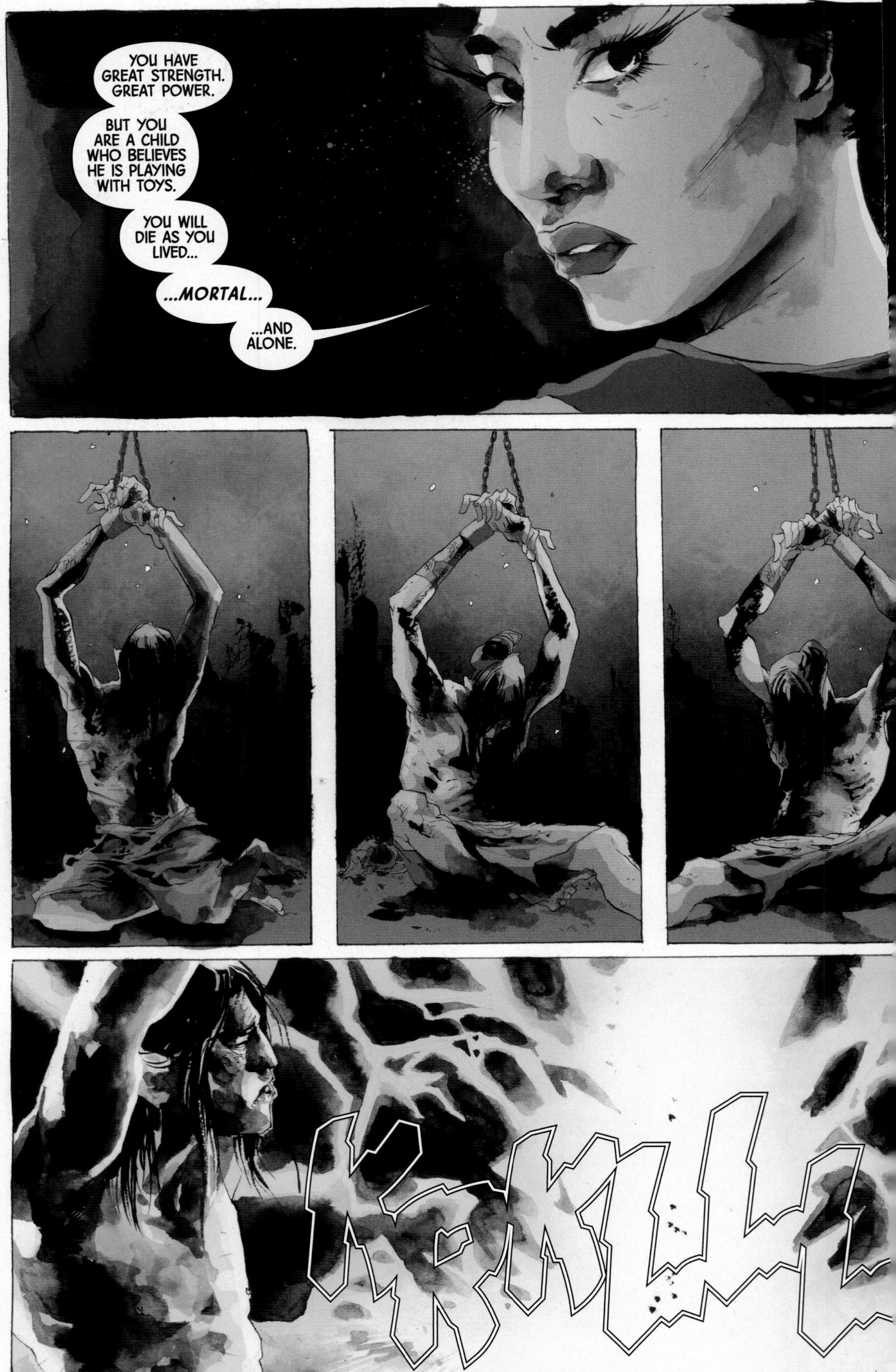
YOU HAVE GREAT STRENGTH. GREAT POWER.
BUT YOU ARE A CHILD WHO BELIEVES HE IS PLAYING WITH TOYS.
YOU WILL DIE AS YOU LIVED...
...MORTAL...
...AND ALONE.

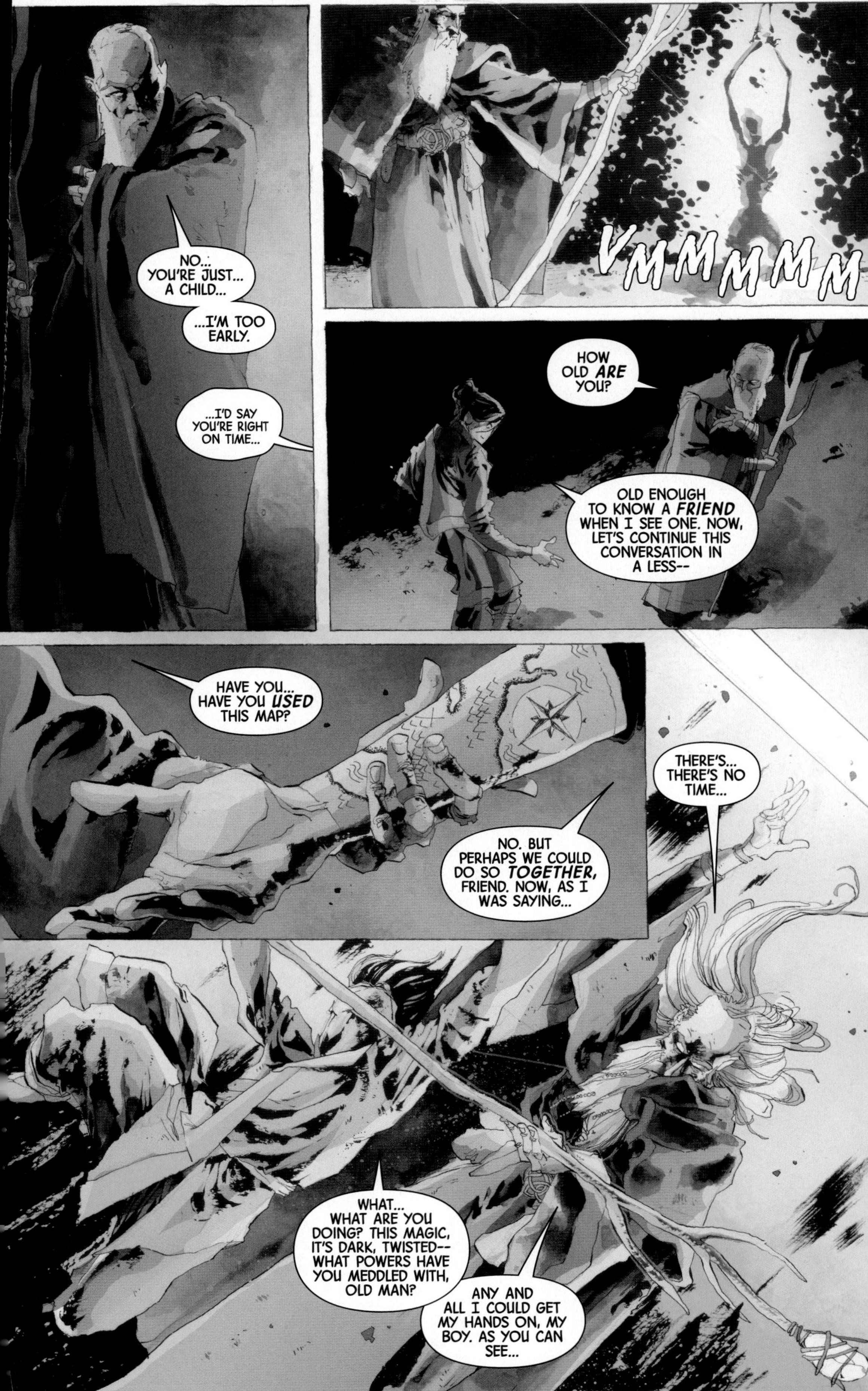
NO... YOU'RE JUST... A CHILD...
...I'M TOO EARLY.
...I'D SAY YOU'RE RIGHT ON TIME...
VMMMMMM
HOW OLD ARE YOU?
OLD ENOUGH TO KNOW A FRIEND WHEN I SEE ONE. NOW, LET'S CONTINUE THIS CONVERSATION IN A LESS--
HAVE YOU... HAVE YOU USED THIS MAP?
NO. BUT PERHAPS WE COULD DO SO TOGETHER, FRIEND. NOW, AS I WAS SAYING...
THERE'S... THERE'S NO TIME...
WHAT... WHAT ARE YOU DOING? THIS MAGIC, IT'S DARK, TWISTED-- WHAT POWERS HAVE YOU MEDDLED WITH, OLD MAN?
ANY AND ALL I COULD GET MY HANDS ON, MY BOY. AS YOU CAN SEE...

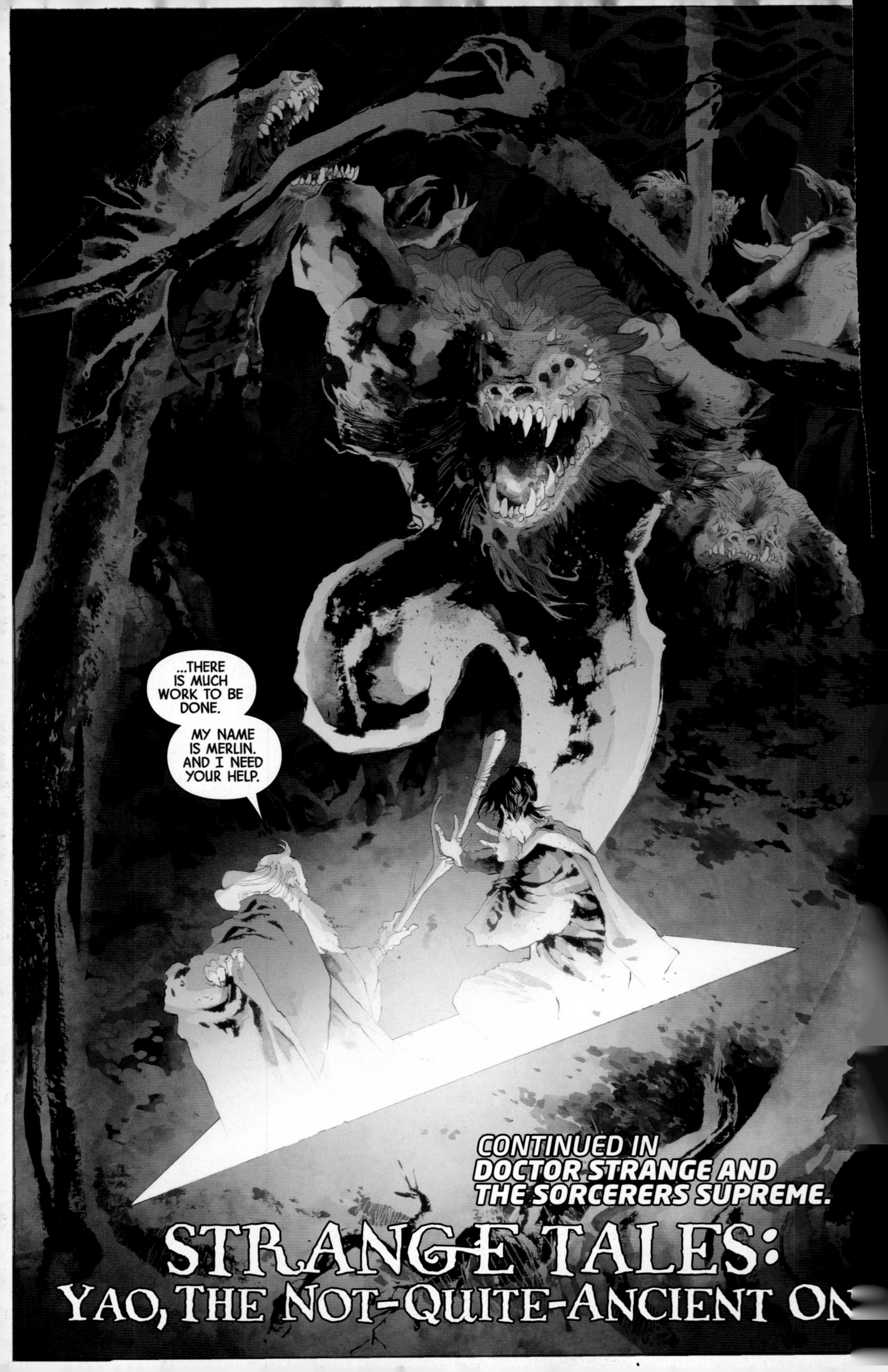
...THERE IS MUCH WORK TO BE DONE.
MY NAME IS MERLIN. AND I NEED YOUR HELP.
CONTINUED IN DOCTOR STRANGE AND THE SORCERERS SUPREME.
STRANGE TALES:
YAO, THE NOT-QUITE-ANCIENT ON

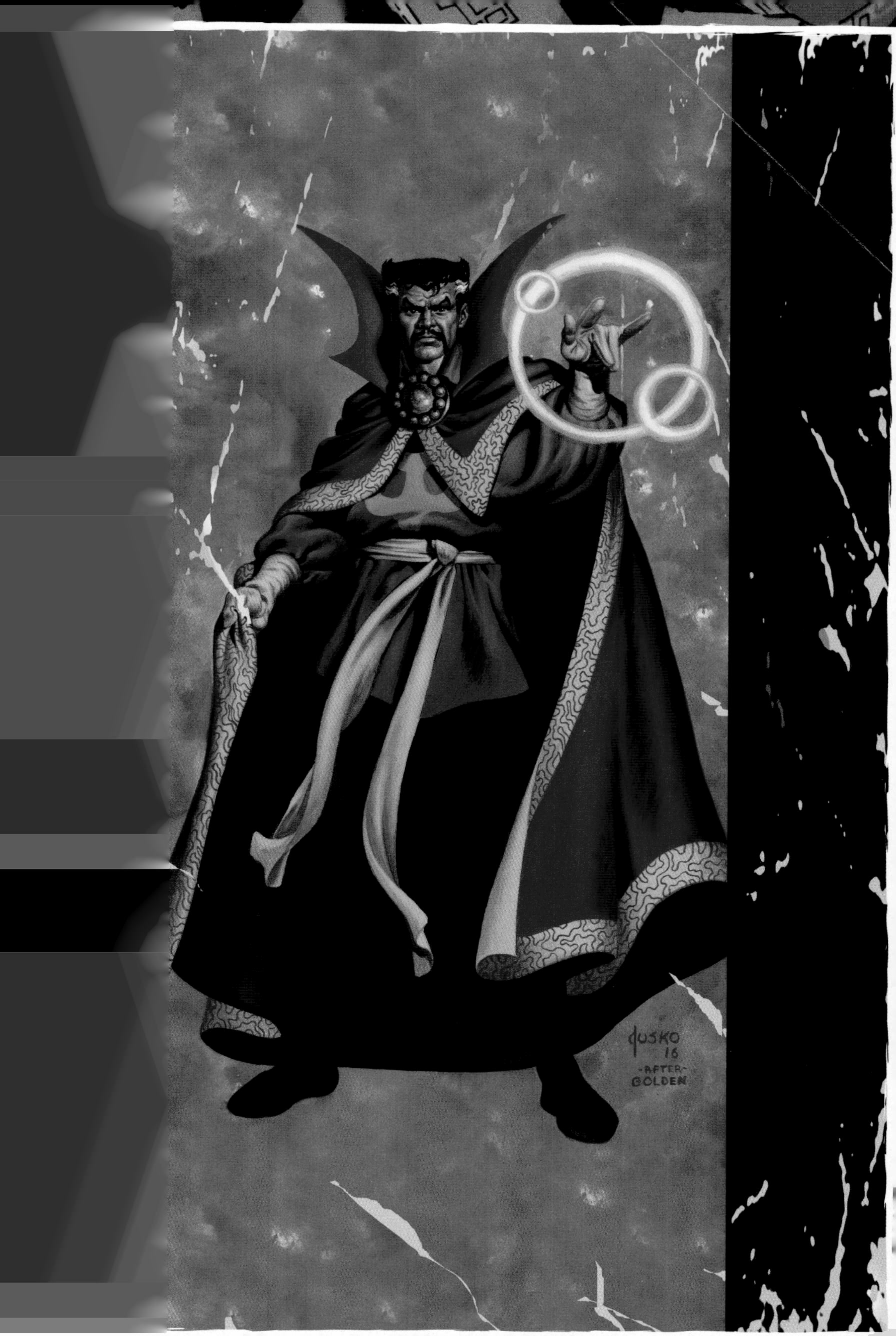
JUSKO
16
-AFTER-
GOLDEN

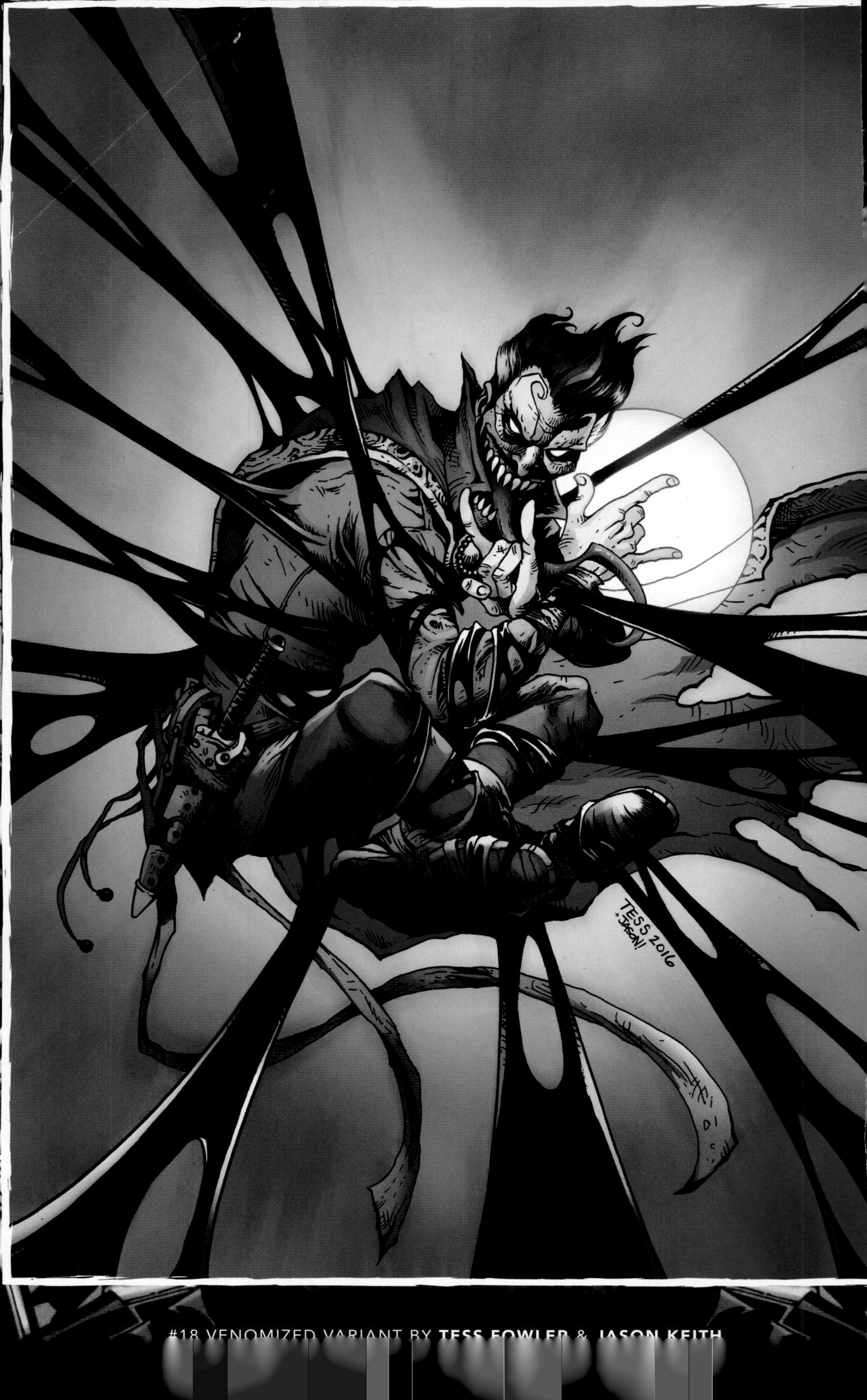
TESS 2016
+JASON!

#18 VENOMIZED VARIANT BY **TESS FOWLER & JASON KEITH**

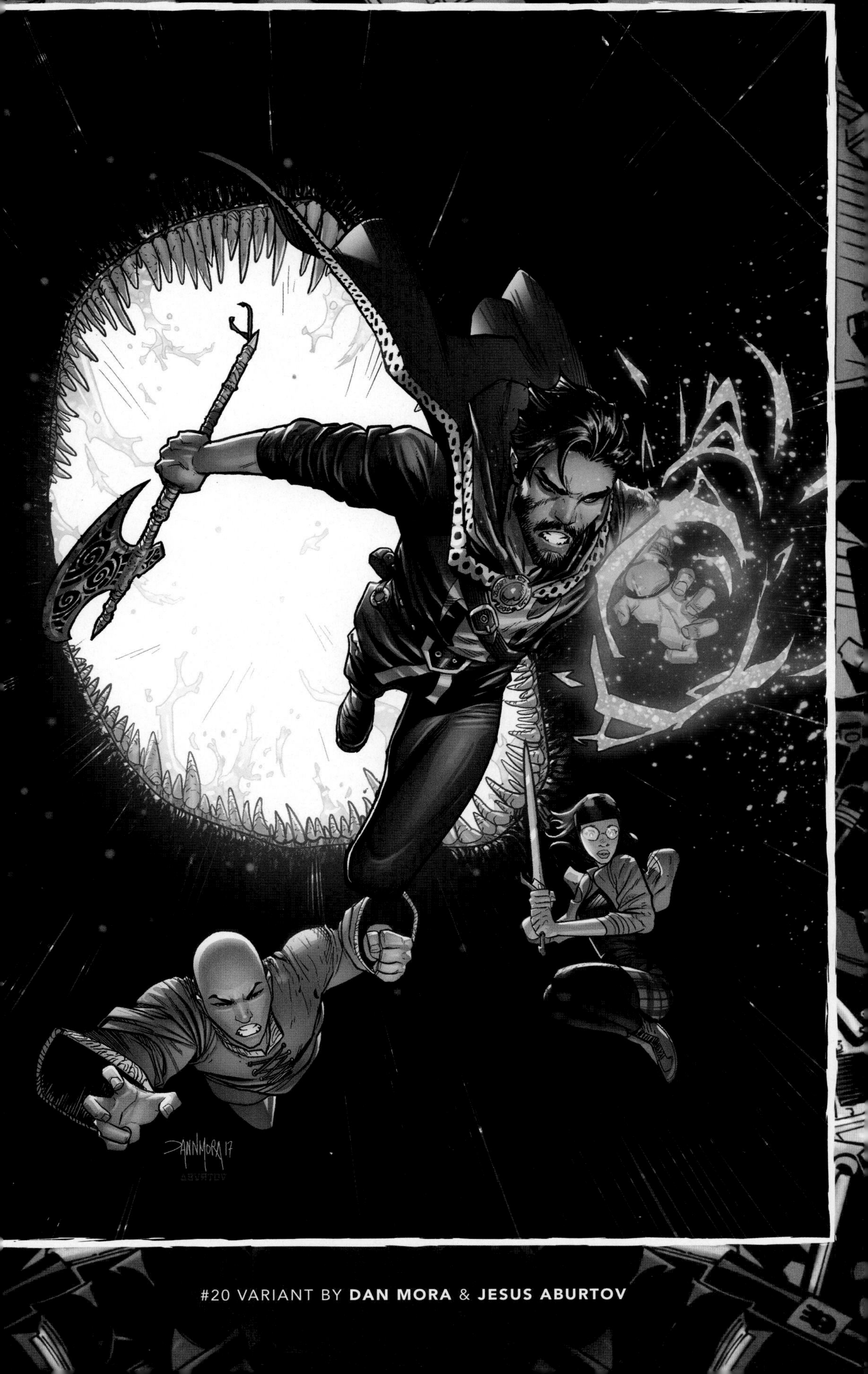

#20 VARIANT BY **DAN MORA** & **JESUS ABURTOV**

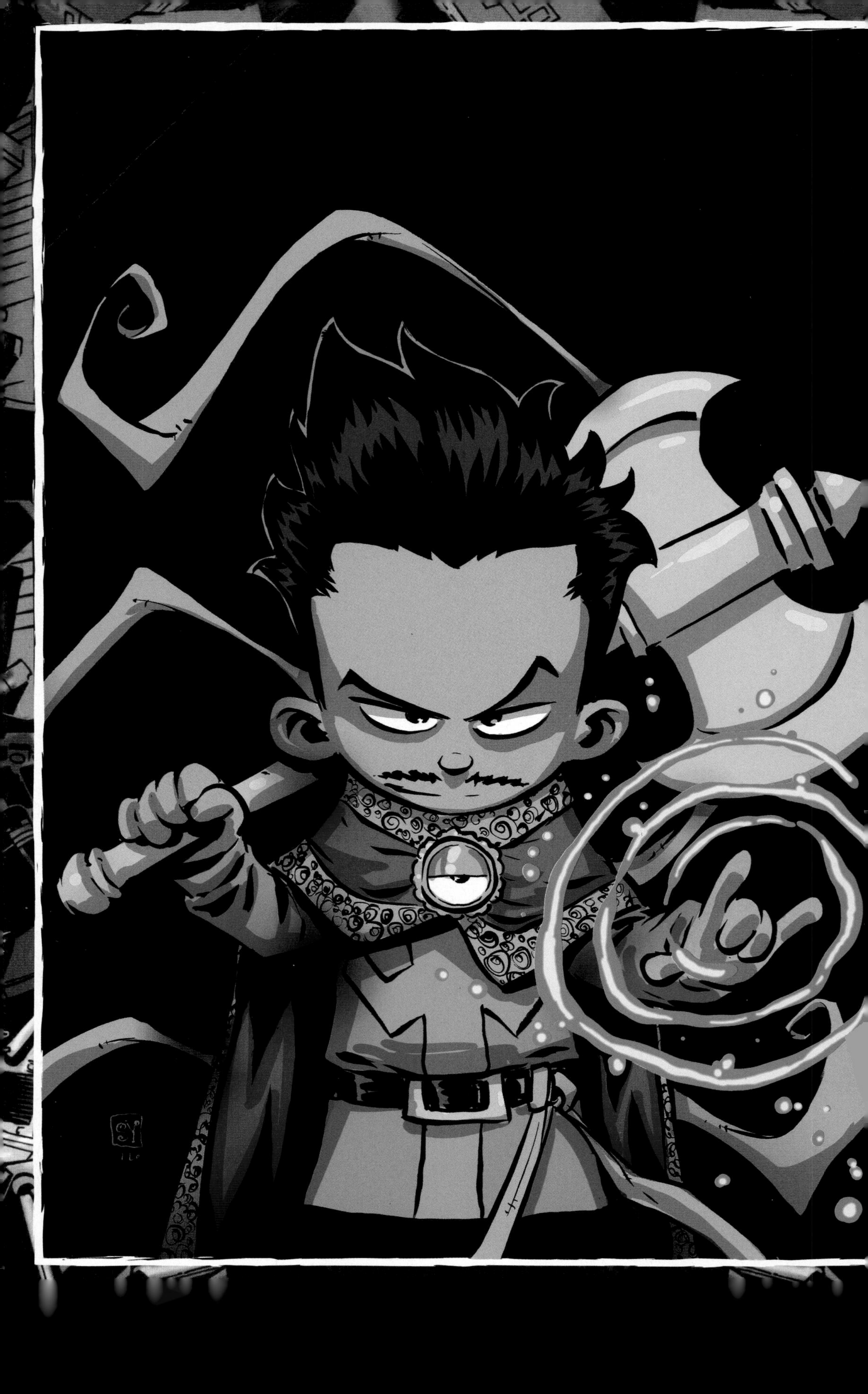

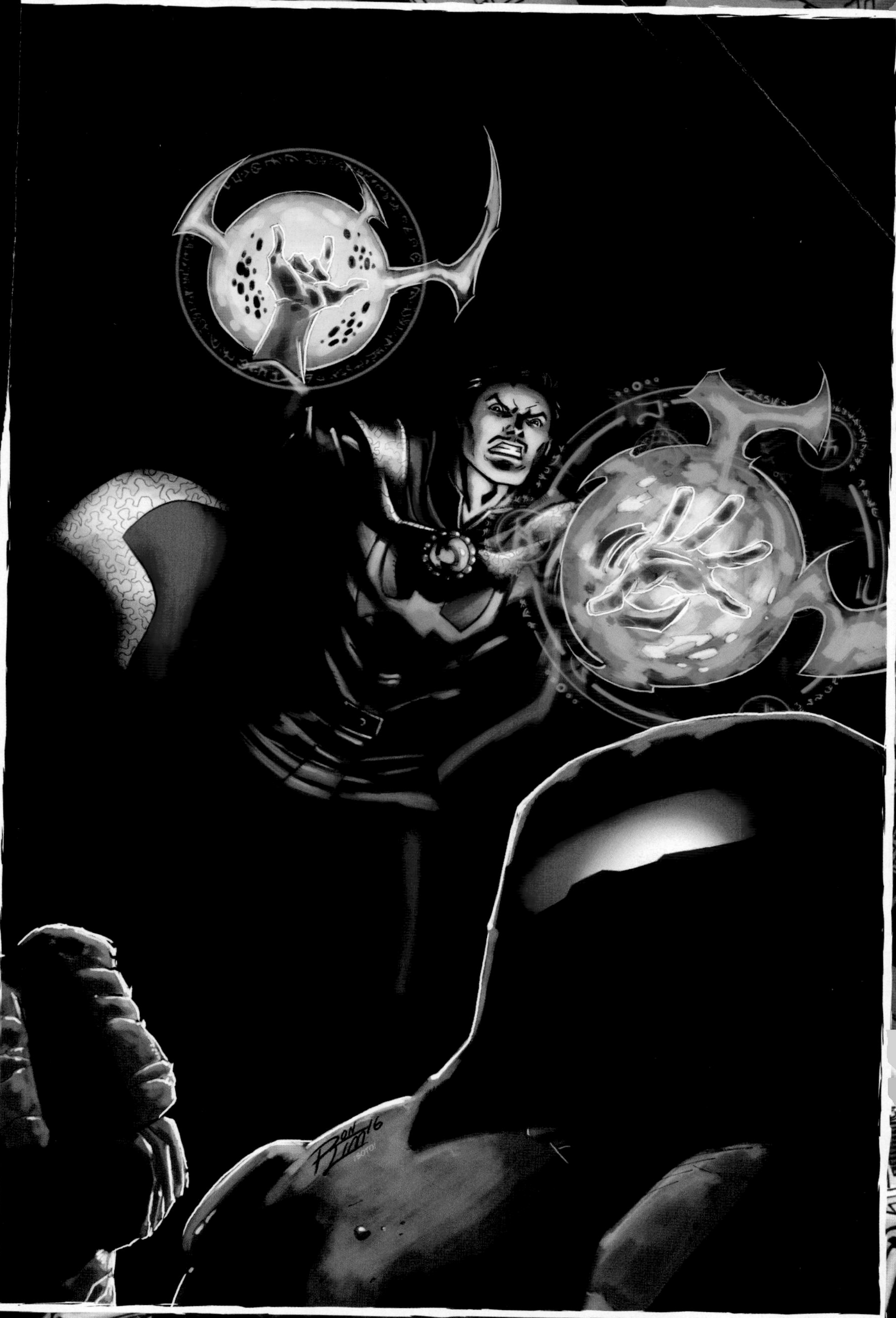

ANNUAL #1 VARIANT BY **RON LIM** & **CHRIS SOTOMAYOR**

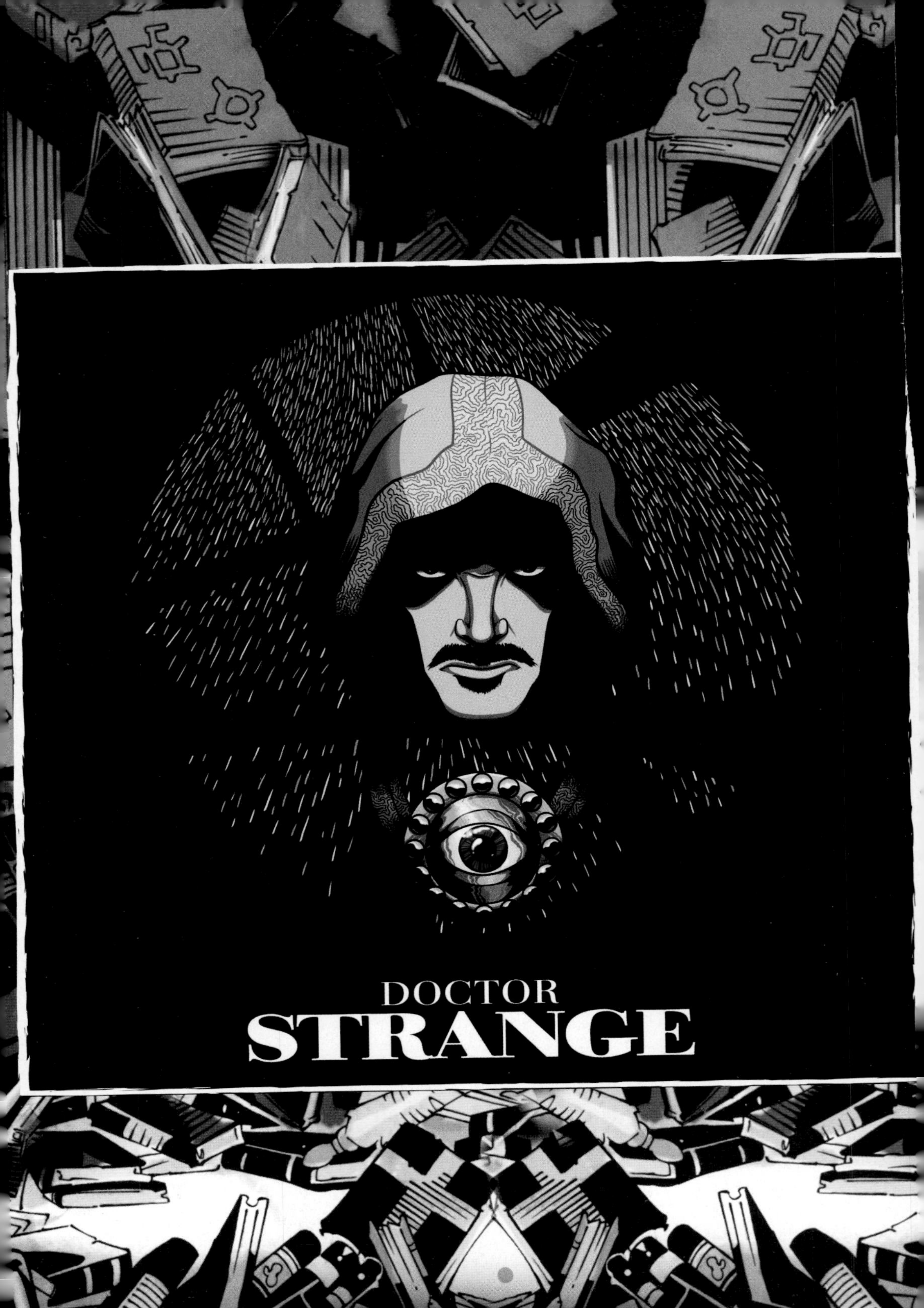
DOCTOR
STRANGE

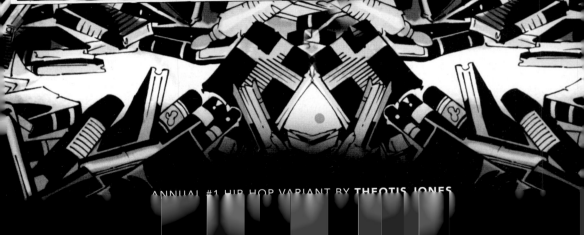

ANNUAL #1 HIP HOP VARIANT BY **THEOTIS JONES**